An Economic History of Europe

This concise and accessible introduction to European economic history focusses on the interplay between the development of institutions and the generation and diffusion of knowledge-based technologies. The author challenges the view that European economic history before the Industrial Revolution was constrained by population growth outstripping available resources. He argues instead that the limiting factor was the knowledge needed for technological progress, but also that Europe was unique in developing a scientific culture and institutions which were the basis for the unprecedented technological progress and economic growth of the nineteenth and twentieth centuries. Simple explanatory concepts are used to explain growth and stagnation as well as the convergence of income over time whilst text boxes, figures, an extensive glossary and online exercises enable students to develop a comprehensive understanding of the subject. This is the only textbook students will need to understand Europe's unique economic development and its global context.

KARL GUNNAR PERSSON is a professor in the Department of Economics at the University of Copenhagen, where he has been teaching comparative economic history and the history of globalization over the last thirty years. He is the author of *Pre-Industrial Economic Growth: Social Organization and Technological Progress in Europe* (1988) and *Grain Markets in Europe 1500–1900: Integration and Deregulation* (1999).

NEW APPROACHES TO ECONOMIC AND SOCIAL HISTORY

Edited for the Economic History Society by
NIGEL GOOSE, *University of Hertfordshire*
LARRY NEAL, *University of Illinois, Urbana-Champaign*

New Approaches to Economic and Social History is an important new textbook series published in association with the Economic History Society. It provides concise but authoritative surveys of major themes and issues in world economic and social history from the post-Roman recovery to the present day. Books in the series are by recognized authorities operating at the cutting edge of their field with an ability to write clearly and succinctly. The series consists principally of single-author works – academically rigorous and groundbreaking – which offer comprehensive, analytical guides at a length and level accessible to advanced school students and undergraduate historians and economists.

An Economic History of Europe

Knowledge, institutions and growth, 600 to the present

KARL GUNNAR PERSSON

CAMBRIDGE
UNIVERSITY PRESS

CAMBRIDGE
UNIVERSITY PRESS

University Printing House, Cambridge CB2 8BS, United Kingdom

Published in the United States of America by Cambridge University Press, New York

Cambridge University Press is part of the University of Cambridge.

It furthers the University's mission by disseminating knowledge in the pursuit of education, learning and research at the highest international levels of excellence.

www.cambridge.org
Information on this title: www.cambridge.org/9780521840095

First published 2010
6th printing 2013

A catalogue record for this publication is available from the British Library

Library of Congress Cataloguing in Publication data
Persson, Karl Gunnar, 1943–
  An economic history of Europe : knowledge, institutions and growth, 600 to the present / Karl Gunnar Persson.
    p.   cm. – (New approaches to economic and social history)
  ISBN 978-0-521-84009-5 (hardback) – ISBN 978-0-521-54940-0 (pbk.)
  1. Europe–Economic conditions.   2. Europe–Social conditions.   3. Europe–Intellectual life.   4. Technological innovations–Economic aspects–Europe–History.   I. Title.
  HC240.P388 2010
  330.94–dc22
  2009048041

ISBN 978-0-521-84009-5 Hardback
ISBN 978-0-521-54940-0 Paperback

Contents

3 Population, economic growth and resource constraints   42

4 The nature and extent of economic growth in the pre-industrial epoch   60

5 Institutions and growth   74

9 International monetary regimes in history
by Karl Gunnar Persson and Paul Sharp   171

10 The era of political economy: from the minimal
state to the Welfare State in the twentieth century   185

Tables

Figures

Maps

Boxes

Foreword

This book evolved over the years from the lectures I have given and give to my students at the Department of Economics in Copenhagen. I have, however, attempted to write a book for a wider audience who are searching for a very concise introduction to European economic history which is in tune with recent research. I make use of a few basic and simple economic tools which turn out to be very effective in the interpretation of history. The book offers a panoramic view rather than close-ups. However, the analytical framework will be useful in further studies of the specialized literature. For readers with little background knowledge in economics I provide a glossary defining key concepts, which are marked by italics and an asterisk, for example *barter**. Economic ideas demanding more attention are explained in the text or in appendices.

This is a work of synthesis, but it attempts to give challenging and new insights. I am indebted to generations of economic historians as well as to a great many of my contemporaries. That normally shows itself in endless footnotes, which not only interrupt the narrative flow but also drown the general historical trends amidst all the details. Instead, I have chosen to end each chapter with a selective list of references which is also a suggestion for further reading. Authors I am particularly influenced by are referred to in the main text.

A large number of colleagues have guided me. Cormac O'Gràda has as usual been a very stimulating critic and Paul Sharp has not only saved me from embarrassing grammatical errors but is also the co-author of two chapters. I would also like to thank Carl-Johan Dalgaard, Bodil Ejrnæs, Giovanni Federico, Christian Groth, Tim Guinnane, Ingrid Henriksen, Derek Keene, Markus Lampe, Barbro Nedstam and Jacob Weisdorf for helpful comments and suggestions.

Mette Bjarnholt was my research assistant during the initial phase of the project and Marc Klemp and Mekdim D. Regassa in the final stage and they have all been enthusiastic and good to have around.

Introduction: What is economic history?

Efficiency in the use of resources shapes the wealth of nations

Economic history is concerned with how well mankind, over time, has used resources to create wealth, food and shelter, bread and roses. Nature provides resources and man transforms these resources into goods and services to meet human needs. Some resources remain in fixed supply, such as land, but the fertility of land can and must be restored after harvest. Over thousands of years of agriculture, mankind learned how animal dung, rotation of crops and the introduction of nitrogen-fixing crops could increase the yearly harvest. Natural resources such as coal, oil and iron ore are, however, non-renewable. Other resources are made by mankind. Capital, for example factory buildings and machinery and tools, is therefore renewable. Labour, finally, is a resource whose supply relies on how well mankind uses the other resources at hand. But labour has been in increasing supply since the transition from hunter-gatherer technology to agriculture about ten thousand years ago. The skills of labour, so-called human capital, were primarily based on learning by doing, and it is only since the nineteenth century that formal education has played an important role.

Efficiency is determined by the technology of production and by the institutions that give access to the use of resources.

Institutions can be understood as the rules of the game for economic life. Institutions or principles such as the Rights of Man matter because if labour is not free to move it is unlikely that labour will find its most productive employment. Workers who are not properly rewarded will have every reason to shirk, that is, not to offer sufficient effort. Owners of capital need assurances from ruling elites that their property will not be arbitrarily expropriated before they will be willing to invest. Inequalities in the distribution of income and wealth tend to trigger off distributional conflicts in nations, which hamper growth because political conflicts create uncertainty about the rules of the game in the future.

Economic history traces the efficiency characteristics of institutions by studying the development of commodity and labour markets, financial intermediaries (banks), the legal framework of contract enforcement, property rights, openness to trade and international capital flows. Property rights over resources can be more or less well defined and they impact on the use and distribution of resources. Markets can be more or less efficient depending on their competitive nature and the speed at which new information about supply and demand conditions is spread. Markets can be thin, that is trade can be infrequent and engage few participants at a time; or thick, which means that markets are almost continuous and involve a large number of traders. In history, markets have tended to become thicker and more efficient over time. Money facilitates trade and exchange and banks can help savers with incomplete knowledge to find good investment opportunities. High risks can deter people from trade, but insurance can reduce these risks. Openness to trade and factor flows has varied dramatically throughout history. Even though there is evidence that openness tends to increase efficiency in the use of resources, there are losers as well as winners within any nations from the practice of international trade. Although the long-run historical trend has been one of increasing openness, there are significant setbacks in this process driven by those who fear to or actually do lose from free trade. Openness can increase risk because open economies are more exposed to shocks originating in the world economy. It is possible that openness is therefore linked to the evolution of specific institutions, such as the Welfare State, that alleviate these effects of openness. Government sets the rules of the game, and tries to uphold law and order. But since governments have a monopoly of force, good and accountable government is far from the rule. Corruption and bad government is a major reason why economies fail.

Technology is knowledge about how to use resources in the production of goods and services. The ability to make iron out of iron ore is based on knowledge originally derived from trial and error. Without that knowledge iron ore would be useless, as it was throughout most of the history of mankind. Modern technologies differ from pre-nineteenth-century technologies mainly by the fact that they are developed from theoretical and scientific inquiry about the world, which over the span of just 200 years has expanded the knowledge base at an ever-increasing rate.

Often such knowledge will be 'embedded' in particular pieces of production equipment and tools. Think of a modern PC. It is a useful tool in a wide variety of operations, and a large amount of prior knowledge is embedded in it in the sense that the operations you can perform with the computer rely on the prior knowledge needed to construct the computer and its software.

Although some natural resources may have been depleted over time, such as oil and minerals, there has been an increase in the efficiency of their use. The general technological trend in history has been that the amount of resources you need to produce a given amount of output has declined. Late nineteenth-century economists all agreed that coal deposits would be exhausted in the near future, which would put an end to prosperity. It did not happen because another non-renewable resource, oil, and renewable energy sources such as hydroelectricity, replaced coal as a major source of energy. In the long run oil resources will be exhausted if no alternative energy resources, renewable or non-renewable, are exploited.

Material resources, such as capital equipment, land and natural resources, are what we can call *rival* goods. You cannot both use the coal and keep it. Your use of a particular machine hinders others from its use. However, the factors that generate efficiency, that is technology and institutions, are non-rival. *Your* use of common knowledge to construct a new efficient tool does not preclude *others* from using the same knowledge. It is true that some knowledge is not immediately and freely accessible to all because of patent protection. Such protection is an institutional mechanism to stimulate research spending, but patents expire, after which private knowledge becomes common knowledge. Knowledge of a new institutional mechanism – say a change in corporate *tax-ation**, which gives investors incentives to invest in sophisticated production technology – can be imitated in any nation. The non-rival nature of know-ledge about technologies and institutions gives it an almost limitless potential to change the efficiency of production.

In recent years, climate change has come to the forefront in the political and economic debate. What role, if any, has climate in the framework sketched here? Climate is best seen as a factor, along with technology and institutions, which determines the degree of efficiency with which resources can be used. Climate change is certainly not new to economic historians, but neither the extent of these changes nor their effects have been sufficiently explored. The so-called Little Ice Age, in the Early Modern period (1450–1650), is according to one line of research responsible for a decline in output produced by given resources and technology. As a contrast, the contemporary discussion focusses on the poten-tial increasing costs of production from global warming, although the impact may differ significantly among regions and sectors in the world.

Resource endowments of nations as far as land and mineral deposits are con-cerned have not changed over time. The dramatic changes that economic histo-rians focus on are how human capital, technologies and institutions develop over time to facilitate the access to and efficient use of resources that permit income and wealth to grow. Initial resource endowments matter, but it is increased efficiency in their use which has permitted economies to enjoy increasing wealth throughout the course of history. At this stage we can formulate a strong proposition which will be corroborated in the subsequent chapters:

Proposition 1: Economies that are richly endowed with resources are not necessarily rich but economies which use resources efficiently are almost always rich irrespective of their resource endowment.

Outline of the chapters

Our story begins at a time when the first European civilization, the Roman Empire, had declined. Chapter 1 examines the surprising geo-political continuity of Europe despite the endemic political and territorial conflicts. One question asked is what shapes regional entities such as Europe. The gravity theory of trade notes that trade is stimulated by proximity and similarity and stresses the gravitational attraction of large core economies. The chapter advances the idea that trade has been a major force of integration, not only economic but also cultural and political. Initial barriers to trade tend to develop into trade-inhibiting border effects which define the limits of regional entities.

Proposition 2: Europe trades, therefore it is!

Before the nineteenth century technological progress was very slow and rested on a thin base of knowledge which was mainly derived from experience acquired from learning by doing and the division of labour. The division of labour was the primary source of efficiency gains in production and triggered the development of institutions, markets, money and contract enforcement rules, which facilitated exchange. Without the exchange of services and goods there was no scope for people to specialize in separate skills. In Chapter 2 I develop a simple explanation of the rise and fall of economies stressing the ups and downs of orderly markets, urban settlements and trade nodes and division of labour. The positive effects of population growth are stressed when the declining trend in the aftermath of the decline of the Roman Empire is reversed. The decline of the Roman Empire is a story of institutional and political breakdown with severe consequences for economic welfare. An interesting question arises here: are modern economies immune to institutional failures? As we will see in subsequent chapters, the answer is no!

Proposition 3: The forces that stimulate division of labour (specialization), that is political order, population growth, money supply and exchange, were essential

*for the revival of the European economy in the early Middle Ages and started a
process of slow growth of welfare based on skill perfection and learning by doing.*

Economics and economic history tell us, first, that more resources per producer generally increase output and income. Second, and more interestingly,
even within the constraints of resources which are in fixed supply, such as land,
output and income per person will increase if a person learns how to increase
efficiency in her use of resources. For example, the yield of wheat per year from
a hectare of land has increased continuously and dramatically in the course
of history. In Chapter 3 I focus on how the fixed supply of land can constrain
growth, but only insofar as technology is stagnating.

*Proposition 4: Technological progress is essentially resource saving, which makes
explanations relying on binding resource constraints insufficient and often
inappropriate for historical analysis except with regard to economies that are
characterized by technological stagnation.*

The lesson from history is that technological change can relieve the economy
of the constraints of a resource in fixed supply. More paradoxically, we find that
an increase in population can stimulate both technological change and division of labour, thereby counteracting the impact of diminishing returns when
land resources per producer fall. In Chapter 4 I explore this finding further.
The pre-industrial economies differed in their capacity to balance negative
and positive effects from population increase. The outcome is not deterministic: some regions and nations experience slow economic growth while others
have periods of growth followed by stagnation.

*Proposition 5: Population growth tends to increase demand and hence division of
labour as well as technological progress (Pepys' rule).*

We often take institutions as given, but in a historical analysis, we cannot
and should not do so. Institutions develop spontaneously or by design; they
regulate use of and access to resources and the conditions for exchange. It is
useful to look for efficiency characteristics in institutions. In the absence of
contract enforcement mechanisms, exchange which involves future delivery
will be severely restricted, for example. However, institutions which regulate
the access to resources, that is property rights, have an impact on the distribution of welfare, and persistent institutions may survive only because they serve
powerful elites. In Chapter 5 I discuss the interpretation and impact of institutions and note that there is often a bewildering variety of institutional solutions to the same economic problem. I ask questions like the following: why

are farms generally small and managed by those who work there, whereas industrial firms are large and managed by those who own the firm rather than those who provide labour services? It turns out that in some cases institutions fail because they are inefficient, but history also tells us that inefficient institutions may survive because they serve vested interests and powerful elites.

Proposition 6: Efficient institutions are often stable, but stable institutions are not necessarily efficient.

The industrial revolution in the eighteenth and nineteenth centuries was founded on a set of modern institutions as well as new mechanisms serving the growth of science. Chapter 6 explores the foundations of modern economic growth and the conditions for technology transfer. During most of the history of mankind technology has been based on knowledge derived from experience in production, which is learning by doing. Such knowledge can develop by chance or by deliberate trial and error. However, these technologies are not based on theoretical or scientific understanding. The great leap forward in technological development is associated with the breakthrough in the nineteenth century of knowledge gained through theoretical and scientific inquiry. This industrial enlightenment, as it has been called, has its roots in preceding centuries but becomes a decisive force only in the second half of the nineteenth century. From being slow, technological progress became the prime mover of economic growth by the end of the nineteenth century. It turns out that the vast majority of products and production processes that came to dominate the twentieth century were invented in the nineteenth century. Since technology is essentially the useful application of knowledge and ideas, which are non-rival in nature (i.e. your use of knowledge does not reduce the availability of it), we would expect transfer of best-practice technology among nations to lead to convergence in the levels of technology and income across nations. We do indeed observe this convergence, but it is not *universal*. This is a paradox since I am arguing that what matters is a factor – ideas and knowledge – which is non-rival. However, being in the public domain does not imply being easily accessible or easily applied. We need to know *why* some nations were not able to use available knowledge of superior technologies and develop institutions which helped the efficient use of resources. It turns out that technology transfer is dependent on institutional and educational pre-conditions which, if absent, will make transfer imperfect.

Proposition 7: Science and R&D (Research and Development*) are recent phenomena in technological development. Fast technology transfer after 1850

*led to convergence based on catch-up among economies that had an appropriate
educational and institutional infrastructure.*

Over thousands of years money developed into an increasingly efficient
instrument of credit and payment. Banks are a more recent phenomenon,
emerging only in the late medieval period and not reaching maturity until
the nineteenth century. Banks are intermediaries between savers and investors (spenders). They reconcile the savers' desire to hold liquid assets with the
investors' need for long-term finance, and they reduce risks by holding diversified asset portfolios beyond the reach of individual savers. Despite the inherently risky nature of banking and finance, it is possible to show how banks over
time reduced risk and costs in transactions. Furthermore, the development of
banks increased savings and investment. The breakdown of a financial system
in twelfth-century Europe would have effects on trade, but in the present world
it threatens all economic activities. The evolution of money, credit and banking is explored in Chapter 7.

*Proposition 8: Banks have developed as intermediaries between savers and
investors by reducing risk in saving, by solving informational asymmetries and by
monitoring borrowers more efficiently than savers would be able to on their own.*

Before the Industrial Revolution, international capital flows and international
trade were limited; the first wave of globalization occurred in the nineteenth
century. The institutional foundations of a functioning international trading
system and monetary regime are explored in Chapters 8 and 9. Although there
are net gains for nations that trade, there are winners and losers within each
nation. Sometimes the losers dictate trade policy and the result will be trade
restrictions and a globalization backlash, as in the interwar period (1920–40).
While it is easy to understand that a majority of losers can dictate protectionist
policies, like landowners in Europe in the closing decades of the nineteenth century, we also face the paradox that small minority groups, such as farmers, can
lobby successfully for tariff protection 100 years later. Explain that!

*Proposition 9: Net gains from trade do not preclude winners and losers. The
protectionist paradox is that both large and small groups can successfully
lobby for protectionism* and win, but for different reasons. Bad times foster
protectionism, but good times help free trade forces.*

International monetary regimes, discussed in Chapter 9, have varied significantly throughout history. The relative merits of fixed exchange rates vs.

floating exchange rates cannot be determined in a straightforward way. The advantages of fixed exchange rates in stimulating trade and capital mobility were noted in the nineteenth century, but these phenomena have also been present in the floating exchange rate regimes emerging since the mid-1970s. Fixed exchange rates tend to restrict the ability of policymakers to impact on domestic economies, and floating exchange rates are therefore favoured when there is a demand for an activist domestic economic policy, as emerged after the breakthrough of democracy in Europe in the early twentieth century. Although economic orthodoxy led Europe back to the Gold Standard, a fixed exchange rate regime, it had neither the equilibrating mechanisms nor the longevity of the classical Gold Standard of the period before the First World War. The lessons from the interwar period were applied in the exchange rate regime introduced after the Second World War, giving nations more say over domestic monetary policy at the expense of free capital mobility. But a system with fixed exchange rates in the short run and adjustable exchange rates in the long run fell victim to its own contradictions. The twentieth century was not made for fixed exchange rates.

Proposition 10: The historical record suggests that widespread democracy seems to be difficult to reconcile with a fixed exchange rate policy because such a policy constrains domestic economic policy options.

Chapter 10 explores economic growth and economic policy in the twentieth century. That century can be described as the era of political economy because it witnessed the transformation of the minimal state to the activist state. The balance between politics and markets differed and the 'over-politicized' economies of the Socialist bloc ultimately failed because they did not deliver the goods promised. The mixed approach favoured in the rest of Europe was more successful in the combination of competitive markets and extensive insurance schemes provided by the Welfare State. We interpret Welfare State provisions as a response to market failures in insurance and the need for life-cycle smoothing of income.

The book illustrates the fragility of free trade policies and fixed exchange rates under pressure from an international crisis. But I also demonstrate the power of economic policies in reviving growth in a depression, and the tragedy of erroneous policy responses, as in Germany leading to the ascent of Adolf Hitler. The interwar period paved the way for a new economic policy regime characterized by more active fiscal and monetary policies of Keynesian persuasion. I shall chronicle its birth, near-death and resurrection.

Proposition 11: The idea that the economy was a self-regulating and equilibrating process was killed by the Great Depression, and after the Second World War Europe worked out a new balance between politics and economics, paving the way for activist fiscal and monetary policies. The Welfare State is primarily an inter-temporal redistribution institution which is explained by market failures and human lack of self-control.

Chapter 11 discusses inequality, past and present. While Europe converged, the income gap between the rich industrialized countries and the rest of the world increased dramatically from around 1800 and has gone on increasing up to the present. The developing nations are poor mainly because they are not capable of creating the institutional and educational conditions for technology transfer. The spectacular growth in recent decades of economies in South East Asia indicates the power of institutional change. Industrialization and modernization usually increase inequality within nations because of bottlenecks in the supply of skilled people. But by expanding human capital investment and easing access to higher education inequality will be reduced, as in Europe in the twentieth century. However, there are persistent wage differences between men and women that are based on discrimination.

Proposition 12: World income inequality has probably peaked after 200 years of increased income gaps. More equality ahead need not be just wishful thinking but will be the result of an increasing number of nations getting the institutional infrastructure needed for technology transfer.

Chapter 12 deals with the challenge and opportunities of globalization. I argue that, on balance, globalization brings net benefits to the world economy. But there are losers and winners. A number of questions will be addressed. Will globalization put downward pressure on (unskilled) wages in the rich countries? Will wages in poor and rich countries converge? Will there be a 'race to the bottom' as regards 'labour standards', that is hours and conditions of work? The preliminary answer to the first two questions is yes, but it is no to the last question – if we are allowed to judge from the experience of the first era of globalization.

Proposition 13: The world economy just before the First World War was as globalized as the world economy today. There was convergence of wages in the first era but not a race to the bottom in 'labour standards'.

The making of Europe

1.1 The geo-economic continuity of Europe

The formation of Europe was a long historical process which involved political, cultural and economic forces. The most striking fact is the geo-economic persistence and continuity of Europe during the last two millennia. We will deal with the integrative impact of trade as well as its border-maintaining effect in shaping and maintaining Europe. Trade was the cohesive force when political and military conflicts threatened to tear Europe apart.

If we let the core of Europe be defined by the borders of the European Union, we can trace back the origins of that geographical entity to the Roman and Carolingian empires, the latter emerging in the ninth century, several centuries after the collapse of the Roman Empire. (See Maps 1.1–1.3). About 80 per cent of the total population of the Roman Empire around the year 100 AD lived within the present (2010) borders of the European Union. It stretched from the Atlantic coast to the Black Sea. Ireland, the northern periphery of Europe, Scandinavia and Russia were touched by neither the Roman nor the Carolingian rulers. Russia's relationship to Europe has remained ambivalent throughout its history, with periods of self-imposed isolation as well as enthusiastic embracing of European ideals, and Scandinavia was late in joining the European Union; in fact Norway is still making up its mind whether to join or not.

The Carolingian Empire represented the revival of political order after the disintegration of the Roman Empire, and also the emergence on the political scene of Germanic peoples, who amalgamated their own traditions with the adopted culture, law and language of their Roman predecessors in their south and westward push. Germanic tribes also advanced towards the east, but kept their own language and pushed the Slavic languages back eastward when they subjected the indigenous peoples and their land. It took centuries, in fact a millennium of conflicts, for the present map of nation states forming the

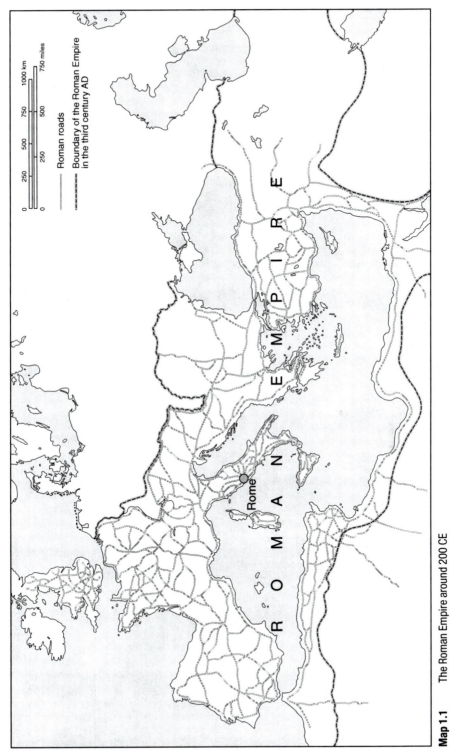

Map 1.1   The Roman Empire around 200 CE

Map 1.2   The Carolingian Empire around 850 CE

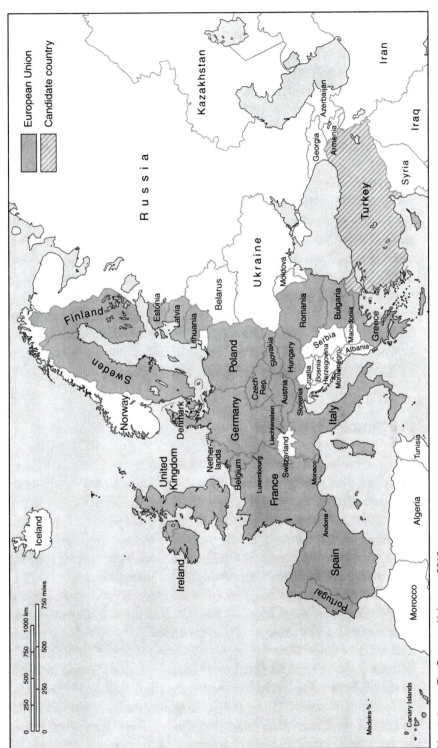

Map 1.3 The European Union year 2010

European Union
Candidate country

Iceland

Finland

Sweden

Norway

Russia

Estonia
Latvia
Lithuania
Belarus

United
Kingdom

Denmark

Nether-
lands

Poland

Ukraine

Ireland

Belgium
Luxembourg

Germany

Czech
Rep.

Slovakia

Hungary

Moldova

Romania

France

Liechtenstein

Switzerland

Austria

Slovenia

Croatia

Bosnia
Herzegovina

Serbia

Bulgaria

Monaco

Italy

Montenegro

Macedonia

Albania

Greece

Turkey

Georgia

Armenia
Azerbaijan

Iran

Andorra

Spain

Portugal

Syria

Iraq

Kazakhstan

Morocco

Algeria

Tunisia

Madeira

Canary Islands

0   250   500   750   1000 km
0   250   500   750 miles

European Union to emerge, and it is worth noting that the heartland of the Roman Empire, that is Italy, was not again a nation state until in the late nineteenth century. After Rome and after the partition of the Carolingian Empire the new nations remained smaller. At one extreme we have the prosperous merchant city states of Italy, for example Venice, emerging in the eleventh century, and at the other extreme a large nation state emerging in France as the western part of the disintegrating Carolingian Empire. The age of empires was not to appear again until the European colonial expansion of the nineteenth century.

We delineate a nation or a union of nations by borders because borders represent the limit of political authority and the capacity of the state to tax and spend on roads and *public goods**, such as defence and law and order institutions. Nations form because they offer *economies of scale** in providing these public goods. The size distribution of nations has varied dramatically throughout history, but the reason for that has probably more to do with politics than with economics. Since the breakdown of the unified Carolingian Empire, national borders have been redrawn repeatedly after bitter and costly conflicts. The great historical paradox is that despite disruptive political forces Europe remained as a unit of cultural and institutional homogeneity because of strong cohesive forces, of which trade was the most important.

1.2 Europe trades, therefore it is!

Throughout history, the intensity of trade has been stimulated by the *proximity* and *similarity* of nations. Nations close to each other trade more with each other than with economies far away. When trade expands, it does so more with those nations already part of the trading network than with those on the fringe of that network. This is true today but was even truer in the past, when land transport costs were often prohibitively high for commodities other than luxury goods: silk was transported over long distances, but bulky commodities like grain were not. Over land a commodity like grain was not normally transported more than 100 km, but since the cost of sea transport was only about 10 to 25 per cent that of land transport, grain could be and was shipped over longer distances by sea, for example from the Baltic coast to the Atlantic ports in Europe. Dried cod (*stoccafisso*), was shipped from Norway to the Mediterranean in the late medieval period. A large economy will typically stimulate trade with the surrounding economies very much like a force of gravity. Trade transmits goods, but also common languages, commercial law, culture, preferences and technology. Intense trade makes economies with initial differences more similar in all the respects listed above. Economies come to share similar technologies and, as a consequence, similar income levels that will also stimulate trade. However, if trade was stimulated by proximity alone we would not see the evolution of regional entities like Europe, because there are always nations at the margin or limit which are close to *some* neighbours. Nations at the margin would therefore tend to extend the limit successively. Why did that not happen? The reason was 'trade resistance' due to lack of *similarity* of nations at the geographical margins as well as the distance from the large trade-generating core economies of Europe.

Although empire building like that of the Romans tended to create homogeneity in language and law, there were limits to the extension of empire. These limits were set by the mounting costs of policing frontier areas as well as the falling revenues from populations at a lower level of income. At the geographical margin, the forces of gravity from the large core economies were too weak to generate sufficient trade. Furthermore, the neighbouring economies differed in income levels and technology, in culture and preferences, in language and law, and these differences remained because they constituted a barrier to trade. When technology and income levels differ among trading partners, trade volumes will be low irrespective of proximity. Relatively rich nations find the export prospects of poor nations too small. A lack of commonly accepted currency units made transactions difficult or based on *barter,** which also reduced the volume of trade. As a consequence the initial lack of similarity was broken down in the proximity of a core economy – but *only* in the proximity. For areas further away heterogeneity was maintained or increased when the frontier area started to adopt the institutions – say the money or contract resolution institutions – of the core economy. The implication is that if the periphery is initially poor it may remain poor because it is left untouched by the knowledge, commodities and institutions that trade is bringing. We call these forces *border effects**. You can think of a border effect as a high transaction cost imposed on trade which is *not* present in trade *within* the region or empire which has a common legal and monetary system and language. Border effects reduce trade and therefore maintain the lack of similarity between neighbouring economies in the border areas. A telling illustration of border effects is the diffusion of late Roman pottery from a particular production site in southern France. The pottery was shipped as far as Hadrian's Wall in Britain, North Africa and all over the Empire, but there are practically no finds north of the River Rhine, as indicated in Map 1.1. So the border of the Empire constituted a formidable obstacle for this type of commodity.

The impact of border effects on trade is illustrated in Figure 1.1, which demonstrates the trade and trading costs of an economy (C as in Core), with

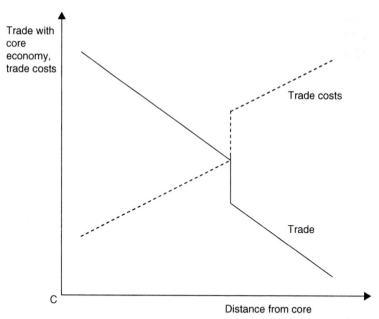

Figure 1.1   The impact of distance and border effects on trade

trading partners scattered along the vertical axis at increasing distance from the C economy. Trading costs, mostly transport costs, increase with distance from the exporting nation. Owing to increasing transport costs, the proximity effect, and the fact that the similarity of nations tend to decrease with distance, trade will diminish with increasing distance from the C economy. A border effect represents an upward shift in the trade cost curve and will be associated with a downward shift in the volume of trade schedule.

We can illuminate the argument by an example from history. The Arab conquest in the eighth and ninth centuries of northern Africa and the Iberian peninsula, once part of the Roman Empire, created a cultural and religious barrier to trade in the Mediterranean. The core of Europe moved away from the Mediterranean world towards western and central Europe. Henri Pirenne, a Belgian economic historian (1862–1935), focussed on what were later called border effects, in this case the negative effects on trade of a cultural and religious divide, in analysing the decline in Mediterranean trade and imports to northern and western Europe after the Arab conquest. Why would religious and cultural differences affect trade negatively? In the context of long distance trade exporters and importers need to trust each other. Trust is needed because a trader in Genoa cannot easily verify that the importer in Alexandria is right in claiming that the shipment from Genoa has been damaged during the passage. Different cultures, which also have different procedures for settling disputes, might discriminate against strangers. By and large trust is easier to build if people share common beliefs and a common code of conduct that develops into common rules of contract enforcement. Within Europe a fairly uniform set of rules and institutions emerged as trade picked up in the medieval period to assist in settling contractual disagreements, honouring promises and protecting foreign merchants from arbitrary actions by local merchants.

Recent research based on the ample finds of Arab coins in Western Europe suggests that the trade between the Arab and European nations probably did not decline as much as maintained by Pirenne; part of the reason for the low trading activity was probably the fact that Europe was just recovering from the decline following the demise of the Roman Empire. Poor nations simply do not trade much. To the Arabs Europe was a backwater. However, Pirenne was right in focussing on border effects and pointing out that previously flourishing trade relations deteriorated as a consequence of a cultural and religious divide. But there were other cultural divides.

The diffusion of ideas and goods and the exercise of authority are helped by a common language. Most of the Germanic tribes which flowed into the Roman Empire were fast learning the language and the law of their hosts, but in the rest of Europe, the local languages remained. Compared to the Roman Empire, tenth-century Europe was much less homogenous in linguistic terms. Many tongues were spoken, but traders and merchants often adopted a regionally uniform language in transactions. For example, varieties of German were generally spoken in the Baltic area, since trade was dominated by Germans. However, with the advance of the Christian faith which also gradually penetrated the Baltic area – often commercial and spiritual missions went hand in hand – a universal language, Latin, was used all over Europe since the Church insisted on its liturgical use. It was also standardized by the Church, but was used not only by the clergy but by the secular elites as well. As a consequence the elites were united culturally by one language, and the schools and universities which emerged from the twelfth century, teaching law and theology, attracted students from all over Europe. For example, the early thirteenth-century bishop Anders Sunesen in Lund (southern Sweden), which was on the periphery of Europe at this time, was educated in France, Italy and England. Much of higher learning relied on results already obtained in Antiquity, and when that learning was forgotten and neglected in Europe it survived among learned men in the Muslim world and was then rediscovered in Europe. *Algebra*, *alchemy* and *algorithm* are words borrowed from Arabic, and with the words came the learning.

Similarity, proximity and the absence of (strong) border effects stimulates trade. Is that prediction corroborated by the data? Table 1.1 conveys the answer

Table 1.1   Intra-European trade and trade with ROW (Rest of the World), in 2005. Percentage of total trade

Importing country / Exporting country	EU25 Norway Switzerland	Denmark	France	Germany	Italy	Netherlands	Spain	Sweden	United Kingdom	ROW
Denmark	76%		5%	18%	3%	5%	3%	13%	9%	24%
France	67%	1%		15%	9%	4%	10%	1%	8%	33%
Germany	72%	2%	11%		7%	4%	5%	2%	8%	28%
Italy	65%	1%	13%	14%		2%	8%	1%	7%	35%
Netherlands	82%	2%	9%	25%	6%		4%	2%	9%	18%
Spain	76%	1%	20%	12%	9%	3%		1%	9%	24%
Sweden	72%	7%	5%	11%	4%	5%	3%		8%	28%
United Kingdom	67%	1%	10%	12%	5%	7%	6%	2%		33%

Source: Total trade data: Eurostat: Europe in figures, Yearbook 2005–2006: epp.eurostat.ec.europa.eu/cache/ITY_OFFPUB/KS-CD-06-001/EN/KS-CD-06-001-EN.PDF
EU25 consists of: Belgium, Czech Republic, Denmark, Germany, Estonia, Greece, Spain, France, Ireland, Italy, Cyprus, Latvia, Lithuania, Luxemburg, Hungary, Malta, Netherlands, Austria, Poland, Portugal, Slovenia, Slovakia, Finland, Sweden, United Kingdom

for present-day Europe. The table indicates that about three-quarters of the trade of individual EU nations is within the EU plus Norway and Switzerland. We also note that for each nation *similarity*, presumably in language and preferences, matters a lot. Denmark has a larger share of its trade with a comparatively small economy, Sweden, than with much larger economies, the UK and France. But *proximity* might explain part of the difference. Denmark's trade with Germany is three times larger than its combined trade with Spain and Italy. European trade as a share of income was smaller in the past but it has always been primarily intra-European trade. When trade among nations expands, it grows roughly in proportion to previous trade. Nations intensive in their trade tend, in other words, to trade more with each other, which is another aspect of the cohesive force of trade. This is the combined effect of similarity, border effects with regard to 'outsiders', and the fact that trade is stimulated by proximity.

1.3 From geo-economics to geo-politics: the European Union

The Europe we have discussed so far is an entity defined by cultural and institutional similarities. Trade can contribute to the breakdown of initial heterogeneity and maintain similarity in these domains, but the formation of the European Union in the latter half of the twentieth century is a new and historically unique experience. In its formative years in the 1950s it was dominated by purely economic concerns and the nations participating were those which throughout the second millennium had been the battlegrounds for endless military conflicts: France, Germany, Italy and the BENELUX nations. Diverging national interests were however still high on the agenda and split Europe into two trading organizations. When the European Economic Community was formed by the Treaty of Rome (1958), the UK was excluded and formed EFTA (the European Free Trade Association) with the rest of Western Europe. However, most EFTA economies traded more with EEC nations than with each other and continued to do so. Hence, EFTA was doomed from its beginning, while the EEC was growing by admitting new members and broadening its agenda. The decisive step was to admit the UK in the early 1970s, which was conditional on reducing Anglo-French discord. The trade-creating effects of the initial tariff reductions, and the subsequent creation of a single market doing away with non-tariff barriers to trade, have been impressive and far greater than the tendency to divert trade from non-members. The relabelling of the European Economic Community as the European Union indicated a wider and more ambitious agenda of political co-ordination. It has been a history of the political elites trying to convince reluctant national electorates of the benefits of political integration, which is however yet to materialize fully. The insight on which this chapter has been organized is that in the past trade has been the cohesive force in a Europe of political and military conflict. Political co-operation in the EU has added a new dimension to Europe. It seems highly unlikely that a military conflict could break out among the former bitter enemies in Europe. At last geo-politics is in tune with geo-economics.

Summary

It has been argued that the limits of larger units such as Europe emerge from initial border effects as well as differences in income levels and technology at the border and the waning of the gravity force of core economies as the distance to the core increases. Since impediments to trade are also impediments to the shaping of similarity in preferences, commercial practices and income, regional entities such as Europe will tend to persist because they are built on self-reinforcing mechanisms. However, border effects are also deliberately created by nations or unions of nations, such as the EU (in particular by its protectionist Common Agricultural Policy), and by the creation of a common currency. The effect will be that trade is diverted from external to internal, intra-union, trade.

Suggestions for further reading

The explanation of trade discussed in this chapter is known as the 'gravity theory' and is explored in all modern intermediate textbooks on international trade theory. It was first applied by Nobel laureate Jan Tinbergen in *Shaping the World Economy* (New York: The Twentieth Century Fund, 1962). There are numerous articles developing the framework. See E. Helpman, M. Melitz and Y. Rubinstein, 'Estimating trade flows: trading partners and trading volumes', *Quarterly Journal of Economics* 123(2) (2008), pp. 441–87.

There is a vast political science literature on state formation, but interestingly economists have recently been focussing on it. See A. Alesina and E. Spolare, *The Size of Nations* (Cambridge, Mass.: MIT Press, 2003).

Henri Pirenne's argument was first expressed in the 1920s and in a monograph from 1937 published in an English translation in 1939 as *Mohammed and Charlemagne* (London: George Allen and Unwin, 1939). Critical reviews of the Pirenne thesis include R. Hodges and D. Whitehouse, *Mohammed, Charlemagne and the Origins of Europe: Archaeology and the Pirenne Thesis* (Ithaca: Cornell University Press, 1983).

A modern classic: E. L. Jones, *The European Miracle: Environments, Economics and Geopolitics in the History of Europe and Asia* (Cambridge University Press, 1981).

Europe from obscurity to economic recovery

2.1 Light in the Dark Ages

The Dark Ages in Europe, the centuries after the decline of the Roman Empire, were not as dark as we used to think, although they did not possess the political, cultural and economic grandeur of the Roman Empire. Nor did Europe match Muslim civilization in terms of wealth and technical ingenuity. Products and technologies for the manufacture of sugar, paper, cotton and fine fabrics, chemicals for dying and glassmaking, would be imported during subsequent centuries. However, modern historians are now rewriting the history of the sixth to ninth centuries, and the prevailing pessimistic view is giving way to a more nuanced view of what happened after the decline of the Roman Empire. Settlements were abandoned and cities lost population and skills; roads deteriorated because of lack of proper maintenance; political maps were redrawn and social order was difficult to maintain; money was scarce and uniform coinage was lacking; income fell for ordinary people as well as the rich. Income declined because traditional trade links had been disrupted and because the social disorder and declining population could not support the infrastructure of public institutions and roads, markets and fairs, or the division of labour and specialization of the previous centuries. Income per head did not attain the peak level reached in the Roman period until the twelfth or thirteenth century in the most advanced parts of Europe.

In one respect this age remains dark: we do not have much written documentation, so we have to rely on archaeological evidence which is difficult to interpret. Historians use numismatic evidence, deposits of pottery and metal utensils; they analyse the nature and extension of settlements and of course the few written documents that are available. By locating coins you can, with a critical eye, trace trade links, for example. The extension of a market network can be revealed by the diffusion of specific types of pottery, jewellery and coins. It is more difficult to document technology because most tools were made of wood, which has not been preserved. Recent advancements in historical research reveal that there was light in the Dark Ages. The contour of a new Europe was evolving and the centre of gravity of that new Europe was shifting in a northwesterly direction from the Mediterranean basin. What remained of the Roman Empire shifted eastwards with Constantinople as the centre, and former Roman lands in the Middle East, North Africa and Spain were gradually coming under Arab and Muslim rule. By and large these parts of the formerly unified Empire fared better economically than Western Europe, at least until the eleventh century. Eventually the Byzantine world, the heir of the Eastern Empire, was replaced by the Ottoman Empire, a Muslim civilization, advancing as far as the Balkans. It was once argued, most famously by Henri Pirenne, that the religious divide also severely affected trade. Trade did decline, for a number of reasons, falling population and income being important factors; but it did not cease.

2.2 Gains from division of labour: Adam Smith revisited

Before we proceed we need to understand the elementary conditions for economic growth in a pre-industrial economy. Unlike a modern economy it relied on a thin basis of knowledge and capital. Knowledge there was, but it was extracted from experience and trial and error rather than theoretical inquiry. Mankind could observe regularities in nature, for example that animal manure mixed with the soil improved yields per acre in grain cultivation, but there was no profound knowledge about how this effect came about until the development of modern chemistry and agricultural science at the end of the nineteenth century.

What is the basis for growth of income per head in an economy where accumulation of human and physical capital has only a minor role? The straight answer is this: there are gains from specialization, which is division of labour, from learning by doing, and from trade based on regional differences in resource endowments and climate.

Imagine an isolated village with households cultivating land. Being isolated, households would typically produce not only their own food but also their cloth; they would build and maintain houses, fences and stables, and the agricultural tools, for example the ploughs, used in cultivation. Adam Smith (1723–90), the classic economist and author of *An Inquiry into the Nature and Causes of the Wealth of Nations* (1776), made the important observation that subdividing production into separate tasks and letting different producers specialize in each will improve the efficiency of all. The gains stem from perfection gained through repetition or practice ('economies of practice' for short), *and* learning by doing. If one household specializes in clothmaking and another in food processing and a third in building houses, these specialists can supply the entire village with cloth, food and housing respectively. Since producers improve their skills in what and when they specialize, they acquire an advantage in terms of labour productivity. This means that the clothmaking household, the Weaver family, will be better off not processing food or maintaining the house, and the Farmer family will be better off not producing cloth and housing and concentrating on what they are best at doing. The basis for exchange is differences in *opportunity costs** among households once they have started to acquire skills through division of labour and economies of practice. By specializing, the Weaver family has obtained a low opportunity cost in producing cloth, which means that they do not have to give up much food when making more cloth. Had they instead chosen to produce more food it would have been very costly in terms of the cloth they had to give up, which means that food has a high opportunity cost for the Weaver family. The household specializing in food production, the Farmer family, has attained a low opportunity cost in producing food. Households typically exchange the good they produce at a low opportunity cost for the commodity they have a high opportunity cost in producing.

Figure 2.1 illustrates the gains from specialization. Imagine two initially identical households which can produce a combination of food and cloth along the convex curve. The shape of the curve is explained by the gains from specialization. If they produce more of one of the goods they have to produce

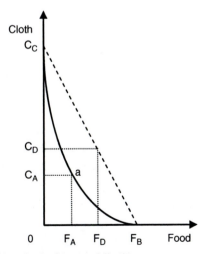

Figure 2.1 Mutual gains from specialization

less of the other. The secret in gains from specialization, that is economies of practice and learning by doing, is that you need to give up less and less of the other good as you specialize in what you are getting better at doing. The opportunity cost of that good will fall. For example, the more cloth the household produces the better it gets at doing so in the sense that each successive unit of cloth can be produced by forsaking less and less food. Initially we can think of the households as self-sufficient, and they will produce and consume a combination of food and cloth, say, at a (as in 'autarky'), which implies $0C_A$ cloth and $0F_A$ food. Exchange between producers will improve the lot of all. Given the gains from specialization, it would be advantageous for the households to specialize fully in only one of the commodities. One household will specialize entirely in cloth – the Weaver family – and another in food – the Farmer family. Weaver now produces $0C_C$ cloth and Farmer produces $0F_B$ food. The households can keep a portion of their produce for their own consumption and exchange the rest. The slope of the straight line indicates the rate at which cloth is exchanged for food so that the entire output is shared between the two households. In this particular example the 'exchange rate' is about 1.5 units of cloth for one unit of food. If Weaver and Farmer can agree on the terms of exchange, that is 1.5 units of cloth for 1 unit of food, Weaver can exchange $C_C C_D$ cloth for $0F_D$ food and can consume what remains of cloth production after exchange, that is $0C_D$. Production and consumption of both goods have increased relative to the situation with no exchange. Farmer has also increased his consumption of both goods. Food consumption for Farmer is $F_D F_B$, that is the production F_B minus $0F_D$, which was offered to Weaver. It is easy to verify that the entire output of food and cloth is consumed.

2.3 Division of labour is constrained by insufficient demand

The nature of the gains from specialization suggests that households or producers typically strive for complete specialization, that is you are either a farmer or a weaver, either a carmaker or a shipbuilder. And indeed, in history specialization has led to an increasingly detailed subdivision of skills and tasks. The technical subdivision of the production process into separate tasks is almost without limits and has proceeded throughout history, but with setbacks. These setbacks are associated with population decline and political disorder, which harmed market exchange. But where we are now is far away from earlier forms of rudimentary specialization. Given markets and money, what constrained division of labour in earlier epochs? The answer is both available knowledge of technological possibilities and economic and social factors. Adam Smith coined the phrase that division of labour was constrained by 'the extent of the market', which in modern terminology must be rephrased: the limit for division of labour is the level of *aggregate demand** in an economy. Take the case of the Weaver family before they reaped the gains from specialization: part-time farmers and part-time cloth workers, as in the example above. If labour efficiency is growing with practice it will be an advantage if the Weavers give up agriculture altogether. However, that is not possible unless the aggregate demand for cloth can support the full-time work effort of the Weavers. Demand for cloth increases if aggregate income is increasing, which will depend on population increase and increase in income per head. If the village is growing by adding new households then demand for cloth will increase. Population increase will help division of labour as long as population growth is also associated with increasing aggregate income.

Aggregate income or demand is defined over a geographical unit and can grow by extending the borders within which social and political order reign. In the era of Roman decline, the effective size of economically functioning regions declined. Roads were poorly maintained, political authority was contested and *taxation** systems became fragile. Transport also became less safe owing to robber bands and foreign raiders and trade was therefore restricted. The restoration of political order would therefore increase the size of the economy and hence the aggregate demand: first, because safety within a given territorial unit increased; second, because the borders of the territory within which trade could take place increased. If market exchange could safely be extended to an entire region and then to several regions, that would extend the scope of the economy and its aggregate income (the sum of the income of all households). If a village smith moved to the nearest town he would not be confined to demand from just one village but could serve many, which would trigger off further specialization: say one smith specializing in products used in agriculture – ploughs – and another in products used in the building trade – hammers and nails and horseshoes. However, as the scope or territory of the economy is extended the preconditions for market exchange are altered. As long as exchange is restricted to known members of a small community the method of settlement need not call for elaborate means of exchange. A peasant household in the isolated village we started with can get a plough from a producer, promising to pay in kind after next harvest. When the economy is extended exchange will take place between strangers, perhaps at monthly and yearly fairs, and promises to pay at a later time, which will be like asking for credit, will be difficult to monitor until specialized financial institutions, banks, emerge.

2.4 Division of labour promotes technological change

Division of labour makes it possible for producers to improve efficiency through repetition, what we have called economies of practice. That means that each individual producer improves her skills over time but possibly at a decreasing rate. That does not necessarily mean that an entire economy will display a pattern of increasing efficiency or output per labourer over time. The age distribution and average age of the labour force of an economy is fairly stable and so is the efficiency level at a given degree of division of labour. If the division of labour is enhanced, the economy will go through a new period of increasing efficiency but will then settle at a stable and higher efficiency level. However, there are other forces which can increase the efficiency in the economy. The gains from practising single tasks a great many times are 'locked into' the individual producer: the perfection acquired from practice cannot be transferred from person to person. However, in production there is also learning by doing, which differs from economies of practice in the following way. In production, experience is enhanced and improved since producers learn from the regularities they observe, and from chance events and trial and error. For example, shipbuilders gradually learnt about modifications in the design and the materials or tools used which improved the capacity and/or seaworthiness or speed of a ship. Although that knowledge was seldom written down, it could be transmitted from one generation of shipbuilders to another. This new and useful knowledge represents an increase in technological knowledge, and will generate an increase in the output and/or an improvement in the quality of the product given the inputs in production. However, the transfer of this type of knowledge is based on the continuity of production and division of labour. If for some reason a fall in demand occurs, as happened after the decline of the Roman Empire, and production is constrained, parts of the accumulated knowledge will soon disappear. This is why history exhibits not only technological progress but regress as well. Furthermore, it is documented that tools used in production improved with division of labour. When the typical artisan repeated a specific operation many times because the volume of output for a particular product increased, it became rational for that artisan to develop and use tools which were particularly well suited for to that specific operation, and as a consequence output per worker was enhanced. This can also be seen as an extension of useful knowledge, an improvement in the level of technology embedded in tools used in production.

The processes just described are illustrated in Figure 2.2.

Output per worker

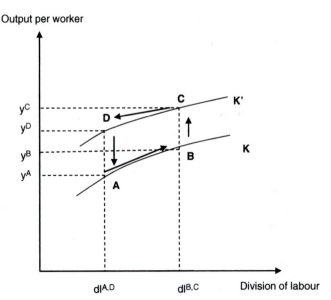

Figure 2.2   Virtuous and vicious processes in technological progress/regress

The efficiency of labour, measured as 'output per workers' on the vertical axis, is positively linked to the degree of division of labour, as measured on the horizontal axis and represented by the K schedule; K represents a given technological knowledge. You can describe a virtuous process as starting at A with output per labourer of y^A given the degree of division of labour $dl^{A,D}$. Imagine an increase in demand, which permits a further subdivision of labour to $dl^{B,C}$, which will enhance output per worker to y^B at B. It is likely that the more sophisticated division of labour will increase learning by doing and the development of specific tools, so there will be a shift in the technological or knowledge level to K', which implies an increase in output per labourer to y^C. Specialized tools represent fixed costs and therefore require a critical minimum level of production to be profitably used; the higher the fixed costs the higher the critical minimum level of production necessary. This is one of the reasons why there is the spectre of technological regress. Imagine that there is a shock to demand due to, say, political disorder making exchange costly and risky, or an exogenous fall in population and production due to epidemics. To start with the knowledge base is preserved but there is a movement along the K' curve from C to D, representing a backward step in division of labour and a fall in output to y^D. However, the high level of specialization at dl^C is essential to preserve knowledge and permit the use of specialized tools. After a generation or so the technological knowledge represented by K' will fade away and the economy shifts back to output y^A. In this very schematic and simplified way, the rise and decline of the Roman Empire can be represented by the counter-clockwise circle just described.

A historical example will illustrate this argument. The falling population and per capita income linked to the decline of the Roman Empire caused a fall in the demand for new housing and buildings. Consequently a technological regress in building technology set in, which was not reversed until the end of the Middle ages. In particular, the hardened cement of exceptional quality that the Romans were able to use was not in use again until the thirteenth century.

The process described in Figure 2.2 explains the relationship between changes in population and market demand, and division of labour and income per head. Income per head increases by a multiple of two or three over a virtuous, that is A to C, process but could also fall back nearly as much in periods of social and political crisis.

Box 2.1　Income levels and division of labour in the pre-industrial era

Income per head can be expressed in constant prices, which need a sense of abstraction, or as multiples of the subsistence income or SI, which is an income sufficient to sustain life with moderate activity. Expressed in constant 1990 prices the subsistence income so defined was 355 so-called $PPP (1990). ('$PPP (1990)' means constant (1990) purchasing power parity adjusted dollars.) This estimate comes close to the often-used measure of absolute poverty, the one-dollar-a-day minimum at which a large but falling number of people in the world still suffer. By this standard A in Figure 2.2 can represent a state with minimum division of labour and an income per head of 1.25 SI or 400$PPP. Estimates of income at C in a sophisticated pre-industrial economy such as the Roman vary between a minimum of 813$PPP and 1742$PPP or between 2.3 and 4.9 SI. An income of around 800$PPP is probably an underestimate because it would imply that the Roman economy, with its known inequality, was in fact at the margin of *maximum* inequality, defined as a state in which a small elite consumes all surplus above the SI, which is left to the remaining population. Modern underdeveloped economies with a similar inequality profile typically have income per capita well above 1000$PPP. An income around 1000$PPP is a fair conjecture which would allow the majority of the population a per capita income of about 2SI given the fact that the richest 3 per cent of the Roman population received a little more than 20 per cent of *national income**. However, there was a decline after the dissolution of the Roman Empire. East Rome, Byzantium, fared much better than the rest and around year 1000 income per head there was estimated at about 80 per cent of Roman income, which can serve as an approximation to income at D. Western Europe fell back to in between the levels of D and A in the figure. English income per head has been estimated at 1.55 SI at about the same time, year 1000. However, in the first half of the second millennium Europe recovered considerably. Italy took the lead and attained the highest European income levels by the fourteenth and fifiteenth centuries but then seems to have stagnated at a fairly high level, about 3 SI. By the end of the sixteenth century, the Netherlands, one of the most successful economies at the time, enjoyed an income per head of almost 4 SI, which was attained about a century later by another sophisticated economy, England.

2.5　After the post-Roman crisis: the economic renaissance of the ninth to fifteenth centuries

Social order, population growth, transport networks, markets and money are prerequisites for growth based on increased division of labour and trade. Social order is necessary for exchange. Transaction costs are lower if roads, rivers and seas are safe. Legal rules and courts that enforce those rules are necessary to make contracts binding and sanctions effective. Population growth is essential in the 'extension of the market' and we will see that this growth induces division of labour and urbanization. Money extends trade from barter to market exchange.

These preconditions were evolving again by the ninth century. We now witness the beginning of a long economic renaissance, centuries before the cultural renaissance of the late medieval period. It is a transition, admittedly slow and hesitant, to a modern economy. However, Europe was lagging behind other civilizations – China, the Byzantine Empire and the Muslim world – in terms of welfare, technology and learning. It took almost the first half of the next millennium for Europe to catch up with the leading civilizations. Can we be sure that given these prerequisites the optimum level of division of labour will be assured? The short answer is no. Despite the proliferation of money, its supply in medieval Europe was often erratic, which muted the volume of trade because the alternative to money as a means of exchange is direct and balanced bilateral barter of goods. Markets were imperfect; information flowed slowly and was distorted on the way. Traders exploited profit opportunities where possible, but they had to have sufficient knowledge to do so. As a rule, we can safely guess that these markets worked below their capacity, as witnessed by seasonal unemployment and missed opportunities. Missing trade is revealed where price differences between geographically separated markets are greater than transport costs, for example. However, there was a gradual improvement of market performance over time, which helped economies to come closer to their capacity constraint.

2.6 Population

The sixth to the eighth centuries witnessed a long period of population decline in Europe and the wider Roman world. Epidemics and invasions from the north took their toll. It is difficult to assess the exact magnitude of the population decline, but in some areas recurrent outbreaks of bubonic plague over 200 years were as grave as the fourteenth-century Black Death when a third or more of the population disappeared. Epidemics of this magnitude were not an isolated phenomenon, in terms of either geographical diffusion or in time. Diseases were endemic for generations before they vanished or their virulence decreased. The political disorder and the redrawing of political maps contributed to the diffusion of epidemics because people on the move carried diseases.

The economic impact was that a smaller population could not support the existing infrastructure of urban settlements and urban amenities such as market places, money exchangers and roads. The 'extent of the market', as Adam Smith called aggregate demand, declined. Land that was taxed was abandoned and sales taxes, which were a source of revenue for local governments, fell when fewer goods were brought to markets. But eventually this long and painful population decline was reversed. From the ninth century Europe experienced an almost unbroken increase in population until the middle of the fourteenth century, when again the cause of the negative population shock was exogenous, the outbreak of the Black Death. In the economic renaissance from 800 CE to 1300 CE population almost tripled, from around 18–20 million to close on 60 million, and then tripled again by the middle of the nineteenth century, to about 180 million. The market size necessary for extended division of labour was now attained.

2.7 The restoration of a monetary system

The decline of the Roman Empire caused the dissolution of a unified minting system; a new attempt to install such a system was made in Charlemagne's reign, in the Carolingian Empire around 800 CE. The advantage of a unified system is of course that it reduces uncertainty regarding the value of the means of payment. A legitimate coin could easily be recognized because it was stamped in a standardized way and its weight of metal, in this case silver, was known and could easily be checked. In Charlemagne's era a silver penny (denarius) was minted, but since the value of a coin was derived from its metal weight older coins and coins from other nations and cities were used alongside the newly minted ones. Over the centuries, mints and denominations multiplied and the metal contents of a penny varied a lot from nation to nation and from city to city. It was not just the major cities that had mints: they were also found in provincial centres. A larger number of coins small and large also developed. The gains from *seignorage** were captured by central or local governments and occasionally by private mints. Settlements of imbalances in international trade were often made in gold coins, while daily transactions used small-denomination silver and copper coins. However, as long as trade was balanced there was no need for transfer of moneys. A merchant in Genoa might have liabilities as well as assets in (say) Antwerp which balanced, and *bills of exchange** were useful mediums of exchange and credit in national as well as international trade. By and large, the increased demand for money resulted in the debasement of coins, that is the precious metal content of a given coin was reduced. Exchange rates between different moneys were derived from the relative weight and purity of the metals used. Money broking became a specialized occupation and can in several ways be seen as the precursor of modern banking. Etymologically the link is obvious, since the word *bank* derives from the Italian word *banca*, the table where a money dealer displayed the monies and scales for weighing, and *bankruptcy* from Italian *banca rotta*, a rotten table. Money dealers often developed into creditors, and it is no coincidence that the terminology stems from Italian because the innovations in financial institutions in the first half of the second millennium emerged primarily in the prosperous and busy Italian city states, which were active in trade and finance and often had their own mints. The monetary system remained based on commodity money, that is on means of payment with an *intrinsic value** deriving from the precious metal content, except for very small denominations which were mere *tokens**, that is money of which the nominal value is greater than its metal value.

2.8 Transport and trade routes

The Roman Empire bequeathed to large parts of post-Roman Europe an extensive road network, which remained the transport infrastructure, although maintenance differed over time and across regions. Bulk long-distance transport of, say, grain and wine was preferably along coasts and rivers in ships and barges. The size and hence carrying capacity of ships increased and navigation techniques improved with the help of new types of sails and rigging which permitted a better use of the wind. Ships in the early part of the second millennium could sail much closer to the wind than at any time earlier in history. Roads were preferred for less bulky and pricey goods using horses and carts and men, often slaves, laden with commodities. Much of the transport over the Alps was performed by un-free men and animals. Where it was feasible the Crown or local lords collected tolls and fees and traders tried hard to evade them, for example by disguising themselves as pilgrims. Major roads were toll free, bridges generally were not, but financing stimulated the dramatic increase in new and improved bridges as trade gained momentum. The passages over the Alps were subject to numerous tolls.

Contact between north-west Europe and the Mediterranean seems to have been unbroken even in the darkest moments of the immediate post-Roman period, but it relied mostly on river transport. Southern and northern Europe were linked commercially by rivers. From the Rhône delta near Marseille on the Mediterranean, commodities continued up the Saône and by overland transport to the Meuse or Rhine, and hence to the western shores of Europe, where they could travel further north along the coasts to Scandinavia and the Baltic. Scandinavia became a link between Western and Eastern Europe. The Swedes operated in an easterly direction and travelled as far as Constantinople and Baghdad. Frisians on the north-western coast of what is now Germany were a link between Scandinavia and England. Although we have no information on the magnitude of trade, it is possible to document trade routes showing that Europe was interlinked and maintained trade relations with the Mediterranean world and the Arab world. Map 2.1 shows documented merchant communications.

Northern Italian cities, which were the important pioneering merchant and financial centres of the first half of the second millennium, already had a prominent role in the trading network as a link between the Mediterranean world and north-west Europe at the close of the first millennium. In Scandinavia Ribe, Haithabau (Hedeby near Schleswig in Germany, in the region bordering on present-day Denmark) and Birka were involved in long-distance trade, and in England York and London traded with the continent. Many of these trading posts remained and grew as urban centres over the coming centuries, while others were replaced by better-located ports.

2.9 Urbanization

The ratio of urban population to total population is an approximate guide to the level of per capita income of an economy. (This insight will be developed further in Chapter 4.) Urban dwellers are active in non-food production, and if the proportion of non-food producers is increasing it means that demand for goods which are not necessities is increasing. The fundamental reason for this phenomenon is the fact that the *income elasticity** of demand for food is lower than for non-food items such as cloth and luxuries: this is known as *Engel's law**. Urban settlements not only excelled in the number of artisan specialists they possessed but also had a large array of service providers, from finance and law to medicine.

The Roman Empire was an urban civilization, essentially based around the Mediterranean, and practically all the major cities existing today in the Roman part of Europe were major cities during the Roman Empire as well. That is true of Milan, Turin, Marseille, Lyon, Paris, Cologne and London, to mention only a few. Some cities were even large by modern standards, at over half a million inhabitants, for example Rome and Constantinople. In some parts of the Empire urbanization ratios were as high as 25 per cent. However,

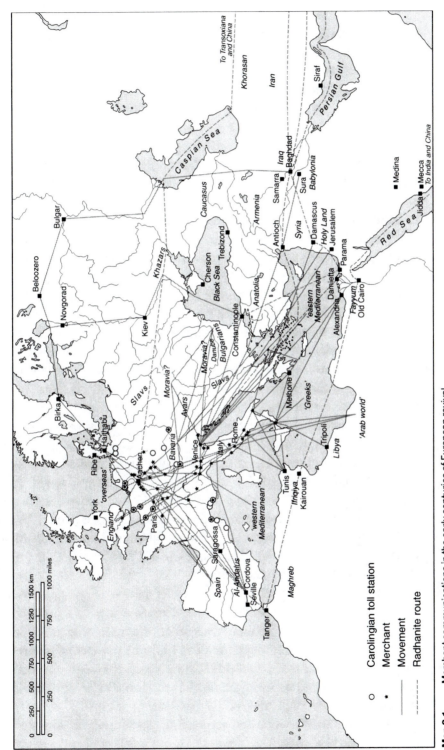

Map 2.1   Merchant communications in the early centuries of European revival

Source: M. McCormick, *The Origins of the European Economy*, Cambridge University Press 2002.

when the Empire was breaking apart and severe shocks to population set in in the fifth century, a period of de-urbanization commenced. Rome it-self declined to about half its former size. The quality of housing declined, large houses were subdivided into smaller units reflecting falling household income, monuments and public areas were not maintained and commercial activity fell back. A period of de-specialization set in, meaning that the vast array of skills and occupations found in cities was no longer available. Technologies were forgotten. We see here the decline described in Figure 2.2 from C to D and finally A. A decline in the variety and quality of goods is well attested by archaeological excavations. The learning-by-doing process we discussed above was reversed: varieties of pottery which used to be available even to humble consumers were now only available in smaller quantities, a sign that they were becoming luxuries. Artisan production did not disappear entirely, but retreated to rural areas and was performed by part-time artisans rather than full-time specialists. Signs of recovery in population and urbanization appear in the eighth century and to a large extent the regenerated cities were built on or near the sites of old Roman cities, or within the walls erected around cities in the turbulent years of the late Empire. In this new era of city growth the need for protection against local robber bands and foreign raiders, be they Vikings or Arabs, made fortification essential. In the larger cities there had been commercial and administrative continuity, but that was not always the case for the smaller provincial cities. In many cases they had been practically abandoned or were functioning only at a low level of economic activity. Cities which got new life often combined commercial functions, such as a mint and a market space for weekly or daily use, and ecclesiastical functions, and also served a hinterland of rural producers who exchanged food for processed goods such as pottery, metal utensils, textiles, salt and spices. However, as cities grew the number of specialized occupations also grew, from a handful in the early phase of urbanization to several hundreds in the thirteenth and fourteenth centuries in large cities like Paris and London. By 1700 London alone supported about 700 occupations.

It is noteworthy that small cities had a smaller number of occupations which is what we would expect from the fact that division of labour is limited by the extent of the market. Furthermore division of labour seems to have declined somewhat after the Black Death, to judge from the number of occupations reported in London in 1300 and 1422. The considerable large difference between Paris and London before the Black Death can also be attributed to the fact that Paris was a much larger city at that date.

New cities were also founded, responding to the need for long-distance trade: so-called *emporia*. These were often quite small, say between 1000 and

Table 2.1   Increasing division of labour as measured by number of occupations

	c. 500 BC	1148	1300	1400	1422	1455	1500	c. 1700
Denmark					72			
UK								
London			175		111			721
Winchester		62	70	57			52	
Norwich			68					
Gloucester						54		
France								
Paris			300					
Middle East	40							

Sources: Old Testament (The Bible); N. Hybel and B. Poulsen, *The Danish Resources c. 1000–1550: Growth and Recession* (Leyden: Brill 2007), pp. 264–65; D. Keene, 'Continuity and development in urban trades: problems of concepts and the evidence', in P. J. Corfield and D. Keene (eds.), *Work in Towns 850–1850* (Leicester University Press, 1990); R. Campbell, *The London Tradesman* (1747; reprint, Newton Abbot: David & Charles Ltd, 1969); ISCO-08: www.ilo.org/public/english/bureau/stat/isco/index.htm
To get a rough idea of division of labour in Antiquity I have made an estimate of the number of occupations mentioned in the Old Testament.

4000 inhabitants, and were mainly or wholly economic centres with fewer occupations. Along the western European coastline, these emporia were to be found as far north as Ribe in Denmark. However, urbanization ratios were still quite low – lower than in the Roman period. In Western Europe, urbanization ratios on the eve of the tenth century were below 5 per cent. However, in the tenth century a long period of intense urbanization set in, leading to urbanization ratios close to 25 per cent by the end of the medieval period in the most advanced areas of Europe. In course of that process manors and estates became less self-sufficient, artisans moved from rural areas to urban centres. There are exceptional regions, such as the northern provinces of the Netherlands, which by c. 1500 already had a modern occupational structure, revealed by a very high urbanization ratio as shown in Figure 2.3.

The Roman heartland, Italy, was the only part of Europe to have a high urbanization rate in Antiquity, and in the first half of the second millennium its cities were advanced by European standards in terms of occupational diversity and income levels. However, Italy lost momentum and as Figure 2.3 indicates, the new centres of urban production and growth were located in the 'Low Countries', an area stretching from northern France to the Netherlands. However, that area also did not maintain its urban surge and was surpassed by Britain in the late eighteenth century. In an international perspective, Europe is

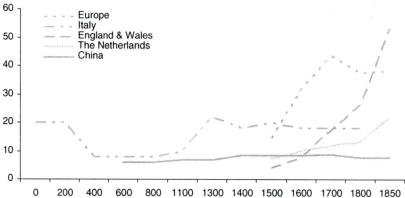

Figure 2.3   Urbanization in Europe and China: urban population as a percentage of total population. Sources and comments: Jan de Vries, *European Urbanization 1500–1800* (London: Methuen, 1984); Paolo Malanima, 'Urbanization and the Italian economy during the last millennium', *European Review of Economic History* 22(1) (2005) pp. 91–133; S. N. Broadberry and B. Gupta, 'The early modern great divergence: wages, prices and economic development in Europe and Asia, 1500–1800', *Economic History Review* 59(1) (2006), pp. 2–31. Urban population is estimated as the number of people living in cities with more than 5,000 inhabitants. Data referring to urban population estimated as number of people in cities with more than 10,000 inhabitants have been adjusted by a factor of 1.3.

more urbanized than the most sophisticated non-European economy, China. These trends in urbanization, approximate as they are, also reveal the ranking of nations in terms of income.

2.10 Production and technology

The long swings in production discussed so far have been deduced from archaeological evidence, degrees of urbanization and population trends as revealed by the extension of settlements and, in more recent centuries, written documentation. Is there supporting evidence of a fall in output with the decline of the Roman Empire and a subsequent upturn by the ninth century? One revealing piece of evidence is the production of metals as measured by lead emissions layered in the Greenland ice cap. Lead was alloyed with other metals, such as silver, copper and iron, and can therefore be used as an approximation of metal production and more generally as a guide to productive activity. Figure 2.4 brings us from Greece in Antiquity to the eighteenth century CE; note that the vertical axis has an exponential scale. The first peak in metal production is at the zenith of the Roman Empire in the first century CE. The gradual decline of the Roman Empire is well indicated, as is the beginning of the revival of the European economy by the end of the first millennium. The second peak is linked

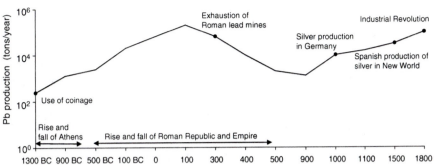

Figure 2.4   An approximation of metal production in the northern hemisphere as revealed by lead emissions found in the Greenland ice cap. The figure is adapted from data in S. Hong et al., 'Greenland ice evidence of hemisphere lead pollution two millennia ago by Greek and Roman civilization', *Science* 265 (1994), pp. 1841–3, and S. Hong et al., 'History of ancient copper smelting pollution during Roman and medieval times recorded in Greenland ice', *Science* 272 (1996), pp. 264–9

to the Industrial Revolution. The figure is only an approximate or rough indicator, but its general outline is supported by other evidence, although it cannot be used to draw precise conclusions about rates of growth, for example.

What sort of technological knowledge permitted this expansion by the end of the first millennium? Initially it was based on technology known already in the Roman period, then forgotten or neglected and eventually rediscovered or transmitted from the Muslim world when the economic recovery started. We need to recognize that the advancement of technological knowhow was piecemeal but nonetheless impressive in its effects. A number of inventions were transferred from Asia and the Arab civilizations, for example paper. Animals were essential as a source of traction power in transport as well as in ploughing. Efficiency in the use of animals improved substantially due to changes in the design of harness and the use of the iron horseshoe. The harness shifted the drag from the throat collar, inherited from Antiquity, to the shoulders of the animal. The original harness tended to hurt and compress the windpipe and is estimated to have reduced the traction power derived from the animal by up to 80 percent compared to the shoulder collar. The design of the plough improved partly because of the availability of iron: it was made to cut deeper and turn the soil, creating a deep furrow since the plough, sometimes equipped with wheels, now had a mould-board. Nutrients deep in the soil were therefore released.

As the pressure on available land increased again in the twelfth and thirteenth centuries land was used more efficiently, for example the fallow periods were reduced. A three-period rotation scheme was introduced whereby a third of the land was left fallow and the other two thirds were used for winter and spring crops. The fallow land was suitable for grazing animals and animal dung helped to renew its fertility. Peasants learned how to restore the fertility of land. For example, a rotation of crops including pulses, used as fodder, actually restored nitrogen to the soil, which is essential for plants to grow. This was learning-by-doing knowledge, which could be carried over from one generation to another. Peasants and their lords became better at selecting the particular varieties of a plant that suited the typical soil and climate of an area. Trial and error is essential in this process of enhancing knowledge.

A particularly good example, revealing the importance of the general principles of technological progress and reversal laid out above, is the proliferation of the water mill. It was first used to grind grain into flour. Although known before the revival of the European economy it did not become widely used in Europe until then. Its fast diffusion from the ninth century onward was due to the increase in the scale of the economy and the application of the technology to a large number of production processes outside flour production. The alternative to the water mill was the hand mill, which was less efficient but dominated as long as the volumes of grain to be ground were small, as in low population density areas. A water mill was a considerable investment, not only in the mill itself but also in building dams to store water and diverting rivers to regulate the flow of water. The high fixed costs required a critical minimum scale of operation to make the mill profitable. In the Dark Ages the opportunity to exploit the *economies of scale** offered by a water mill was simply not present because of scattered and low population density, and the technology was neglected. The existence of high fixed costs and economies of scale gave the owners of the mills, often landlords, *market power**, as witnessed by complaints from peasants of the high tolls they had to pay when using them. In China the water mill was used in a wide variety of productive activities, for example operating bellows to increase the heat necessary for metal processing. The proliferation of these mills in activities other than grain milling came later in Europe. But from the tenth century onwards, and particularly in the twelfth and thirteenth centuries, mills were operating in an increasing number of production processes. In textiles the mill was used in fulling, which is the process of cleansing and thickening cloth by beating and washing, and also in tanning hides. In wood processing mills drove mechanical saws, and in iron production mills drove hammers to stamp out impurities in the de-carbonization process to produce wrought iron. By converting the vertical motion of the water wheel, often with a diameter of 2–4 metres, to the upward and downward movement of a hammer, ore could be hammered into small pieces; and to obtain the heat required to melt the ore in furnaces, mechanical bellows driven by water power were used. Most of these innovations were labour saving, and there were cases of labour unrest caused by the fear of 'technological unemployment'. The development of the wind mill offers a good example of what small innovations can do to increase efficiency or capacity. To operate a wind mill you needed to turn the entire body of the mill until its sails were against the direction of the wind. As a consequence the size of the mills was constrained. By attaching the sails to the upper part of the body of the mill, a movable top, you simply had to turn the top in the right direction. Thereby the size of the wind mill was increased and so was the power generated.

This example illustrates that the technological basis for the pre-industrial period was a process of gradual learning. Similar examples can be mentioned from almost every type of activity. In the next chapter we will demonstrate a process of land-augmenting technological change. There was advancement in knowledge about how to restore the fertility of depleted soil which enabled a more intensive use of land by reducing the fallow periods. Peasants selected superior varieties of plants from spontaneous natural mutations and to some extent from deliberate trial-and-error breeding of better varieties of plants and cattle. Inter-regional trade made specialization possible so that crops and plants were selected to maximize yields in different environments.

Paper manufacturing is of particular interest because it literally ended the 'Dark Ages', if we interpret the term as indicating an era without much written documentation. Papyrus and parchment were of course used even in the 'Dark Ages', but the former had to be imported from Egypt and went out of use because paper became cheaper. The increased supply and improved quality of paper in the first centuries of the second millennium enhanced the documentation of prices, wages and rents, sales and purchases in the accounts of estates, city authorities, monasteries and the state. Written documentation of trade and payments between bankers and merchants also become more frequent from the eleventh and twelfth centuries. Although the skill of papermaking was imported from the Middle East the process was mechanized in Europe, where water mills were used to produce pulp, reducing the price of paper and making it more widely used. Large-scale paper production preceded the new printing technology using movable type by about two centuries. Design of and experiments with movable type occurred in several cities in the middle of the fifteenth century, which may explain why printing shops were set up in all major European cities over a few decades after the publication of Gutenberg's Bible in 1445. Paper and printing are two of the more precious gifts from the late medieval world to the modern era. The wind mill finally got a well-deserved renaissance in the closing decades of the twentieth century, although that revival needed the additional understanding gained in the nineteenth century of how a rotary movement can generate electricity.

Summary

This chapter has singled out the most essential mechanisms behind economic decline and its reversal, which is the dramatic historical process Europe went through in the Middle Ages. Market size, as measured by aggregate demand, mattered and markets needed a social order that protected traders, ensured that contracts were honoured, and provided the means of payment. There was technological progress, slow but persistent, and there was institutional development in finance that facilitated trade over long distances. There was also an increasing consumption of goods produced outside the agrarian sector, witnessing to the fact that economies were leaving behind the bare subsistence economy of the past.

Suggestions for further reading

There is an ever-growing literature on the recovery of the European economy after the decline of the Roman Empire. The topic engaged the leading economic historians of the past. M. McCormick, *The Origins of the European Economy: Communication and Commerce A.D. 300–900* (Cambridge University Press, 2001) is an impressive new study using archaeological and numismatic evidence and written documents to give a nuanced view of the recovery of the European economy, focussing on trade. It also builds on a long tradition of research, which is generously referred to, and the book is therefore a good guide to the relevant literature. Shorter monographs include R. Hodges, *Dark Age Economics: The Origins of Towns and Trade, 600–1000* (London: Duckworth, 1989). On urban revival see A. Verhulst, *The Rise of Cities in North-West Europe* (Cambridge University Press, 1999).

A modern classic is C. Cipolla, *Before the Industrial Revolution: European Society and Economy 1000–1700* (London, Routledge, 1977 or later editions).

Angus Maddison has contributed to the comparative work on income in a number of books. His most recent contributions include *The World Economy: A Millennial Perspective* (Paris: OECD Development Centre Studies 2001), and *Contours of the World Economy: The Pace and Patterns of Change, 1–2030 AD* (Oxford University Press, 2007). On the Roman era income see also Raymond W. Goldsmith, 'An estimate of the size and structure of the national product of the early Roman Empire', *Review of Income and Wealth* 30(3) (1984), pp. 263–88.

B. Milanovic has studied Byzantine and Roman income in 'An estimate of average income and inequality in Byzantium around year 1000', *Review of Income and Wealth*, 52(3), 2007, pp. 449–70. In a working paper with the same title published by the World Bank Milanovic gives a full range of estimates (Table 5a) including what he calls an implausibly high estimate of Roman per capita income at 2500$PPP.

For a short introduction and interpretation of the history of technology with relevant references to the specialist literature see Joel Mokyr, *The Lever of Riches: Technological Creativity and Economic Progress* (New York: Oxford University Press, 1990).

A rare example of a theoretical model discussing technological regress is S. Aiyar, C.-J. Dalgaard and O. Moav, 'Technological progress and regress in pre-industrial times', *Journal of Economic Growth* 13 (2008), pp. 124–44. Technological regress as well as the conditions that make an economy operate below its potential are analysed in G. Grantham, 'Contra-Ricardo: on the macroeconomics of pre-industrial economics', *European Review of Economic History* 3(2) (1999), pp. 199–232.

3 Population, economic growth and resource constraints

3.1 Historical trends in population growth

Economics is sometimes called the dismal science because many of its pioneers expressed pessimism about the possibility of sustained economic growth in a world of limited resources. We meet this view today in the worries about shortages of raw materials, such as oil, eventually putting an end to economic growth. Late nineteenth-century economists worried about coal shortages, but the concern today is rather that coal generates too much CO_2, which might in the long run harm growth. The first economist to develop a coherent theory of limited resources as a binding constraint for sustained long-term economic growth was Thomas Malthus (1766–1834), whose *An Essay on the Principle of Population* was first published in 1798. The date of publication is not without interest, since it falls within the first decades of the Industrial Revolution in Britain, which combined unprecedented population growth with increasing (or at least constant) income per head. Malthus argued that given limited land the supply of food would eventually constrain income and population growth. We will soon return to a detailed exposition of the Malthusian view, but we will first review the evidence on long-term population growth in Europe. Reasonably precise population estimates are available only from the sixteenth century onward; before that, populations are estimated from projections based on scarce data and conjectures of the carrying capacity of a given area using the prevailing technology.

Cultures based on hunter-gatherer technology, which preceded the breakthrough of agriculture and sedentary civilization in the Middle East some 12,000 years ago, are very demanding in terms of land, and this limited world population to an estimated 6–8 million. A hunter-gatherer culture satisfies its food requirements from nature without actually controlling it: consequently an equilibrium between the stock of animals and the stock of men will evolve. If mankind over-exploits the animal stock the reproduction of both will be disturbed. As the animal stock declines the size of the human population will also fall. Technological progress in a hunter-gatherer culture (better arrowheads, say) will therefore not spill over permanently into higher food consumption or a larger population but only generate more leisure. The high proportion of leisure in surviving hunter and gatherer cultures has sometimes been romanticized by anthropologists, but is really imposed by the peculiar character of hunter-gatherer technology. The effect of technological progress on agricultural and on industrial societies is fundamentally different; it not only saves labour time but other resources as well. The threat that modern economies pose to non-renewable resources is due to the high level of income and consumption.

The *Neolithic revolution**, that is the transition from hunter-gatherer cultures to agriculture, which started about 12,000 years ago, introduced a growing element of control of nature and gradually reduced the land required to feed one man. For example, cattle breeding in agricultural societies involves the possibility of increasing the size of the herd. As a consequence agricultural civilizations were accompanied by a permanent growth in world population and the possibility of sustained increases in income levels depending on the rate of technological progress. From an estimated 6–8 million at the dawn of the Neolithic revolution, world population increased to some 250 million by the beginning of the first millennium, one billion when Malthus published his *Essay on Population* and six billion in 2000 CE.

Figure 3.1 illustrates the population of Europe over the last 2400 years. The first 1000 years in the figure smoothes the actual variations because the curves are based on estimates given in intervals of 100 to 200 years. In between the estimation points political crises, epidemics, harvest failures and wars had severe effects on population. However, the figure catches the major characteristics of pre-industrial European population: as slow growth until the middle of the eighteenth century, interrupted by two major setbacks, and with a significant increase in population after 1750. The first major setback in population growth is associated with the decline and crisis of the Roman Empire, which was triggered off by internal political conflicts, invasions, massive migration flows and recurrent epidemics. Between 200 and 600 CE Europe's population may have been reduced by half until it started to grow again. The next setback is again linked to an exogenous shock, the Black Death in 1347, a highly contagious plague. This plague was not a single event but ravaged Europe and Asia for about 100 years, reducing the population in Europe by at least a third. Europe did not regain its pre-plague population until the middle of the sixteenth century. China has more reliable population data for the pre-industrial period, but the general

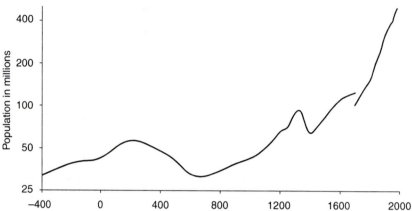

Figure 3.1 European population 400 BCE to 2000 CE. Millions. Sources: –400–1700: J.N. Biraben, 'Essai sur l'évolution du nombre des hommes', *Population* 34(1) (1979), pp. 13–25;1700–2000: Netherlands Environmental Assessment Agency, http://www.mnp.nl/hyde/Images/pop_summary_tcm63–22929. xls. The discontinuity in the curve is caused by the change of source.

pattern of positive growth interrupted by exogenous events such as invasions and war, epidemics and political disintegration, is supported by the data. It is possible that the increase in the rate of population growth started somewhat earlier than in Europe.

Apart from the large exogenous shocks to population, there were also short-term shocks, driven ultimately by variations in harvest outcomes, which in turn were largely influenced by unforeseen climatic shocks or plant diseases. A poor harvest was often associated with epidemics because hard times triggered off migration, which carried diseases. However, the excess deaths in a crisis, mainly children and the elderly, were followed by excess births and lower mortality after the crisis so that population reverted to its long-run rate of growth.

Until the eighteenth century population growth was slow, but then a 'demographic transition' set in, leading first to a sharp rise in population growth from the late eighteenth and in the nineteenth century and then to a slow down in the twentieth century. Since its medieval peak, the European population has increased by a factor of five. If we concentrate on the 200 years since the publication of Malthus' influential book, the fears that he expressed seem to be utterly misplaced. World population has increased by a factor of six, world food production by a factor of ten, and still not all land fit for agriculture is currently being used. According to the Italian economic historian Giovanni Federico, between 80 and 90 per cent of all cultivable land is now used.

However, that Malthus was wrong about his own period and the future need not imply that he was wrong about the past. In fact his analysis is routinely invoked by economic historians as a meaningful model explaining pre-industrial economic history, so we need to take a closer look at the Malthusian view.

3.2 The Malthusian theory of population growth and stagnation

One reason for the continuous appeal of Malthus' view is its seemingly irresistible logic and simplicity. However, as we will see, logic does not necessarily imply historical relevance.

The Malthusian view can be neatly summarized as follows: population growth correlates positively with income per head, but population growth will ultimately reduce income and population growth will then come to a halt. The prospects for sustained growth are dim. The irresistible logic referred to above is that there is no escaping from the fact that there are physical limits to the amount of cultivable land. As population increases the land available for agriculture per head will ultimately fall, that is, diminishing returns set in, which will lead to falling income and ultimately to a subsistence income which will be associated with stagnating population. The argument assumes implicitly that there is no technological progress in agriculture, that is, there is no increase in the efficiency of the use of land. But the big question remains unanswered: when exactly was this land constraint binding? It certainly was not a real constraint after the demise of the Roman Empire or after the Black Death, when vast areas of cultivable land were deserted. Was it at the end of the eighteenth century, when population growth increased after four centuries of slow growth? If so, we should be able to document falling income per head driven by population growth. We will return to that crucial test in Section 3.3. Malthusians are right in pointing out, however, that it is not only the availability of land that matters but also the quality. If so, the argument can be restated to say that at some point, the quality of marginal land will deteriorate, causing diminishing returns. But the question remains, when does marginal land become of inferior quality?

The issue of a binding land constraint is elusive because technological progress in agriculture increases yields from land per unit of time (years, say) in that yields per harvest increase as well as the number of harvests per year.

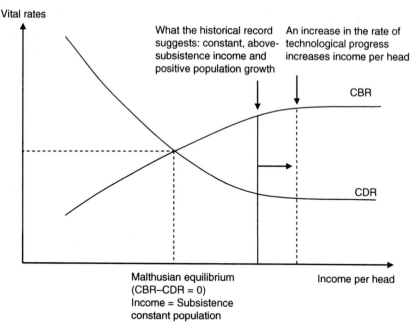

Vital rates

What the historical record   An increase in the rate of
suggests: constant, above- technological progress
subsistence income and   increases income per head
positive population growth

CBR

CDR

Malthusian equilibrium   Income per head
(CBR–CDR = 0)
Income = Subsistence
constant population

Figure 3.2   Malthus graphically speaking. If income per head is above subsistence, that is, to the right of the Malthusian equilibrium, population growth will be positive, CBR (birth rates) will be larger than CDR (death rates) but due to diminishing returns from labour income will fall and the economy will finally settle in the Malthusian equilibrium with constant population and zero population growth.

Box 3.1 Some basic demographic concepts

So-called vital rates are crude birth rates (CBR) and crude death rates (CDR) and they are normally measured per thousand and per year. CBR is referred to in the text as fertility and CDR as mortality. Population growth per thousand is equal to CBR-CDR.

   Positive check: Falling income will worsen human nutritional status and increase mortality (CDR), and so permanently reduce population to its equilibrium level (or equilibrium growth rate).

   Preventive checks are related to voluntary restraints on fertility. When income falls young people marry later and this reduces the number of pregnancies per marriage.

   Total fertility is the expected live births per woman.

Let us now see what Figure 3.2 is telling us. Initially income per head is above subsistence, that is, to the right of the Malthusian equilibrium, because land is in abundant supply. This implies that population growth is positive, that is, CBR (the birth rate) is greater than CDR (the death rate). However, as population increases the land-to-labour ratio will fall or the quality of marginal land will fall. That will lead to diminishing returns from labour, and income and population growth (CBR-CDR) will fall. It is still positive, but in the long run the economy will finally settle in the Malthusian equilibrium with constant population and zero population growth. However, this reasoning ignores the possibility of technological progress. If there is a permanent positive rate of technological progress, it will balance or counteract the forces of diminishing returns. The economy will settle at a point, described in the figure as 'What the historical record suggests', where income is above subsistence and population growth positive. If the rate of technological progress increases but the rate of diminishing returns remains constant, then both income and population will increase and the 'What the historical record suggests' point will shift to the right, further away from the Malthusian equilibrium.

In the Malthusian world view CBR is at its maximum when income is high, because households need not worry about economic constraints. *Preventive checks**, which imply a deliberate reduction in fertility, will set in as income falls, however. In modern parlance, we would say that Malthus assumed fertility to be very income elastic. Demographic research suggests that falling income reduces the proportion of a generation that gets married and/or delays the age of marriage and makes women have children later, thereby reducing total fertility. CDR increases with falling income because populations become more vulnerable to poverty related diseases and premature deaths since the nutritional standard deteriorates with falling income: the so-called *positive checks**.

3.3 Is the Malthusian theory testable?

Long-lived theories paradoxically evade proper testing. Is that also the case with the Malthusian theory? The British economist Mark Blaug famously dismissed Malthus' theory as 'a perfect example of a tautology masquerading as a theory'. This harsh judgment is based on the view that Malthus did not specify a precise outcome that could be refuted or corroborated. The Italian demographer Massimo Livi-Bacci, however, proposes a long-term Malthusian population trajectory along the lines explored in Figure 3.2. Population will grow fast initially, then at a falling rate when land scarcity sets in until zero population growth rate is reached, which is the Malthusian equilibrium described in Figure 3.2. If we take Livi-Bacci at his word, we can safely dismiss the Malthusian theory as a prediction of long-term population growth. Figure 3.1 indicates a long-term positive trend in population interrupted by large exogenous shocks. However, long-term population growth can be included in a Malthusian model if technological progress is taken into account. Mark Blaug was right insofar as there is ambiguity in Malthusian predictions depending on the choice of assumptions. If there is a technological shock which increases income per head above subsistence, population growth will become positive

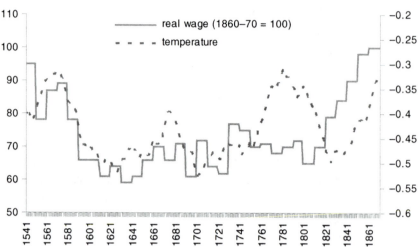

Figure 3.3   Real farm wages in England and fluctuations in northern hemisphere temperature, 1560–1880
Sources: Real day wage rate for farm workers from G. Clark, 'The long march of History', *The Economic History Review*, 60 (2007), p. 100. *Real wage** is indexed to 1860–9 = 100. Temperature is the deviations in degrees Celsius, measured on the right-hand side of the graph, from average temperature between 1960 and 1980. The temperature data is a 25 period moving average. Higher temperatures are indicated by a rise in the curve and vice versa. From Keith R. Briffa, 'Annual climate variability in the Holocene: interpreting the message of ancient trees', *Quaternary Science Reviews* 19, Issues 1–5 (1 January 2000), pp. 87–105; Jan Esper, Edward R. Cook and Fritz H. Schweingruber, 'Low-Frequency signals in long tree-ring chronologies for reconstructing past temperature variability', *Science* 295 (March 2002), pp. 2250–3.

again. Because of diminishing returns, the economy will be forced back to subsistence level in due course. In the Malthusian world, an income increase can only be transitory and the only permanent effect of technological change will be to increase the level of the population.

The century-long decline in real wages in England from a high level at the beginning of the sixteenth century as population increased again after the mortality shocks of the Black Death, has been invoked as a proof of the idea that population growth will inevitably bring down wages. However, the evidence is open to a different interpretation. Climate change may be part of the story, as is suggested in Figure 3.3.

Formal testing of the response of grain output to temperature change has confirmed that in pre-industrial societies a decrease in mean temperature did indeed have a negative impact on output. That impact might spill over into effects on rural wages. What is remarkable in Figure 3.3 is the close association between the fall in mean temperature that set in at the end of the sixteenth century and the fall in real wages. Wages then stabilized, as did temperature. A century-long rise in wages set in by the end of the seventeenth century, which was initially accompanied by a rise in temperature.

It cannot be ruled out that 'global chilling' was what caused the decline in wages, but there is no consensus among economic historians that climate really mattered much in this period.

In the past, empirical tests of the Malthusian theory were limited by the absence of long-term data on income or real wages as well as death, birth and marriage rates. The publication of E. A. Wrigley and R. Schofield's ground-breaking work on England's population history (see Suggestions for Further Reading at the end of the chapter) changed that, and a number of increasingly sophisticated tests have since been published, investigating whether birth and death rates react in the expected way to changes in real wages, that is, whether there is a positive relationship between real wages and population growth and whether – in the long run – population growth tends to depress real wages. The general conclusion from these studies is that the Malthusian model performs poorly. The most important result is that population growth does not – in the long run – depress real wages. This is the crucial criticism because it suggests that a positive shock to technology and wages can have permanent effects not only on population but on real wages as well.

There are three major problems in the Malthusian model which explains its poor predictive power: (i) it ignores or underestimates technological progress, or at best technological progress is seen as isolated shocks rather than a perma-nent characteristic; (ii) it characterizes the economy as closed, that is it neglects the efficiency gains from regional and international specialization and trade; (iii) it lacks a theory of fertility strategy for households based on optimizing forward-looking behaviour, which should include a concern for not only the quantity but also the quality of children.

3.4 The secrets of agricultural progress

The focus on land as a limiting resource ignores the fact that the quantity of cultivable land – say a hectare – is an extremely poor predictor of the yield of that land in the long run. In the history of agriculture, the crop ratio, which is the number of crops per year and per unit of land, has increased from a ratio of 0.05 in primitive land use where land was left fallow for generations after a few harvests to close to one crop per year in Europe (but higher in horticul-ture) and two or more in some regions outside Europe when it comes to cereals such as rice. The crop ratio has, in other words, increased by a factor of forty in the very long run. Furthermore, the yield per unit of land has also increased meaning that the combined yield per unit of land multiplied by crop per year has increased even more over the long history of agriculture. This is what technological progress does to agriculture. Technological progress is based on the accumulation of useful knowledge, which in pre-industrial economies was slow, often by chance but sometimes by deliberate experimentation or trial and error. However, needless to say, the knowledge gained from learning by doing has no scientific basis. Pre-industrial producers could see that manure increased yields but did not know that the essential elements involved were nitrogen, potassium and phosphorus. Farmers also noted that some types of seed-corn were better than others but they had no knowledge of genetics.

In agriculture, experience was linked to the management of soil fertility, mainly the maintenance and release of nitrogen. The nitrogen in the air cannot be taken up by plants directly. The stock of nitrogen in the soil is only slowly released by mineralization, which makes nitrogen water-soluble in the form of ammonium and nitrates. You need to add directly accessible nitrogen as well by means of manure. The nitrogen in grain fed to animals or men will be recycled as manure, and the residues of harvested crops, for example the roots, will have the effect of a fertilizer when they are decomposed. Soil fertility is also dependent on the choice and rotation of crops and the extent of fallow, which is a period where the land is not used for tillage but for stock rearing, or left to rest. Some crops, for example clover, are better than others at fixing nitrogen and if included in a crop rotation enable better use of land and an increase in yields. It is not the plant itself that fixes the nitrogen but bacteria which live in symbiosis with the plant, or its roots to be precise. Other crops, such as beans and peas, had a long-term effect on grain yields because they increased the stock of nitrogen in the soil. Control of soil humidity and ploughing technology are both essential for the release of nitrogen. Nitrogen was left in roots and other plant residues and needed to be decomposed to be of any use. Too much rain may wash away nitrogen in the form of water-soluble nitrates. Yields will also depend on the control of competing plants – weeds – and the administration of animal and human manure, and more recently, chemical fertilizers. Increases in nitrogen will increase yields over a fairly large input range and the response in terms of yields is very high. A supply of manure requires a balance between tillage and animal husbandry, which can be difficult to maintain if land is scarce. However, in densely populated areas human manure ('night soil') from neighbouring cities was used as a substitute for animal manure. The stock of nitrogen in the soil is released only slowly and will be depleted in the long run if land is not properly fertilized or was not sometimes left fallow.

The characteristics of soil differ, just as plants have different needs, when it comes to location and climate. The complementarities of soil, climate and plants cannot be exploited without trade, and trade contributes to better land use, which has a positive effect on yields. By and large densely populated regions in pre-industrial Europe, such as the Low Countries, south-east England and the Paris basin, were characterized by high agricultural productivity, as will be further explored in Chapter 4. At first sight, this seems to be a paradoxical finding. However, proximity to urban centres gave agriculture in densely populated regions a number of productivity-enhancing possibilities. The shortfall in nitrogen from land-intensive stock rearing could be made good by night soil from the cities. New knowledge is also diffused more swiftly in densely populated areas. The varied demands from cities enabled peasants to diversify into poultry, horticulture and non-food crops for example flax and plants used for dyeing. Furthermore a diversified crop 'portfolio' was an insurance against natural accidents, since harvest failures were often specific to a single crop or plant at a given point in time. Again, trade helps in putting scarce land into best use, and the densely populated regions were usually dependent on cereal imports from other regions and nations. Land and capital markets were much more developed in the proximity of urban centres, which contributed to getting land into its most profitable use compared to remote sparsely populated areas with little access to consumer markets and little scope for diversification of crops.

If we return, for a moment, to Figure 3.2 we can spell out the implication of technological progress and more efficient land use facilitated by trade. Malthusians have tended to focus on limited land supply, neglecting the fact that output per unit of land is dependent on crop ratios and yields which change, albeit slowly, over time. This being the case, we can easily imagine the economy settling in an equilibrium to the right of the Malthusian equilibrium. In that equilibrium, real wages are constant and above subsistence, population growth is positive and although the physical quantity of land per farmer continues to decrease the output per farmer is constant. Since technological progress increases the crop ratio we can say that it is 'land augmenting', in the sense that the 'effective' land is increasing and at the same time the efficiency of land is increasing as witnessed by increasing yields.

Box 3.2 An example of increasing productivity: more grain from less land

Initially each farmer has 5 units of land, a crop ratio (harvest per year) of 0.3 and a yield of 500 kg of grain per unit of land, which means that the yearly output is $5 \times 0.3 \times 500 =$ a yearly output of 750 kg.

After a period of population increase and technological progress affecting the crop ratio and the yields we have the following configuration:

Each farmer has now just 3 units of land, a crop ratio of 0.5 and a yield of 650 kg, which generates an output of 975 kg.

In the particular case described in the box it is assumed that the decline in the amount of land per peasant household caused by population growth is more than compensated for by the combined effect of increased crop ratios and yield increase, leading to a greater real output per head. What happens to output and real income in the long run will depend on the rate of change of population relative to the rate of change in technological progress. If the latter is strong, income per head might in fact increase, that is output may increase faster than population. The long historical trend of increasing population with constant, and in some areas and periods increasing, income is best explained in the framework discussed here in which pressure on the land is relieved by slow progress in yields and crop ratios.

3.5 Understanding fertility strategies

Malthus, like his contemporaries, did not base fertility strategy on the optimizing behaviour of the household, though modern economists and economic historians do. Natural instincts leading to excessive procreation dominated his thinking even if he also admitted the possibility of moral restraints. It is commonly accepted that no known society has fertility rates at the level of the biological maximum. Also, despite the absence of modern fertility control methods like the pill or condoms there were means of controlling total fertility, even though these methods were less efficient. One fairly efficient one was postponement of marriage, since births out of wedlock were rare – which in itself is quite remarkable, and suggests that sexuality was controlled by norms and cultural habits. The low rate of illegitimacy is in itself a sign that men and women were able to control their sexual desires. Coitus interruptus, long periods of breast-feeding and/or taboos on sex during breastfeeding as well as abortions were other methods of controlling fertility. The fraction of the population that was seriously malnourished probably increased in difficult times. The impact on fertility was direct since the seriously malnourished were infertile or suffered spontaneous abortions.

Table 3.1 illustrates some of these fertility strategies in a Tuscan village but the general pattern was fairly universal throughout Western Europe. The troubled period between 1650 and 1750 was characterized by a high age at marriage and a short period of in-marriage fertility measured as the interval between first and last child, which reduced the number of births to about four per married woman. When marriage age fell in the two subsequent periods that fall was also associated with a longer period of in-marriage fertility leading to a rise in the number of children. The forces that shaped fertility behaviour in the

Table 3.1   Number of live births per married woman, age at marriage and survival chances of children, 1650–1950

Year of birth of childbearing woman	Age of woman at marriage	Number of births per married woman	Number of years between first and last child	Number of children who survived first year	Number of children who survived to age 10	Survival chances up to age 10 (per cent)
1650–1749	23.3 (9.4)	3.85 (2.8)	7.67 (6.6)	2.74 (2.7)	2.12 (1.7)	55
1750–1849	22.1 (7.1)	5.04 (3.6)	10.82 (8.0)	4.06 (2.8)	3.30 (2.5)	65
1850–74	21.4 (6.7)	5.43 (3.7)	11.73 (7.8)	4.62 (2.9)	4.27 (2.8)	79
1875–99	24.8 (9.7)	3.93 (2.8)	9.38 (7.6)	3.59 (2.4)	3.43 (2.3)	87
1900–20	24.5 (6.1)	2.40 (1.8)	6.55 (6.6)	2.40 (1.6)	2.38 (1.6)	99

Source: Own estimates from family reconstitution data in Renzo Ronchi, *Le radici e la memoria: Buriano e le sue famiglie, Origine, genealogia e tradizione* (Rome: Begliomini, 2004). *Standard deviations** in brackets.

two final periods, that is after 1900, were entirely different as they were based on a reduction in the number of children to concentrate resources on the education and training of a smaller number, as well as a response to the increased opportunity costs of having children, as explained in Section 3.6.

An economic approach to understanding the fertility strategy of households suggests that *numbers* of children cannot be all that matters if a household experiences an increase in income. Pre-industrial mankind was, like modern mankind, capable of seeing that there was a trade-off between consumption of other goods, the quality of children (their nutritional status, say) and the *number* of children. Since both numbers and quality of children are associated with costs, there will be a trade-off in the sense that given the income constraint of the household it cannot have both more and better children. To assume, as Malthusians tend to do, that income increases necessarily spill over into an increasing *number* of children is an arbitrary restriction of the choices available to households. That assumption stems from the erroneous belief that humans have reproductive habits exactly like those of other animals. However, humans have the faculty of being forward-looking, capable of planning and, to some extent, being able to avoid undesirable outcomes. The empirical finding that population increase did not suppress wages in the long run is entirely consistent with the view expressed here that households were forward-looking and understood the trade-off between family size and the prospects of maintaining a given living standard. Over time households can be expected to develop a preference for quality of children at the expense of quantity as entry into the labour market becomes increasingly demanding in terms of educational attainment, which we will discuss in the next section.

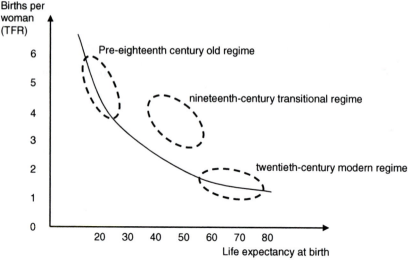

Figure 3.4   Old and new total fertility regimes relative to a population growth isoquant of 0.1–0.4 per cent per year

3.6 The demographic transition

Until the end of the eighteenth century the demographic regime in Europe was characterized by high fertility and high mortality and consequently low population growth. A third or more of all children died before the age of ten. Total fertility, that is the expected number of live births per fertile woman, was very high, on average between four to six. But given the high mortality rates, in particular for those under five years of age, the rate of increase of population was not very high, around 0.1–0.5 per cent per year. Paradoxically, the rate of population growth under the old regime was not very different from that of Europe at present. However, total fertility, as defined above, is now down to fewer than two. That process has been accompanied by a sharp rise in life expectancy, from 25–35 years to 70–80 years.

The nature of that transition is illustrated in a simplified way in Figure 3.4. The convex curve is an iso-growth curve of population at 0.1–0.4 per cent per year. The old regime has high total fertility and low life expectancy while the modern regime has low total fertility and high life expectancy.

The decline in total fertility started first in France, reached the UK around the middle of the nineteenth century and the rest of north-western Europe a little later, but not until after 1900 did it affect most other European nations.

The demographic transition includes a period of rapid population growth caused primarily by a fall in infant mortality and by an increase in life expectancy for those who survived the difficult first years. All European nations went

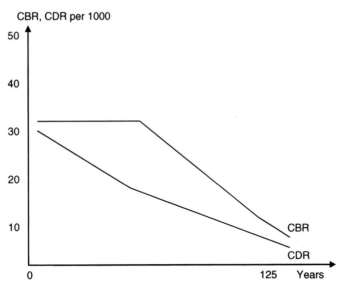

Figure 3.5   Fertility and mortality in the demographic transition

through a demographic transition starting with a fall in mortality followed, after a delay of some fifty years, by a fall in fertility. The whole process took about 150 ($\pm$ 50) years, starting as early as the mid or late eighteenth century in some countries like England and Sweden and a little later in the rest of Western Europe. However, fertility rates remained high for several generations before a decline occurred. Table 3.1 suggested that for the Tuscan village we analysed, total fertility was at a peak for the parents born in 1850–75, but from then on fertility and consequently population growth converged on modern rates. The timing is consistent with the general Western European pattern, give or take twenty-five years. The mass migration to the New World at the end of the nineteenth century must be understood as a push caused by the fast population growth, especially in the second half of the century. By the middle of the twentieth century, both fertility and mortality rates converged on their present low rates, as is demonstrated in Figure 3.5. It is worth noting that the demographic transition as described by Figure 3.5 seems to be a worldwide phenomenon: economies like Taiwan, Japan, China and Mexico entered into it much later but also experienced a much faster transition from the old to the modern regime. Most economies today are in the final stage of the transition, with the exception of a large number of African nations, which are midway through it, exhibiting high fertility and low mortality, even though mortality is on the rise again due to the AIDS epidemic.

The fall in mortality in twentieth-century developing countries can be explained by better access to medical services, but that was not the case in mid or late eighteenth-century Europe. Public health measures did not play an important role until the early nineteenth century. In fact the early decline in child mortality is still an unresolved historical puzzle. It is known that an improvement in the nutritional standard of pregnant women can contribute to higher survival probabilities in the newborn, but the fall in child mortality was not necessarily accompanied by rising income levels. However, given a stable income level a redistribution of food resources to women might have occurred. It is known that females generally were less well fed than males, because of outright discrimination and/or because men did physically more demanding work. The hypothesis that women were all of a sudden able to gain access to a larger share of the household's food resources is at best unproven. Purely accidental exogenous factors such as the development of a less aggressive disease environment cannot be ruled out; neither can an acquired immunity against prevalent diseases. The other puzzling issue in our understanding of the demographic transition is the fact that fertility remained high despite falling mortality for several generations before the former started to decline. One might expect that in the old demographic regime household fertility strategy would anticipate the high incidence of child mortality. If so, the high total fertility should be interpreted as a necessary, and for women in particular very demanding, task: to bring two or three children out of four to six births to adulthood. If two to three surviving children is the target size for a family, a decline in child mortality should induce families to reduce the number of births when child mortality declined. But that does not happen initially. A plausible interpretation is that households initially believed the decline to be only transitory. Such a misperception is understandable given the huge variations in mortality rates from year to year due to harvest failures and epidemics, especially in the early phase of the demographic transition. If this interpretation is correct, households continued their traditional total fertility strategy over a few generations until convinced that the fall in child mortality was a permanent change. This hypothesis might seem far-fetched but we have to recognize that the old demographic regime had been in operation for a long time and might have been locked into cultural norms. If we look at Table 3.1, it is clear that the survival chances of children increase from about 50 per cent in the first period to 30 per cent in the eighteenth century and then to about 20 per cent in the middle of the nineteenth century. With unchanged fertility strategy that led to a dramatic increase in family size. However, the *standard deviation* in the number of children surviving their first ten years is very high, which makes it difficult to disentangle permanent from transitory effects. The generation born in 1875–99 may, however, finally have learned that the traditional fertility strategy resulted in families that were too large to cope with the struggle for a decent standard of living.

The decline in fertility occurred before the widespread use of contraceptives; it coincided with the early phases of urbanization and industrialization and with increasing household income, which is contrary to the Malthusian theory and is related to the fact that there is no trade-off in fertility strategy between number and quality of children. Numbers rule! As discussed below, it is in fact not at all surprising that household size fell when income increased.

It is important to focus not just on the *income effect** on the demand for children but also on the *substitution effect**. Since one of the major costs of having children is the income forgone in giving birth and staying out of the labour market in order to take care of children, any income increase will also automatically increase the *opportunity cost** of having children. Modern fertility strategies in high-income nations can therefore be explained by the drift in preferences towards *quality* rather than *quantity* of children as well as strong substitution effects when wages increase, which are apparently strong enough to counteract the income effect on the desire for numbers of children.

In the past as well as the present fertility strategies of households depend on whether it is possible for households to externalize the costs of children. For example, if households have access to shared resources the costs will be diffused among the entire community, which may lead to fewer restraints on fertility compared to a context in which households bear the entire cost. It is known that, in the past, national differences in total fertility might be linked to laws governing the inheritance of property. If all offspring have equal access to property, as in France after the enactment of the Code Napoléon, family size will be lower than in nations where only the first-born male has legal or customary access to the property. The logic is here supposed to be the desire of households not to split landed property into smaller units.

Modern European nations differ in that some, for example the Scandinavians, externalize the costs of raising children by offering subsidized child care financed by taxes paid by parents and non-parents alike. It is not clear, however, that total fertility in Scandinavia differs significantly from that of nations without comprehensive child care at a similar level of economic development. It is an issue worth looking into.

Summary

The history of Europe has conventionally been framed as a discussion of the spectre of population outstripping resources. But we have not found strong evidence for so-called Malthusian stagnation meaning a drift towards subsistence income as population grows in the pre-industrial era. Technological progress, however slow, and diversified land use made possible by trade permitted a more efficient use of land. The most enduring characteristic of agricultural civilizations, as opposed to hunter-gatherer cultures, has been slow but steady population growth interrupted by exogenous shocks. This slow growth was a result of deliberate fertility strategies, such as variations in the marriage rate, as well as largely exogenous forces, epidemics, acting on child mortality. After centuries of slow growth, a demographic transition began at the end of the eighteenth century whereby fertility remained high while mortality, in particular child mortality, fell. However, by the middle or the end of the nineteenth century fertility rates also started to fall, leading to a regime with low fertility and mortality rates. Population growth in Europe is now at about the same rate as in the old regime, but it is associated with a radical decline in child mortality and a fall in total fertility caused by a shift in households' preferences from large numbers of children to better-educated children, as well as an increase in the opportunity cost of having children when income increases for both men and women.

Suggestions for further reading

Nobel laureate R. W. Fogel is an influential researcher on historical demography: *The Escape from Hunger and Premature Death 1700–2100: Europe, America, and the Third World* (Cambridge University Press, 2004).

Robert C. Allen offers a penetrating study of the impact of nitrogen on agricultural yields in 'The nitrogen hypothesis and the English agricultural revolution: a biological analysis', *Journal of Economic History* 68(1) (2008), pp. 182–210.

G. Clark offers a slightly dogmatic restatement of the Malthusian hypothesis as a general theory for pre-industrial economies in *Farewell to Alms: A Brief History of the World* (Princeton University Press, 2007). The book has provoked an intense debate; see the symposium in *European Review of Economic History* 12 (2008), pp. 149–95.

Economists have made efforts to analyse fertility strategies in a context of optimizing behaviour, but there is as yet no consensus as to the empirical validity of these models. See Matthias Doepke, 'Child mortality and fertility decline: does the Barro-Becker model fit the facts?', *Journal of Population Economics* 18 (2005), pp. 337–66; O. Galor and D. Weil, 'Population, technology and growth: from Malthusian stagnation to the demographic transition and beyond', *American Economic Review*, 90(4) (2000), pp. 806–28.

The dynamic nature of agricultural production worldwide is covered in G. Federico's *Feeding the World: An Economic History of Agriculture* (Princeton University Press, 2005).

One of the first demographers to develop a more sceptical view of the Malthusian theory on the basis of econometric analysis was Ronald Lee. He has published a large number of papers and the literature is well summarized in his 'The demographic transition: three centuries of fundamental change', *Journal of Economic Literature* 17 (4) (2003), pp. 167–190.

A team of young researchers at University of Copenhagen has taken the econometric analysis a step further and is presently involved in extending it to a number of countries. Check their results at Paul Sharp's homepage: www.keynes.dk

M. Livi-Bacci, *A Concise History of World Population*, 3rd edn (Oxford: Blackwell, 2001) is very useful introduction to population history.

E. A. Wrigley and R. Schofield, *The Population History of England, 1541–1871: A Reconstitution* (London: Edward Arnold, 1981) sets the standard for historical demography.

On famines and population see C. O'Grada, 'Making famine history', *Journal of Economic Literature* 45 (2007), pp. 5–39.

A modern classic is W. Abel, *Agricultural Fluctuations in Europe from the Thirteenth to the Twentieth Centuries* (London: Methuen, 1980; first German edition 1966).

4 The nature and extent of economic growth in the pre-industrial epoch

---

4.1 Understanding pre-industrial growth

We will now combine elements in Malthusian and Smithian explanations as developed in Chapters 2 and 3 to enhance our understanding of the nature of pre-industrial economic growth. This new view acknowledges diminishing returns from labour in agriculture as the rural population grows and if the tilled land/labour ratio falls, but we also explicitly acknowledge technological change, that is, the useful application of new knowledge. Furthermore there are Smithian gains from specialization triggered off by division of labour stimulated by increasing 'the extent of the market', that is an increase in aggregate demand. If we have resource constraints *and* technological change the story will become fundamentally different. Technological growth is present if we can produce more goods today than were produced yesterday, with the resources used in production held constant. Technological progress and division of labour enable the economy to have both positive population growth and constant or increasing per capita income. The intuition here is that the effects of diminishing returns are offset by technological change. Figure 4.1 below explains in a simple way how the mechanism works.

Positive population growth has two effects with opposing signs, plus or minus, as to the impact on output or income per head. If the economy is using all available land there will be diminishing returns from labour, which will affect output and income per head negatively. However, as long as positive population growth is increasing *aggregate demand** (= income per head times the number of people) in the economy, division of labour will be stimulated and hence income per head. There are good reasons to believe that population growth actually increases aggregate demand because, as we noted in Chapter 3, there is strong persistence in wage levels. Furthermore, as discussed in Chapter 2, the extent of division of labour will enhance learning-by-doing based technological change which has a positive effect on income per head. The rate

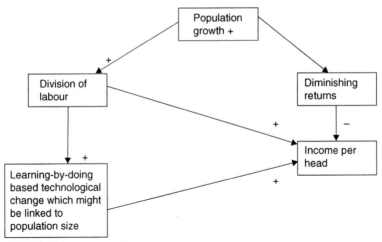

Figure 4.1 Malthusian and Smithian forces in economic growth

of technological progress can also be correlated with the level of population. That idea has recently been explored in growth theory but it is in fact an old notion. The seventeenth-century English diarist Samuel Pepys (1633–1703) famously remarked that a population of four million people is more likely to produce a genius than a population of 400,000, that is the rate at which new ideas emerge is positively linked to the size of the population.

The explanatory scheme in Figure 4.1 is compatible with a number of outcomes. We can think of a neat balance between Malthusian and Smithian forces leading to constant but above-subsistence income combined with positive population growth and hence an increase in aggregate income. This scenario seems to be a good characterization of many regions of Europe in the pre-industrial period. But we also pointed out that some regions experienced slow but sustained growth in income per head in the period, say, from 1000 to 1800 CE or in sub-periods of that interval. For example, Italy was growing from the twelfth century until well into the sixteenth century but then seems to come to a standstill, while the Netherlands was growing in the sixteenth and seventeenth centuries. Some regions, for example parts of Britain and the Netherlands, went through an agricultural revolution in the centuries before the Industrial Revolution. However, we cannot exclude, a priori, that Malthusian forces might wipe out the Smithian effects leading to falling income per head. Falling per capita income in the pre-industrial period was usually associated with a breakdown of social order or climatic or epidemic shocks, which effectively shrunk aggregate income in the economy and imposed periods of technological regress. It is worth repeating that it seems counter-intuitive that households should deliberately follow a fertility strategy which reduces income per head.

Can we also explain why societies remain in low-income equilibriums despite not seeming to be constrained by limited natural resources, for example after the decline of the Roman Empire? To do this we just change the sign in the population growth box in Figure 4.1 to a minus, which may then lead to falling aggregate income and a decrease in division of labour and learning by doing. This may lead to technological regress, which, if it does not outweigh the effects of easier access to land, may lead to stagnating or falling income. This process was discussed in relation to Figure 2.2 in Chapter 2.

4.2 Accounting for pre-industrial productivity growth

Growth in income per head is generated by the increasingly efficient use of greater resources, such as capital and land. The capital/labour ratio did not change much in the pre-industrial period and the land/labour ratio stagnated or fell. So increasing income will be dependent mainly on improved efficiency in the use of the inputs in production. Trade and division of labour, as well as technological change, are efficiency enhancing processes. An approximate measure of these efficiency gains is so-called total factor productivity.

Growth in total factor productivity (henceforward TFP), is routinely measured in modern economies, which have statistical agencies producing detailed and fairly accurate national accounts of economic activity, such as the value and volume of inputs and output in the economy. These measurements generate estimates of *national income*, usually denoted Y.

The intuition of TFP is straightforward: it is the difference between the growth of output in the economy and the growth of inputs. A formal statement is found at the end of this chapter but for our present purpose, an intuitive presentation will do.

$$TFP = \text{increase in output} - \text{weighted increase in}$$
$$(\text{labour input} + \text{capital input} + \text{land input})$$

Imagine that output (in real terms) increases by 5 per cent and the number of hours worked increases by 6 per cent while the units of capital increase by 5 per cent and the number of hectares of land used by 1 per cent.

The weightings given to labour, capital and land are 0.5, 0.3 and 0.2 respectively. Hence the weighted increases in inputs are $0.5*5 + 0.3*5 + 0.2*1 = 4.2$. That implies that TFP, see above, is 0.8 per cent, that is, the increase in output (5 per cent) minus the weighted increase in inputs (4.2 per cent).

The weightings take account of the fact that the relative contribution of different inputs in production differs.

If TFP is positive then the economic process is generating a higher growth than the growth in the weighted sum of inputs, presumably because the inputs are being used in a more efficient way.

But the extent and precision of the data needed in order to measure TFP this way are simply not available for pre-industrial economies. Modern economic historians have succeeded in reconstructing historical national accounts for the nineteenth century, or at least its second half, with reasonably high precision. These reconstructions are based on rather limited data and with the help of simplifying assumptions; but we need to go further back in history, where we lack even imperfect reconstructions of national accounts.

There is another equivalent method, called the *dual approach*, which is more suitable for the measurement of TFP in pre-industrial economies, because it requires only data on the growth of prices and factor incomes, that is, wages, rents and factor shares.

Imagine a predominantly agrarian economy and that your job is to measure TFP in the agricultural sector. There are farm workers who receive a wage and landowners earning a land-rent. (Self-employed farmers can be assumed to earn a weighted average of rents and wages.) The sum of wages and rents is the total income of that sector and must, by definition, equal the value of the value added or output of that same sector. If the sum of the rent *per unit of land* and *real wage per worker* increases from one year to another then land and/or workers are being used more efficiently, since any income increase *per unit of inputs* must correspond to an increase in output. The average worker with a given amount of land is producing more, and this is revealed by an increase in the income of landowners and farm workers.

Box 4.1   Total factor productivity growth in pre-plague English agriculture

The prelude to the Black Death has often been described as a period of falling productivity. However a TFP analysis indicates that existing resources were being used more efficiently. On the basis of price and wage data collected and published by D. L. Farmer (in J. Thirsk, ed., *The Agrarian History of England and Wales*, vol. 2 (Cambridge University Press, 1988), pp. 716–817) we can calculate the growth trend in nominal farm wages as 0.32 per cent per year in the period 1250 to 1347. There are no data on rents for the same period, but we can safely assume that rents increased at least at the same rate as wages because the period was one of land scarcity and hence the bargaining power of landlords must have increased. We assume nominal rents to increase at a rate similar to wages, but we need to deflate both by the rate of inflation, which, using a price index composed of wheat, rye, pigs, wool and cheese, amounts to 0.15 per cent per year. Assuming weight $a = 0.6$ and weight $b = 0.4$ the TFP estimate using the *dual approach* then becomes

$$TFP = 0.6*0.32 + 0.4*0.32 - 0.15 = 0.17.$$

As we will see, a TFP of about 0.2 per cent per year is in line with the upper bound estimates for pre-industrial economies reported later in this chapter.

Table 4.1   Total factor productivity in French agriculture, 1522–1789. Per cent per year

Region	Years covered	TFP growth rate (per cent/year)	
		Overall	Late eighteenth century
Paris basin	1520–1789	0.13	0.31
North-east (Lorraine)	1550–1789	0.13	0.13
Normandy (near Caen)	1520–1785	0.01	0.01
West	1611–1790	−0.16	−0.16
South-east	1580–1790	0.21	0.21

Source: P. Hoffman, *Growth in a Traditional Society, The French Countryside 1450–1815* (Princeton University Press, 1996), Table 4.8, p. 130.

A California Institute of Technology-based economic historian, Philip Hoffman, has made TFP estimates for French early modern or *ancien régime* (1522–1789) agriculture, and the pattern is not very different from the results discussed in Box 4.1. He notes, however, periods of growth and stagnation and large regional differences. The densely populated Paris basin, which might be expected to be the most dynamic region, is surpassed by the equally densely populated south-east of France, which is close to Mediterranean ports. Table 4.1 indicates that growth averaged around 0.13 per cent per year in the Paris basin and increased to 0.31 in the late eighteenth century. One major region, the West, had negative growth and one, Normandy, was characterized by stagnation throughout the *ancien régime*. Hoffman argues that exogenous shocks, religious wars and disorder severely interrupted the growth process and resulted in the low long-term averages. The results referred to above in our analysis of medieval English growth are primarily based on data from the south-east of England, quite close to London, which in many respects was similar to the Paris basin in that it benefited from a large urban market.

All in all these attempts to measure pre-industrial growth leave us with the impression that TFP growth in the major sector, agriculture, could reach 0.1 to 0.2 per cent per year in the pre-industrial era provided that resources and opportunities were reasonably well exploited, which required regional trade and proximity to major urban areas. The results highlight great regional differences. As in the modern world, growth was not shared by all.

Needless to say, these estimates are subject to uncertainty. Can we find some other alternative method of estimation? If so, it could serve as an independent check. There is another way of *indirect* estimation, which is based on the following commonsense observation, first developed by E. A. Wrigley. To simplify the exposition, consider a closed economy with an agrarian sector feeding its own workers and an urban population, that is a non-food-producing population.

Now it seems obvious that if there is an increase in the non-food-producing population relative to the agrarian population without a decline in the per capita consumption of food, then the increase in the size of the urban population must have to do with a productivity increase in the agrarian sector. Each farming household is producing food for a larger number of townspeople.

Box 4.2 Urbanization means higher labour productivity

Imagine an economy which is self-sufficient in food. There is a total population of 100 of which 95 work in agriculture and 5 in urban professions. Each person consumes one unit of food, so total consumption (output of food) is 100. Agrarian labour productivity is total output divided by the number of agrarian workers, that is $100/95 = 1.053$.

Then there is a technology improvement in agriculture so that 85 farmers can produce 100 units of food, and that releases 10 workers to work in urban professions. A total of 15 now work in urban jobs and exchange their products for food. As a consequence the increase in urban population reveals an increase in agrarian labour productivity. Total output is as before, 100 units of food, but it is now produced by only 85 farmers, so labour productivity in agriculture is $100/85 = 1.18$.

This commonsense argument can easily be formalized to include foreign trade, changes in patterns of consumption of food and non-food, and income differences between town and countryside. Why is it necessary to control for imports of food? If we observe that the proportion of workers in urban occupations in a certain economy has increased, it might, in principle, only be due to the fact that the urban manufacturers are exporting their goods against imported food, and if so, this increase in the relative size of the urban sector need not reveal a productivity change in the domestic economy's own agricultural sector. Likewise, relative wages must be controlled for. Again, urban growth might be due to the fact that wages and agrarian consumption in cities are declining, in which case the inference that urban growth always implies agrarian productivity growth is not correct.

Do the results from an analysis along these lines lend support to the previously reported estimates? Yes, they do. K. G. Persson – that's me – investigated agricultural labour productivity changes in Tuscany (Italy) and the historical Low Countries, now northern France and southern Belgium, in the two centuries before the Black Death. Both areas were fairly advanced and similar to the Paris basin and south-east England. Yearly growth of agrarian labour productivity estimates for the period 1100 to 1300 ranged between 0.1 to 0.25 per cent per year. It must be stressed that labour productivity is identical to TFP only on the assumption that land and capital per labourer are constant. If land per labourer declines over time then TFP is actually larger than the estimate of labour productivity. In pre-industrial economies, we can assume that labour productivity estimates are roughly similar to TFP estimates, because land and capital per labourer do not change much.

It is worth stressing that these results do not imply that growth was equally strong in all parts of Europe. On the contrary, remote areas poorly integrated into urban networks probably fared less well and were stagnating. Hoffman's research also suggested that variations in growth were very sensitive to social disorder. Wars and social unrest had a negative impact. A stable institutional framework was a prerequisite for growth.

R. C. Allen, an Oxford-based economic historian, used a similar approach, but for the period 1300–1800. He confirmed that there were different growth patterns in different regions. Belgium – not at that time a nation state, but part of the highly urbanised Low Countries region – starts out as an early leader in terms of the level of agrarian labour productivity, but with negative growth in the period. Unlike the Netherlands (or the United Provinces as it was then called), Belgium could not free itself from the stifling political domination and religious intolerance of the Spanish crown, which harmed growth. Spain and Italy were also in the top layer of European economies in the sixteenth century, but fell in relative terms thereafter. Belgium lost one precious resource, skilled labour, which migrated to the Netherlands because of religious persecution. Not surprisingly, the Netherlands, which combined political independence around 1600 with religious tolerance and a welcoming attitude to immigrants with scarce skills, as well as growth-promoting institutions, became, in the words of Jan de Vries, the first *modern* economy. The first *industrial* nation, England, with an institutional set up similar to that in the Netherlands, also advanced in terms of agrarian labour productivity, almost doubling its output per agricultural worker between around 1650 and 1800.

Other results are less good. For example, France stagnated, according to Allen, which seems to contradict Hoffman's results reported above. However, Allen's choice of large territorial states as units averages out the different growth performances of sub-regions. In fact, Hoffman reported regions with negative and zero growth as well as positive growth.

This highlights the idea advanced previously, that regions and nations may operate below their technological capacity and resource constraints. There is little evidence that resource endowments or access to technology were fundamentally different in, say England and France, or not to the extent that a 2:1 difference in labour productivity can be explained. In other words, we should look elsewhere for an explanation of why parts of France were left behind. Growth-inhibiting institutions and periods of internal disorder are probably part of the answer. On the other hand, Allen's results underline that a surge in agricultural labour productivity started in the Netherlands and England, which were more densely populated than economies such as Spain, which had a dismal growth record in the seventeenth to nineteenth centuries.

Figure 2.3 in chapter 2 presented a general view of the development of urbanization. It will be recalled that there were large national differences in Europe. Around 1100 urbanization was uniformly low, Italy being an exception, but from then on, the growth of urban professions took off, reaching 35–40 per cent in the most advanced areas by 1500; but these regions partly relied on imports of food. For Europe as a whole urbanization was more modest, increasing from about 3–4 per cent to about 12 per cent between 1100 and 1700.

How much must agrarian labour productivity grow to support an increase in the urban population of 10 percentage points? The answer is necessarily an approximation because the estimates are sensitive to assumptions about income distribution, the urban–rural income gap, and the (marginal) propensity to spend on food as income grows. However, the likely answer is a two to threefold increase in agrarian labour productivity. In fact, a one percentage point increase in urbanization at low levels of urbanization implies approximately a 10 per cent increase in agricultural labour productivity. The reason is primarily that the urban population, in which the landed and urban elites must be included, had income levels far above that of the agricultural population.

4.3 Wages and income distribution

A number of economic historians have used *real wage* data to infer income growth and growth of productivity. The logic is simple and at first sight appealing. If real productivity increases, we should expect wages to increase. It is also true that the most urbanized areas of Europe, with ample supplies of skilled workers, had the highest wage levels. For example, between 1500 and 1700 wages in London and Amsterdam were about twice the level in Warsaw. Despite the differences in levels, it is worth stressing the similarity in movements across cities located in all parts of Europe. The similarities of movements in, for example, London and Istanbul, are noteworthy: both entered a phase of slow increase some time in the seventeenth century, which speeded up in the eighteenth century. However, the synchronization of wage movements between different parts of Europe must not be interpreted as a sign of integration in the European labour markets. The phenomenon is rather the effect of a combination of fairly rigid *nominal wages** and rudimentary integration of European food markets.

In general the development of *real wages** of urban workers, that is nominal wages deflated by the price of consumer goods, gives a gloomy picture of the seventeenth and eighteenth centuries in Europe, apart from the leading centres in the west.

However, we need to be careful about interpreting changes in the development of real wages as indicating changes in *income* per head, because wages are affected by the distribution of income. National income is composed of wage income and income from capital, that is profit, and land, that is rent. That means that national income per head in real terms can increase despite stagnating real wages, simply because rents and/or profits increase.

Real (day) wages reached a first historical peak by the middle of the fifteenth century, driven by the general labour shortage as a consequence of a century of declining population after the first outbreak of the Black Death. Workers not only negotiated higher wages and shorter hours, they also benefited from low agricultural prices. As the labour shortage eased from 1450 to 1600, real wages generally dropped, mainly because prices increased while nominal wages did not. However, labourers probably adjusted to that by changing their diet, which was high in meat in the fifteenth century, and ate more bread and porridge in the sixteenth century. Consumers enjoying an income well above subsistence might be induced by the relative rise in food prices to shift to non-food commodities. These changes in the diet are ignored in the real wage estimate, since the commodity composition of the real wage deflator is fixed. Furthermore, real wages usually record day wages. However, the number of days worked did increase from a historical low in the fifteenth century until well into the Industrial Revolution, which may explain what a number of economic historians document as a 'consumer revolution'. The increased yearly income enjoyed by those working more days endowed them with a surplus income to be spent on goods other than necessities, which is part of the reason for a demand driven increase in the goods made by urban producers. This explanation is consistent with the observed increase in urban occupations relative to food-producing workers.

Despite these clarifications, we have to conclude that the development of real wages, especially the century of decline between, say, 1550 and 1650, is difficult to reconcile with a positive rate of total factor productivity unless there were shifts in income distribution away from workers. The observed increase in labour supply lends support to such a redistribution of income, but we have no evidence as to the magnitude of that shift.

4.4 When did Europe forge ahead?

One of the perennial questions in economic history is why the Industrial Revolution happened in Western Europe and not elsewhere. As we have argued, Europe lagged behind the leading civilizations until well into the second millennium, and some historians argue that Europe did not get ahead of China or India until the late eighteenth century. If that is so, the question why the Industrial Revolution happened in Europe and not in other equally advanced economies is highly motivated. However, the most advanced areas of Europe were ahead of China and India (and southern and eastern Europe) well before the eighteenth century, which makes the geographical location of the Industrial Revolution less of a mystery.

Despite the problems associated with interpreting the development of wages as discussed in Section 4.3, we have to rely on wage data in cross-country comparisons of welfare for the pre-industrial epoch. The reason is that there are no national accounts giving us information about income per head. But the problem does not end there, because we have problems constructing an appropriate real wage. Comparing so-called grain wages, that is the nominal wage divided by the price of grain, it turns out that the difference in wages between the core centres of Europe, which later housed the Industrial Revolution, and India and China were quite small around 1550 and remained small until c.1700, but from then on grain wages were considerably higher in England. The logic of using the grain wage is that it catches the purchasing power of the nominal wage over an important part of daily consumption. Ideally we should have the price of a basket of consumer goods as a deflator instead of just grain, but it is very difficult to get reliable price data for other consumer goods. Looking instead at silver wages, that is nominal wages deflated by the price of silver, it turns out the English lead over China and India was already substantial in around 1550: Indian silver wages were about 20 per cent (of the English wages) and falling, and Chinese silver wages started slightly higher but were declining as well relative to English wages. Figure 4.2 gives the details of the evolution of wages in India and China as a percentage of English wages.

What is the interpretation of the diverging results? First, we need to understand that when comparing England, China and India, grain must be considered a non-internationally traded good in this period, unlike silver and other traded goods such as textiles and spices. An internationally traded good is subject to *the law of one price**: that is, unlike non-traded commodities it is sold at (about) the same price in all markets. A meaningful *real wage* deflator should include both traded and non-traded goods because people consume both. The *real wage* curve is constructed to reflect that requirement, in that silver is supposed to represent the price of traded goods and is given a weighting of 0.2, that is, 20 per cent of income is spent on internationally traded goods, while grain is supposed to represent non-traded goods with a weighting of 0.8. Since the deflator is composed of both silver and grain prices it is not surprising that the real wage curve falls in between the grain wage and the silver wage.

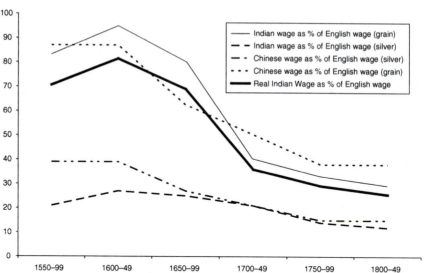

Figure 4.2   Silver, grain and real wages in Britain, China and India, 1550–1850. Wages as a percentage of English wages. Source: Based on the data presented in S. Broadberry and B. Gupta, 'The early modern great divergence: wages, prices and economic development in Europe and Asia, 1500–1800', *Economic History Review* 59(1) (2006), pp. 2–31 (see tables 6–8). The Indian to English real wage ratio curve is estimated by assuming that silver represents traded goods, and is given a weight of 0.2, while grain represents non-traded goods with a weight of 0.8.

It is a well-known finding that developed economies have uniformly higher wages and prices compared to less developed economies. In particular, non-traded goods command lower prices in less developed economies, because they are not traded internationally. In Europe, peripheral and less advanced nations like Sweden had considerably lower grain prices around 1500 than the Netherlands or England, for example. So the combination of roughly equal grain wages and inferior silver wages around 1550–99 only means that grain prices *and* nominal wages were low in China and India while grain prices *and* nominal wages were high in England. And what was true for England was true also for other advanced parts of Western Europe. The intuition should be clear by now. If the relative prices of traded to non-traded goods are higher in China and India than in England, then real wages must be lower in India and China, assuming that consumption is composed of both traded and non-traded commodities. It is in itself a sign of economic development that wages are high enough to permit consumption of both food (grain) and industrial goods. It is therefore little use maintaining that Indian workers could afford to buy almost as much food as the British workers. To the extent that Indian consumers were buying non-traded (grain) as well as traded items (for example textiles and spices), the *real wage* was lower than the grain wage, as is demonstrated in Figure 4.2. The major implication of these results is that initially rather small differences in real wages became magnified in the seventeenth and eighteenth centuries and before the Industrial Revolution. The nineteenth century saw a much more dramatic divergence, however. The results also shed light on the level of real wages in the most advanced areas of Europe. If we assume that Indian workers just earned a subsistence income around 1700, say, and that income was just a third of the English *real wage*, the latter must have been three times a subsistence income. This fits well with the existing estimates of real income per head in England at about this time, as discussed in Chapter 2.

We have argued that wage series are incomplete and sometimes poor guides to the development of income per capita if there was a redistribution of wage income to property income, for example. Can we maintain that Figure 4.2 gives an approximate picture of income per head differences between England and Asia as well? The answer is 'yes'! The magnitude of divergence of real wages is such that it cannot plausibly be caused by changes in income distribution away from wage earners in India and China.

Summary

The pre-industrial economy tended to balance the negative and positive effects of population growth to the effect that income was maintained on a level well above subsistence and increased slowly over long periods in some of the more advanced areas of Europe. Population growth, although potentially associated with diminishing returns on labour when the land constraint was binding, stimulated both division of labour and technological progress, mainly through learning by doing. Upper bound estimates of TFP and labour productivity growth suggest yearly growth rates of about 0.2 percent.

Appendix: The dual approach to total factor productivity measurement

The real value of output in an economy – national income at constant prices – is called Y and is equal to the payments in real terms to the factors of production: K (capital), L (labour) and T (land).

Hence

$$Y = rK + wL + iT \tag{1}$$

where r is profit per unit of capital, w is wage per labourer and i is the land rent per unit of land.

The proportional change in a variable is denoted by * and by log differentiation gives

$$Y^* = s_K(r^* + K^*) + s_L(w^* + L^*) + s_I(i^* + T^*) \qquad (2)$$

where s stands for the share of national income going to labour and owners of capital and land respectively.

Rearranging this expression gives

$$Y^* - (s_K K^* + s_L L^* + s_I T^*) = s_K r^* + s_L w^* + s_I i^* \qquad (3)$$

The left-hand side of this expression is the formal definition of the traditional TFP expression as it was expressed in the text on page 62:

$$TFP = \text{increase in output} - \text{weighted increase in}$$
$$\text{(labour input + capital input + land input)}$$

That is, TFP is the growth in output minus the growth in the weighted sum of inputs. The right hand side of (3) is equivalent to the left hand side and is called the dual approach to TFP:

$$TFP = s_K r^* + s_L w^* + s_I i^* \qquad (4)$$

Suggestions for further reading

Useful attempts to measure the level and growth of labour and total factor productivity include R. C. Allen, 'Economic structure and agricultural productivity in Europe, 1300–1800', *European Review of Economic History* 4 (1) (2000), pp. 1–26. This article combines Persson's method (see below) with independent estimates of per capita income.

An important study of France already referred to is P. Hoffman, *Growth in a Traditional Society: The French Countryside 1450–1815* (Princeton University Press, 1996).

A way to infer productivity changes in agriculture from changes in the urbanization ratio is explored in K. G. Persson, 'Labour productivity in medieval agriculture: Tuscany and the Low Countries', in B. M. S. Campbell and M. Overton (eds.) *Land, Labour and Livestock, Historical Studies in European Agricultural Productivity* (Manchester University Press, 1991), pp. 124–43. This chapter develops a precise formula for deriving labour productivity in the agricultural sector. The data required include changes in urbanization ratio, the ratio of urban to rural per capita income, the net trade in food and the marginal propensity to consume food. The results reported in the text derive from an assumption that the urban to rural income ratio is 5/1 and that the marginal propensity to consume food is 0.5, that is half of an income increase is used for food, and the rest for urban goods.

On real wages and income distribution see P. Hoffman, D. S. Jacks, P. A. Levin and P. Lindert, 'Real inequality in Europe since 1500', *Journal of Economic History* 62 (2) (2002), pp. 322–55. This article suggests a U-shaped development of inequality in the period from 1500 to 2000: it increases up to about 1650, at which time it stabilized and there is then a drift towards more equality after 1800.

Two useful articles on the long-term evolution of real wages in a comparative perspective are: R. C. Allen, 'The great divergence in European wages and prices from the Middle Ages to the First World War', *Explorations in Economic History*, 38 (2001), pp. 411–47, and S. Özmucur and S. Pamuk, 'Real wages and standards of living in the Ottoman Empire, 1489–1914', *Journal of Economic History* 62 (2) (2002), pp. 277–321.

A fair amount of the reasoning in Chapters 3 and 4 is developed more rigorously in K. G. Persson, *Pre-Industrial Economic Growth* (Oxford: Basil Blackwell, 1988). The Dutch economic historian Jan Luiten van Zanden has written extensively on the spectacular accomplishments of the early modern Netherlands. See e.g. 'Taking measure of the early modern economy: historical national accounts for Holland in 1510/14', *European Review of Economic History* 6 (2) (2002), pp. 131–64.

5 Institutions and growth

5.1 Institutions and efficiency

Institutions are the rules of the game. Some are upheld by law, others by mutual and spontaneous consent and a few by the (brute) force of privileged elites. Some institutions are informal, such as trust and commitment, while others – say, the limited liability corporation – needed co-ordinated action by lawmakers to get established as they did by the end of the nineteenth century.

Modern economic historians tend to explain institutions by pointing at their efficiency-enhancing effects. That works well for a large number of institutions and this is how we shall explain the emergence and persistent use of money as well as the evolution of banks in Chapter 7. Welfare state institutions are explained by the way they resolve potential market failures in private insurance and capital markets (Chapter 10). Private property rights can be seen as solving the inefficiencies of communal property rights; this is known as the *tragedy of the commons*. The *tragedy of the commons* is a metaphor for the waste of resources that may occur if there are no restrictions on the use of resources. If all have access to a resource – a forest, say – it will be over-exploited unless there are centrally planned restrictions on its use. The over-exploitation stems from the fact that each individual user generates a cost to others, what is technically known as an *externality**. If an individual logs timber for her own use, she will reduce the future availability of timber not only for herself but for others as well. But the cost to others does not affect or restrain the individual user because that cost does not enter as a private cost. The social costs of individual action are larger than the private costs. Deforestation is a serious problem in large parts of Africa at present because households need wood for cooking their meals.

A problem facing the entire world at present is the problem of access to fishing waters which has tended, historically, to erode fish stocks, despite attempts to regulate fishing rights. Throughout history, and as land and other resources have become scarce, the commons have been privatized. This process was intensified as population growth increased from the eighteenth century. However, privatization of the commons highlights a problem with institutional change. Although a new institution may solve an inefficiency problem, it often also creates an unwelcome distributional effect. The poorer sections of society in the eighteenth and nineteenth-century privatization of the commons were more dependent on common resources and were therefore also affected negatively when they were denied access after the closure of the commons.

Once we acknowledge that institutions often have specific effects on welfare and distribution of income we need to dwell on the meaning of the efficiency concept we use. Economists tend to stick to so-called *Pareto-efficiency**, which denotes a situation in which no one can become better off without someone else becoming worse off. Since institutional change often involves distributional effects, we find that concept limiting for historical analysis. Consequently, when we talk about an efficiency-enhancing institutional change we will include any change which confers a *net* increase in welfare. For example, the abolition of serfdom made landowners worse off, but these losses were smaller than the gains from a labour market where labour had the freedom to choose the best employment.

A fallacy committed by quite a few economists and economic historians is to assume that an institution is efficient just because it is persistent. However, institutions can survive because they serve the interests of social groups which happen to have the political power to resist change. Serfdom and slavery, discussed below, are an example. Other persistent institutions in European economic history, such as the craft guilds, are the subject of conflicting interpretations. Guilds were associations of producers in a particular field – say bakers – which restricted competition from outsiders and regulated entry into their profession, took care of the training of apprentices, fixed prices, and maintained certain quality standards in products. A well-articulated interpretation looks at guilds as efficient institutions in an economic context where markets were thin and did not work efficiently. The common critique of craft guilds maintains that they were just *rent-seeking** clubs, a sort of *cartel** which rigged prices and exploited consumers and delayed technological progress. The origin of that critique can be traced back to early liberals such as Adam Smith, who criticized guilds for their collusive behaviour and restrictive practices. However, there are dissenting voices suggesting that guilds solved inefficiencies in thin markets where some agents had market or political power.

The accusation that craft guilds delayed technological and product innovations has been challenged. This scholarly debate will probably never end. However, when Adam Smith attacked guilds they were already losing importance, and in the nineteenth century they were eventually dissolved in most of Europe, after having been in operation since medieval times. Merchant guilds such as the German Hansa, which was active in north-west Europe and the Baltic throughout the medieval period, had a distinct role in defending the rights of members against violations of rights in foreign cities. A single merchant could not credibly threaten to stop supplying a city, but the Hansa as a collective of merchants could and did. The Hansa did proclaim embargos against cities and could get valuable concessions from cities when vital supplies were cut off. This service to members was essential in a trading environment when foreign merchants were often treated in a discriminatory and arbitrary way.

5.2 The peculiarity of institutional explanations

When institutions are explained by their alleged efficiency-enhancing characteristics, arguments are based on a special type of causal structure. Look at the following explanations.

> 'Because the government cut taxes (at t_0) consumption increased (at t_1).'

This proposition suggests that an action of the government in period 0, a cut in taxes, happened prior to the effect, an increase in consumption which occurred in period 1. The cut in taxes caused increased consumption.

Explanations of institutions which invoke the efficiency-enhancing effects of an institution are fundamentally different. For example

> 'Private property rights evolve at (t_0) because they evade the inefficiency problem of common access to a resource (at t_1).'

The peculiar nature of this explanation is that the time structure is reversed. What you want to explain, that is the institution of private property rights, happens *before* the beneficial effect, that is the solution of an inefficiency problem. We call this causal structure a consequence explanation, because what you want to explain is explained by its beneficial consequences occurring at a later stage. If handled carefully it is not an inappropriate type of explanation. Evolutionary biology in the Darwin tradition is based on consequence explanations such as the following:

> 'Birds have light bones because that characteristic improves their capacity to fly and hence to escape predators'.

However, that explanation is based on a specific mechanism, natural selection, which ensures that the survival chances of a species with light bones will improve. The specific trait we want to explain, such as light bones, can develop through random mutation and natural selection, and is the process whereby species with life-enhancing traits such as light bones survive. The survival of the fittest, as it is popularly known.

To generate legitimate consequence explanations in history and social sciences we need mechanisms that guarantee that efficiency-improving institutions are selected and survive. In the following sections of this chapter, we will try to explore the mechanisms that may be at work. An analogy between natural selection and the competitive selection of markets may sometimes be appropriate: for example, when explaining why some firms are run by owners of capital and others by the suppliers of some essential input, as with producer-directed co-operatives. Statements about the efficiency of an institution are often based simply on its persistence, without specifying a plausible mechanism that selects efficient outcomes, and are therefore illegitimate. However, we also need to recognize that deliberate design of institutions is and has been practised in history, for example bank regulation, although innovative financial institutions always seem to be a step ahead of the regulators. We will not always be able to find a rationale for an institution other than that it serves vested interests, or even worse, that it is just accidental.

5.3 The characteristics of a modern economy

We have observed that income levels and growth rates differed among nations in pre-industrial Europe. Resource constraints, and in particular land constraints, were as a rule not negatively correlated with income. Densely populated areas in Europe were generally more affluent. These areas had access to regular commodity markets with a diversified demand. There were also efficiently functioning markets for land, capital and labour which were poorly developed in less densely populated areas. The Dutch economy (what we today call the Netherlands) in the sixteenth and seventeenth centuries was nominated as the 'first modern economy' by Jan de Vries and Ad van der Woude because it possessed all the institutional characteristics of a modern economy: free access to efficiently functioning markets, advanced division of labour, and a government that respected and enforced property rights – even intellectual property rights, i.e. patents. The idea that markets for factors of production promote growth is based on the plausible assumption that free labour seeks the best reward, that is, the most productive opportunity.

A similar argument would apply to capital and land. If land is used in an inefficient way, someone who imagines she can make more effective use of the land will be willing to offer a price for the land which the original owner cannot refuse.

A culture of thrift prevailed in the Netherlands because status was linked to effort and not to rights obtained by birth. The early development of markets for land and labour had to do with the fact that the feudal aristocracy never dominated the rural economy as in other parts of Europe. A tolerant mentality made the Netherlands a safe haven for talented immigrants forced from their homes by religious and political persecution. It is true that other economies, such as the city states of northern Italy, or England, had many of these traits and that Italy in fact had been the pioneer in capital market innovation and in contracting and contract enforcement. But the Dutch economy was unique in its sixteenth and seventeenth-century dynamics, when Italy was stagnating at a sophisticated level of division of labour. The former was rightly admired and considered as a model economy by no less an authority than Adam Smith and many others among the enlightened elites in Europe. But the Dutch case also demonstrates that the right institutions are necessary but not sufficient conditions for sustained growth. By the early nineteenth century, the model economy was no longer the Netherlands but Britain, which did not hesitate to borrow what was considered progressive from the Dutch.

The Netherlands and Britain shared another institutional characteristic conducive to economic growth: constraints on the political executive. A constitutional monarchy was established in England with the Glorious Revolution (1688–9), whereas until the end of the eighteenth or early nineteenth century most nations in Europe were ruled by absolutist monarchies with almost unlimited rights to tax citizens and grant trading privileges to people in an arbitrary way. It is true that the tax burden as a share of *national income* was quite low, but what disturbed commercial activity was the arbitrary and erratic nature of tax assessment. Uncertainty about future taxes and government privileges to some and barriers of entry into economic activity for others affected investments negatively in those nations where parliaments did not succeed in limiting the power of the monarchy.

The different development of the northern and southern Low Countries, which today constitute Belgium and the Netherlands, tells an interesting story. The northern part broke away in the late sixteenth century as the Dutch Republic. The war of independence was largely financed by merchant groups and the Dutch economy rose to pre-eminence. The southern part of the Low Countries remained under Spanish rule with its oppressive political and religious structures. While the Dutch Republic prospered, the initially richer south lost many of its most talented merchants and bankers, who fled to London or the Netherlands, and entered a long phase of economic decline.

There seems to be an important lesson from history already in the Early Modern period: sustained economic growth is not compatible with predatory cleptocratic government.

5.4 Market performance in history

The idea, derived from the basic principles of economics, that markets generate efficient outcomes is an important insight, but we need to qualify this optimistic message with the doubts and complexities of history. On the one hand, it is clear that markets tend to emerge spontaneously, and also that when they are suppressed they typically reappear as 'black markets'. We should therefore be in no doubt that people prefer markets because of their efficiency. Spot markets can operate without much formal or legal structure. Markets that include future delivery and deferred payment, or delivery to other markets, will need more legal structure as well as contract enforcement, though trust among traders is often preferable because it is less costly. So while it is obvious that market exchange, if it appears spontaneously, is preferable to no exchange or other forms of exchange such as *gift exchange**, it does not follow that all market exchanges work in the way prescribed by textbook economics.

Markets are rarely perfect and the performance of markets has varied in history. One of the major problems with attaining market efficiency is the fact that information about goods and services is difficult to get and costly to process. The price is supposed to summarize all relevant information about a good, but economics do not tell us much about how prices are actually set. We learn that in equilibrium a price will prevail which clears the market, so that supply equals demand. Looking at the price-setting process in markets separated by geographical distance offers some insight into the setting of prices. If we study the price of wheat in, say, Danzig (Gdansk) on the Baltic coast and Amsterdam we notice that there was an equilibrium price in Amsterdam that can be expressed as the price at the export location, that is Danzig, plus transport costs to Amsterdam. This equilibrium relationship is called the *law of one price**. It turns out, however, that the equilibrium price was rarely attained, but nonetheless it worked as an 'attractor' in the sense that the price difference between Amsterdam and Danzig did not permanently diverge from the transport cost, that is the law of one price. Deviations there were, but the law of one price conditioned prices so that there was convergence to a price gap which was equal to the transport cost. This adjustment process was very slow before the introduction of an efficient postal system, but the decisive step was taken with the introduction of the telegraph and the commercial press by the middle of the nineteenth century. Before then it could take several months before prices in one market, say Pisa, reacted to price changes in, say, Marseille. But when the telegraph linked Europe in the 1850s and the entire world in the 1860s and 1870s prices in Copenhagen could react immediately to price changes in far-away markets such as Chicago.

What happens when prices are far away from the market-clearing price? The answer is simple: markets do not clear! Trade and exchange is inhibited, post-poned, or constrained while the haggling over prices continues. If the price is above the *market clearing price** demand can be constrained, that is smaller than at the market-clearing price. However, a price above market clearing will lead to excess supply and it is in this very process that prices may adjust down to the market clearing price. If the price is below the market clearing price there will be excess demand but supply will be constrained. The market clearing price is a sort of attractor, like the law of one price. Throughout most of history, markets have been thin, meaning that participants were few and widely scattered, and information was hard to get and travelled slowly. We can easily imagine that potential trades were often inhibited or constrained and left trade and production at levels below full potential. It is difficult to measure the economic costs of constrained trade, but we observe that merchants and manufacturers addressed the problem by assembling scattered producers and their agents at yearly or seasonal fairs. Some of these fairs were truly pan-European, such as the fairs held in the Champagne area from the middle of the twelfth century; others were more local and held several times a year. The problem that the fairs were addressing was that without them markets would be thin with too few participants, so the risk of not getting on with the price-setting process was pressing. Fairs with thousands of participants were obviously thicker and the likelihood that deals could be concluded increased, which enhanced production and trade.

Have markets become more efficient over time? There is no simple answer to that question. Efficient markets need many participants and a cheap, fast and reliable flow of information. In that respect the conditions for market efficiency have improved considerably and irreversibly. The major changes in this respect occurred in the first era of globalization in the second half of the nineteenth century with the introduction of the telegraph and the commercial press. In international trade, the law of one price was more often and more seriously violated before 1870 than later, for example. But before the information revolution in the nineteenth century slow changes in information transmission occurred. A postal system with regular dispatches of commercial information developed from the beginning of the seventeenth century. On the negative side, economies of scale are more pronounced in the modern economy, so that firms have become larger and larger over time, particularly in the twentieth century. As a consequence quite a few large firms can exert market power if unrestrained by competition authorities, national and supra-national. To conclude, market efficiency has historically been impeded by slow and unreliable information, but is now more in peril because of the market power of large corporations.

5.5 The evolution of labour markets: the rise and decline of serfdom

As noted above, a common mistake made by economists and historians alike is to ascribe efficiency characteristics to institutions because they are pervasive and long-lived. The logic here seems to be that nothing inefficient will survive the judgment of history; it will have to go. However, institutions often have distributional consequences in that they favour particular classes in society – say, owners of land – and they can persist over long periods despite not being efficient. Serfdom in Europe is one example of a long-lived institution without apparent efficiency-enhancing characteristics. Serfs and their offspring were heavily dependent on their landlord. Serfdom typically developed in historical contexts of labour shortage such as the period after the population decline following the demise of the Roman Empire. The landowning elite, which also possessed a monopoly of physical power, had difficulties attracting labour to till the land in their possession because there was frontier land available which was as fertile as the land owned by the landlords. If labour was free to move it would and could negotiate a wage equal to its *opportunity income** on frontier land. But if labour was as productive at the frontier land as on the landlord's estate, the workers' pay would exhaust the entire output or value added on the estate. Consequently the land rent would be zero. Therefore landlords needed to restrict the mobility of workers, and that is exactly what serfdom is about. The peasant or farm worker was tied to the landlord's estate and could not exert the bargaining power inherent in a right to move and seek work elsewhere.

There are several reasons why serfdom and un-free labour was not an efficient use of labour: these reasons have to do with shirking and high monitoring costs. Peasants often had a small plot on which they could grow a subsistence output, and also performed labour services on the lord's estate. However, working on the plot for their own subsistence was self-monitoring in the sense that the work was performed in their own interest. Work on the estate was not. If there was a shortage of labour, the landlord's threat to evict poorly performing peasants was not credible and therefore peasants had every reason to shirk, which meant that the landlord had to monitor the work closely. Landlords still obtained a land rent, however, because they made peasants work on the estate and the value added exceeded monitoring costs.

This is a simplified story, first told comprehensively by the pioneering growth economist E. Domar, but it nonetheless encapsulates the historical dynamics, including the gradual dissolution of serfdom in Britain and most of Western Europe in the course of the later medieval period. When population growth picked up and continued into the second millennium, land shortage forced free labour to cultivate less fertile frontier land. That meant that the peasants' *opportunity income* fell, eventually to or below the wage offered by landlords. Now landlords could negotiate with free peasants and obtain a positive land rent. In this process peasants were liberated from their bonds of serfdom and gained customary rights to the land they tilled and for which they paid a rent to landlords instead of performing labour services. Although this process was well on its way before the Black Death, the ensuing labour shortage triggered off a wave of 'second serfdom' in some parts, particularly in eastern Europe.

While most of Western Europe entered the Early Modern period with reasonably efficient labour and land markets for sale and lease, the emancipation of the peasantry came much later in Denmark and Bohemia, at the end of the eighteenth century, even later in Prussia, in the first quarter of the nineteenth century, and not until the end of the nineteenth century in Russia. It is also worth noting that the end of serfdom in Britain was a spontaneous market-led process, while the late emancipations were initiated by reform-minded elites inspired by liberal ideology. This process suggests a specific and widespread form of institutional change: *imitation* of institutions which were judged to function well in other and more successful economies. The declared intention of the liberal elites working for land reform and emancipation of the peasantry in Prussia was to catch up with the leading European economies. The late emancipation of the peasantry had severe repercussions for the modernization of agriculture and industrialization. As long as labour mobility was restricted, industry was cut off from a potential supply of labour. In Germany, the belated emancipation of the farm workers increased supply and enabled industry to use low-cost labour in the early phase of industrialization. The proportion of self-monitoring owner-occupied agricultural units also increased because of land reforms.

5.6 Firms and farms

As a consequence of agricultural reforms the relative importance of the household-based farm increased while the big estates fell back. It is important to point out here that the share of estate production in total agricultural production has often been exaggerated because the estates were the only producers which kept records. Medieval England, which is usually considered an economy dominated by big estates, had a substantial share of peasant household production. Peasants who were leasing land and owner-occupiers produced most of the agricultural output, probably as much as 75 per cent even in the medieval period. Land ownership remained very unequal, but big landowners gradually chose to lease their land to farming households using family labour and a few hired hands. Consolidated farms run by households are an eighteenth and nineteenth-century phenomenon in Western Europe. Before the concentration of landholdings in single large plots, so-called open field agriculture prevailed in major parts of Europe, in which a household owned or leased land scattered in a large number of narrow strips around the village.

The open field layout allowed or forced farmers to co-operate in ploughing, sowing, weeding and harvesting. Historians have been puzzled by the endurance of this seemingly impractical system of having small plots of land scattered over a large area. There have been numerous attempts to find an efficiency-enhancing characteristic in open field agriculture. One explanation, associated with the economic historian D. McCloskey, suggests that by having its land scattered over the entire village the household minimized risks associated with local harvest shocks that could materialize if all land was concentrated in one location. Others have noted that small communities, such as a farming village, were built on mutual assistance, and the co-operation enforced by the field layout enabled members to monitor the efforts of others in order to maximize the output of all. An element of technological determinism lurks in the explanation that the heavy plough introduced in early medieval times was well suited to long strips of land and a co-operative work effort, since the heavy deep-cutting plough with a mould board needed several oxen to operate efficiently, and each household could muster at best one ox. These explanations are not mutually exclusive, but despite ingenious attempts to find a rationale in open field agriculture quite a few economic historians still find it more of a puzzle, and are entitled to feel that way.

As farming households were abandoning open field agriculture, sometimes forced to by ambitious and modernizing reformers, and consolidated their farms, manufacturing firms broke away from small-scale production. Why was it that in one sector, agriculture, the producing unit or institution remained linked to the household, while in another, industry, units were becoming larger?

Furthermore, in agriculture the worker (the peasant household) owns or leases land and is the *residual claimant**, that is the one that receives the remaining income, if any, when all expenses including rents have been met. In industry workers do not own or hire capital but are employed by the factory owner at a fixed wage, and the factory owner is the residual claimant. Why do workers not do as peasants do, that is own or hire the means of production?

Let us postpone the answer to this question and concentrate on why agriculture and industry developed along different lines as regards the size of the producing units. Agriculture differs from most other sectors in that nature dictates the conditions and pace of production. Work is performed in large fields and the quality of the effort by workers cannot be fully appreciated until harvest. However, natural accidents, both negative and positive, are likely to intervene between sowing and harvesting and it is difficult to disentangle the effects of labour effort and of nature. Thus agricultural workers will neither be fully rewarded for their effort nor be fully punished for shirking. Had economies of scale been sufficiently large it might have been possible to increase monitoring, but the potential for scale economies seems to be smaller in agriculture. Landowners therefore tend to lease or sell their land to farming households for which monitoring costs are by definition zero. That is, if you work for yourself you do not cheat yourself. Monitoring work effort in industry is easier. Workers are on the factory floor and in many cases machines and production design, say the conveyor belt, determines the pace of production. The quality of products is routinely assessed and malpractice by workers can be detected fairly easily. Systems of reward and control of work effort are not cost-free, but economies of scale in industry are larger because the production process is constrained only by human ingenuity and not by nature, as agriculture is.

In early industrialization, the economies of scale stemmed from the need for a critical mass of fixed investments. Textile mills, as the name reveals, initially relied not on steam-powered weaving but on water mills as the source of energy, and there are obvious scale effects in building water mills. These differences may explain the large and growing difference in the size of production units, but not necessarily why owners of capital employ workers rather than the other way around. It would be possible to imagine a world in which workers borrowed capital to set up labour-managed firms, but that has rarely happened. One obvious reason why it did not happen was that capital markets were poorly developed and imperfect in the first phase of industrialization. Early industrial entrepreneurs relied on borrowing from family and friends, and bank managers were likely to be among the friends of the rich rather than the poor. Modern research on the few examples of labour-managed firms that exist also indicates that such firms face credit constraints which are more binding than those facing capitalist firms. Furthermore, managing firms is inherently risky and the rich can endure risk better than the poor. The richer you are the more can you diversify your investments. Workers were poor and could not diversify if they put their meagre wealth into a labour-managed firm. The high risk exposure might discourage the formation of such firms. In this explanation, *path dependence** rules. In explanations based on path dependence a particular institution need not be the most efficient; it only needs to be sufficiently efficient to become established. Once established, perhaps by unique, even accidental, historical conditions, it will breed its own success and even exclude alternatives that are more efficient. In the context of a capitalist firm, the initial conditions – say, capital market imperfections and risk aversion – favour a particular institution, which then tends to be affirmed because the alternative option gets less and less likely. The path dependence constrains alternatives when owners of capital have acquired management skills and entrepreneurial ideals which they pass on from generation to generation.

But it is not the full explanation in this case. Capitalist firms proved more adaptive than labour-managed ones in competitive environments because they had one single aim, which was to maximize returns for the owners. Labour-managed firms had a diverse set of goals, including not to make the initial owners redundant, which retarded the introduction of labour-saving machinery. However, fast technological progress was necessary for long-term survival in a competitive environment with labour-saving technological change. Investment strategies also differed because labour-managed firms had shorter time horizons, usually limited by the working life of the owners. The historical failure of labour-managed firms in this perspective is therefore a case of market selection of the 'fittest' organizational type. There is no reason for undue celebration, however. A large number of capitalist firms fail every day, and those that survive do so because they are good at sacking employees if necessary.

5.7 Co-operatives and hold-up

In many areas the dominance of capitalist firms, that is firms managed by (representatives of) owners who were residual claimants, was challenged in the late nineteenth century by co-operative firms, managed by (representatives of) the suppliers of a major input processed by the firms. Well-known examples are the dairy co-operatives in Scandinavia, owned by farmers. In most cases these firms were latecomers, they crowded out already established capitalist firms within a few decades, by the end of the nineteenth century, as demonstrated by a Copenhagen-based economic historian, Ingrid Henriksen.

Why do co-operatives prevail in some lines of production and not in others? There are, for example, co-operative sawmills and paper producers, meat producers, dairies and wineries, but not car manufacturers or steel producers. The explanation offered here focusses on a problem that all firms face when relying, as they have to do, on others supplying them with inputs. A typical firm has to rely on tens or hundreds of input suppliers. Some of these suppliers may be able to exploit what is commonly talked about as hold-up power. That means that they can exert power over prices and the quality of the inputs they provide, or stop supplying at short notice.

The evolution of dairy co-operatives is an informative case. When they emerged and eventually crowded out capitalist dairy firms, transport technology and techniques for assessing the quality of the input, milk, were poorly developed. Firms had to rely on a critical mass of suppliers within a limited geographical area because milk is a perishable product. The scope for opportunistic behaviour by suppliers was great owing to the imperfection of methods for assessing the quality of the delivered milk. The dairy firms had difficulties exerting a credible threat to punish a supplier which did not deliver milk according to the agreed standards (for example by adding water to the milk), because each firm depended on the supply from a limited geographical supply area. A firm was 'locked in' by the investment in fixed capital with no alternative uses, whereas farmers could switch from dairy farming to meat production or tillage. So whereas dairies have an interest in long-run delivery contracts, farmers do not. When a firm is faced with suppliers who can exert hold-up power by refusing to supply agreed quantities according to long-term contracts, it normally tries to integrate that supply chain within the firm: so-called vertical integration. For example, a car manufacturing firm might choose to integrate the production of the steel it formerly bought from external suppliers if the supplier becomes a monopoly.

Vertical integration was not an option in late nineteenth-century agriculture, given the ownership structure in agriculture, since there was a multitude of independent farmers who had no interest in selling their property in order to become farm workers. Farming is a way of life as much as an economic activity. The co-operative dairy firms explicitly faced the risk of opportunistic behaviour on the part of the member-owners as well as the need for long-term commitments from the suppliers. A co-operative dairy was in fact a vertically integrated firm owned by the farmers who supplied the milk. Members had to commit themselves to long-term contracts but became the residual claimants. The problem of opportunistic behaviour was solved by severe punishment for those who were detected breaking quality requirements, and co-operatives used informants to monitor members' behaviour. Since members were the residual claimant, they had an interest in monitoring the other members and reporting misconduct. A member breaking the rules could be stripped of his membership rights, including the money he had invested in the co-operative. In a capitalist dairy firm the owner was the residual claimant and therefore suppliers had no interest in monitoring and reporting the misconduct of other suppliers.

5.8 Contracts, risks and contract enforcement

Contracts more often than not developed spontaneously, and tend to reduce risk and constrain the opportunistic behaviour of contracting parties.

In commerce, manufacturing and shipping, a way to reduce risk was partnership contracts. A person with liquid funds could invest in a number of commercial pursuits and each merchant then typically had a number of investors. The investors took a risk that the merchant would fail to make a profit, but contracts often stipulated a handsome return on the profits. Long-distance trade necessarily involved information asymmetries between merchants and investors. Partnerships developed further with the need for long-term capital in the nineteenth century: the limited liability model is an excellent example of an efficiency-enhancing institution. Investors get an expected positive return on their shares but take the risk of losing the money invested. However the investors were not liable for the damage or debts accumulated by the company they owned shares in.

Old-style partnerships could be associated with unlimited liability, which restricted the partnership to people who trusted each other. In early industrialization, members of partnerships were therefore often recruited from family and friends, which restricted the amount of capital that could be raised. Credit co-operatives, a type of savings bank which sprang up in rural areas in the nineteenth century, also had unlimited liability among members. In other words, a member could be liable for default by other members, and members therefore had to trust that others did not behave in an opportunistic way, that is, exploit the trust of others in their own interest. Trust relationships are extremely important for making societies work because contracts are rarely complete and are expensive to enforce. Trust is in a sense a self-enforcing unwritten contract for what in modern jargon is called *social capital*. A society cannot work adequately with widespread mutual distrust. It has been argued that the different development paths of credit co-operatives in northern Italy, where they prospered, and southern Italy, where they failed to take root, has to do with the fact that southern Italy, the *Mezzogiorno*, lacked the necessary social capital.

There is a large variety of contract types in labour markets and in commerce. The suspicion that there is no one single contract type that is supremely efficient but rather that several sufficiently efficient contract types co-exist is supported by the historical record. One particular institution, which has attracted the attention of theorists as well as historians, is the output-sharing contract, so-called sharecropping.

In agriculture, unlike in industrial firms where workers were paid a fixed wage, it was common practice for peasants to lease land not by paying a fixed rent but by surrendering a share of the output (*metayage* in French, *mezzadrìa* in Italian), often as much as half.

A share contract reduced labour effort compared to a contractual arrangement where the tenant farmer paid a fixed rent. In the latter case the incentive to produce a larger output was higher because the tenant could keep the entire output once the fixed rent was paid, whereas the sharecropper received only a share of the marginal output.

Box 5.1   Why sharecropping reduces work and output

Let us look at two producers identical in all respects except that one is paying a fixed rent and the other a share of output to the landlord. The fixed rent is 14 pence and the share contract stipulates that the producer pays half the output in rent. The output per hour of work is valued as worth 4 pence. The fixed rent producer keeps the entire marginal product having paid the rent of 14 pence from the first 3.5 hours of work. What will determine the total number of hours worked? The answer is that the limit is set by the opportunity cost of work, which is the value of leisure and rest. The more you work the higher the value you attach to an hour of leisure. Let us assume that the eighth hour of work has an opportunity cost (leisure value) of 2.5 pence. Clearly, the fixed rent producer will work that eighth hour because the value of output, 4 pence, is larger than the opportunity cost of work, 2.5 pence. However, the sharecropper will not work that eighth hour because half of the output of 4 pence must be paid to the landlord, and what remains, i.e. 2 pence, is smaller than the leisure value, that is the opportunity cost of work, which is 2.5 pence. Fixed rents promote work effort compared to share contracts, but in this particular example the landlord is indifferent because the rent extracted from the two producers is equal, 14 pence – which can easily be verified.

Faced with this apparent effort-reducing effect of the sharecropping contract, and observing the widespread use of the sharecropping contract from Antiquity to the present, theorists and historians have searched for hidden efficiency characteristics. One strand of thought has pointed out that sharecropping reduced the risk for the tenant farmer because in a bad harvest season rents would be reduced automatically, since only a fixed *share of the output* was paid rather than a fixed rent. However, it was common practice to allow tenants under fixed rent contracts to postpone rent payments until a year came with an abundant harvest. It is therefore not at all obvious that over an extended period of time the fixed rent tenant needed to pay more rent than the sharecropper. Other authors have made a virtue of necessity, pointing out that the output-reducing effect of the sharecropping contract stopped tenants over-exploiting the land. A fixed-rent tenant under a land-leasing arrangement could be expected to over-exploit the land (or the vine) in the short-term with negative long-term consequences. However, this was true only if the lease was a short-term contract. If the landowner extended the lease, tenants would not be tempted to obtain short-term gains which had long-term negative consequences. Tenants often obtained hereditary rights to a lease, giving them incentives to improve their land.

However, even if we are to believe that the share-contract was efficient for the contracting parties, it was not an output-maximizing institution from a social point of view, since it was associated with lower output than under the alternative institution, the fixed-rent contract.

5.9 Asymmetric information, reputation and self-enforcing contracts

Markets for spot exchange develop spontaneously and need only a minimal institutional framework. Since spot exchange is often local, buyers and sellers get to know each other and trust can emerge. Likewise traders who do not honour contracts will be punished by losing reputation and eventually be forced out of business. Long-distance trade is different because payment and delivery of commodities do not coincide. Specific problems arose because merchants typically used agents to complete an exchange in another market, and therefore we get a so-called *principal–agent problem**, which means that the agent can exploit asymmetries in information in his own interests against those of the principal, in this case the merchant. The agent knows something the principal does not know and has trouble verifying.

The Stanford economic historian Avner Greif has studied a wide variety of contracts in medieval trade, at a time when information travelled slowly and was difficult to assess. Given the difficulty of monitoring appropriate behaviour in agents, an ideal contract needed to be self-monitoring. That is, it should be in the agent's own interest to be honest, or, to put it another way, the long-term gains from honesty must be higher than the short-term gains from cheating. To secure that, reputation has to matter. An agent must know that cheating can be detected, if not by his merchant, then possibly by someone else in a fellowship of merchants. Therefore merchants joined forces, reported any misconduct by agents, and agreed not to employ agents who had been discovered to behave dishonestly. Since agents knew that reputation mattered for future employment, they had an interest in complying with agreed standards of behaviour.

Ethnic groups – Jews, Lombards from northern Italy, Flemings and the German Hansa – operated throughout Europe and formed close and exclusive networks. Most major cities had a Rue Juive or a Lombard Street. One possible interpretation of merchants or financiers sticking together along ethnic lines is that ethnicity facilitated the dissemination of information about members' conduct, since an ethnic group shared common beliefs and language. Reputation is built and destroyed by repeated contact within a fairly tight group of people who meet frequently in commerce as well in social life.

Summary

The ingenuity of researchers in explaining apparently inefficient institutions is impressive but not always successful. Institutions are explained by their consequences, but the selection mechanism may be biased towards vested interests unlike the natural selection mechanism in evolutionary biology which is blind or unbiased. But even if we have difficulty explaining some institutions, the conclusion is not pessimistic. It is only that sometimes history plays tricks on us.

All in all, a large number of institutions exist because of their efficiency-enhancing properties: co-operatives, limited liability corporations, trust, property rights, money, banks, checks and balances on the political executive, and the regulation of monopolies, to mention just a few.

Suggestions for further reading

The Nobel laureate Douglass C. North has been an influential writer on institutions and economic growth. See for example his *Institutions: Institutional Change and Economic Performance* (Cambridge University Press, 1990). A detailed and well-researched case that explores, among other things, the importance of modern institutions is J. De Vries and A. van der Woude, *The First Modern Economy, Success, Failure and Perseverance of the Dutch Economy, 1500–1815* (Cambridge University Press, 1997).

For an insightful overview of the potential fallacies in the historical analysis of institutions see S. Ogilvie , 'Whatever is, is right? Economic institutions in pre-industrial Europe', *Economic History Review* 60 (4) (2007), pp. 649–84.

Open-field farming is a topic with an ever-growing literature. See D. McCloskey's influential article 'English open fields as behaviour towards risk', *Research in Economic History* 1 (1976), pp. 124–70.

The two views on craft guilds referred to in the text are well represented by the background literature cited in S. R. Epstein, 'Craft guilds in the pre-modern economy: a discussion' and the response by S. Ogilvie, 'Rehabilitating the guilds: a reply', in *Economic History Review* 61 (1) (2008), pp. 155–74 and 175–82.

On sharecropping, see F. Galassi, 'An econometric model of farm tenures in 15th century Florence', *Economica* 65 (1998), pp. 535–56, which also has references to the theoretical literature.

Co-operatives have been discussed by Ingrid Henriksen: see for example 'Avoiding lock-in: co-operative creameries in Denmark, 1882–1903', *European Review of Economic History*, 3 (1) (1999), pp. 57–78.

Medieval trading contracts have been analysed in an innovative way by Avner Greif in a number of journal articles and in *Institutions and the Path to the Modern Economy: Lessons from Medieval Trade* (Cambridge University Press, 2006). For an analysis in Greif's spirit see Y. Gonzalez de Lara, 'The secret of Venetian success: a public-order, reputation-based institution', *European Review of Economic History* 12 (3) (2008), pp. 247–85.

E. Domar developed a simple theory of serfdom in his 'The causes of slavery and serfdom, a hypothesis', *Journal of Economic History* 30 (1) (1970), pp. 18–32.

6 Knowledge, technology transfer and convergence

6.1 Industrial Revolution, Industrious Revolution and Industrial Enlightenment

The pre-industrial era witnessed a number of ground-breaking innovations and improvements, but they were typically generated by learning by doing. Producers learned that things worked, but had limited understanding of *why* things worked. From the seventeenth century, decisive efforts were directed towards gaining more and better knowledge of the 'laws of nature'. However, it is wrong to believe that the British Industrial Revolution, the period 1770–1830, was based on a scientific understanding of production processes. Decisive steps were taken in that period towards a more profound understanding of nature, but these accomplishments had little immediate impact on production technologies. The iconic invention of the eighteenth century, the steam engine, is the exception that confirms this rule. The steam engine developed by Thomas Newcomen (1663–1729) relied on the results of scientific inquiry from the preceding century by the Italians Galileo Galilei (1564–1642) and Evangelista Torricelli (1608–97), the Dutchman Christiaan Huygens (1629–95), and Otto von Guericke (1602–86), a German, regarding atmospheric pressure, the weight of air and the nature of a vacuum. In the first generation of steam engines, the steam was condensed in a cylinder, which created a vacuum, and then the piston was pushed into the cylinder by atmospheric pressure.

The massive breakthrough of technologies, which sprang out of abstract theoretical inquiry coupled with empirical testing, did not arrive until the second half of the nineteenth century and mostly in the closing decades of that century. There is no denying, however, that systematic experiments, often combined with limited or flawed theoretical knowledge, became more common before and during the Industrial Revolution.

These misconceptions regarding the role of science contributed to very optimistic assessments of economic growth in the traditional historical narrative of what made Britain 'the first industrial nation'. The lethargy of the pre-industrial era was contrasted with an alleged rapid surge in growth. This view was fundamentally revised by revisionist scholarship initiated by Nicholas Crafts and Knick Harley during the closing decades of the twentieth century. They argued that there was more of an industrial *transition* than an industrial *revolution*, and the focus on Britain has concealed the fact that there was a pan-European intellectual enlightenment going on. That industrial enlightenment, as Joel Mokyr calls it, was a prelude to the ground-breaking scientific revolutions of the nineteenth century which not only transformed the economies of the second half of that nineteenth century but continued to dominate most twentieth-century production technologies as well. Furthermore, the Industrial Revolution was preceded and triggered off by what the Berkeley economic historian Jan de Vries calls an Industrious Revolution, a fundamental change in consumer behaviour. He documents a higher degree of market involvement by all household members either as producers of marketable goods or as expanded labour supply during the century before the Industrial Revolution. Increased income spilled over into an appetite for new commodities. This demand-side vision of the preconditions of the Industrial Revolution serves as a correction to supply-side bias in the traditional interpretation, according to which technological progress makes the goods accessible to a broader spectrum of the population.

The concept of an Industrial *Revolution* suggests a radical and sudden transformation of economic life. It is part of the folklore of the Industrial Revolution that it was associated with rapid growth and the widespread introduction and rapid diffusion of new technologies and energy sources such as steam. While nobody living through the French Revolution, say the period 1789–95, could fail to notice it, and quite a few lost their heads, most contemporaries of the Industrial Revolution were unaware of it. The economists active in the period were convinced that sustained growth was impossible due to resource constraints. In fact, the concept of an Industrial Revolution was not coined until around 1850, when the consequences of decades of higher growth were discernible in higher living standards.

Economic historians have, in recent years, become increasingly dissatisfied with the traditional view of the Industrial Revolution. Some suggest that the concept itself is a misnomer. It is true that new technologies were introduced, but the pace at which they were adopted was much slower than previously believed. Most of these technologies were sector-specific rather than 'general-purpose', i.e. applicable to a large number of different industrial activities. A possible exception was, again, the development of the steam engine. For most of the eighteenth century it was used almost exclusively to pump water from coal mines. The location in coal mines was appropriate because early steam engines were extremely energy inefficient and needed cheap fossil fuel. Since coal is a bulky good it could not be transported over long distances using prevailing transport technology. The introduction of fossil resources as a source of energy and power had revolutionary implications because they replaced human and animal muscle power, and (more slowly) wind and water power. Before that could happen, however, energy savings were necessary.

There was, indeed, a continuous reduction in coal consumption per horse-power-hour as the steam engine was improved. Over about 175 years from the early eighteenth century, the coal used to generate one horsepower hour fell by a factor of almost 45. During the initial phase of the Industrial Revolution, the major energy source for industry remained water power, and that is why the factories were called *mills*, i.e. machines were driven by water *mills*. Not until the middle of the nineteenth century did steam engines have an impact on transport; and sail, which continued to increase in speed and efficiency, remained the dominant mode of long-distance sea transport until the late nineteenth century and was not phased out until the early decades of the twentieth century.

What has recently been recognized is that the Industrial Revolution was limited to a revolutionary change in certain sectors, specifically the textile industries, and to be more precise, the spinning and weaving of cotton cloth. In that process cotton replaced linen, a fibre not as easily adaptable to mechanized spinning as cotton. However, spinning had been developed continuously since medieval times. With hindsight, some of the pre-industrial innovations might seem simple, such as introducing a foot treadle to drive the spinning wheel, which released one hand previously used to set the wheel in motion; or the mechanical winding of yarn using a flyer. This reinterpretation of the Industrial Revolution also indicates that the technological changes that occurred were the result of trial and error rather than scientific discovery. The innovators were skilled craftsmen rather than scientists, and again it was not until the second half of the nineteenth century, almost a century after the Industrial Revolution in Britain, that science entered as a major innovative force in production processes and the development of new products. However, the fact that skilled craftsmen were not trained as scientists does not mean that they did not have a scientific mentality, a rational attitude to nature, an urge to mend it, and a will to learn from experiments.

All this seems to stress the continuity rather than the revolutionary impact of the economic changes from 1770 to 1830. And indeed, growth accounting has revised growth figures considerably. Table 6.1 lists the conventional view, represented by the pioneering work by W. A. Cole and P. Dean and the new

Table 6.1   TFP growth and new and old estimates of national product growth in Britain during the Industrial Revolution. Per cent per year

	TFP	Revised estimates		Dean & Cole	
		National product	Per head	National product	Per head
1700–60		0.69	0.31	0.66	0.45
1760–80	0.14*	0.70	0.01	0.65	-0.04
1780–1801	0.14*	1.32	0.35	2.06	1.08
1801–31	0.41	1.97	0.52	3.06	1.61

Sources: N. F. R. Crafts, *British Economic Growth during the Industrial Revolution* (Oxford: Clarendon Press, 1985), and for TFP estimates based on Crafts' and Harley's revisions, J. Mokyr, 'Accounting for the Industrial Revolution', in R. Floud and P. Johnson (eds.), *The Cambridge Economic History of Modern Britain* (Cambridge University Press, 2004), pp.1–27.
* The TFP growth of 0.14 is estimated for the entire period 1760–1800.

results from the work of 'revisionist' economic historians such as N. F. R. Crafts and K. Harley. The results of recent revisions actually stress that there was not much difference between pre-industrial growth and in the early phase of the Industrial Revolution.

As can easily be seen, the major revisions concern the alleged industrial breakthrough period, i.e. 1780–1830, where per capita growth rates have been reduced to about ⅓ of the previous estimates. In fact, the output growth per head is only slightly higher than in the pre-industrial period. The total factor productivity (TFP) growth is at par with the numbers we found in medieval and Early Modern agriculture as reported in Chapter 4. The main reasons why the new results differ from the old are (i) that previous estimates gave too much weight to the new and fast-growing industries (for example cotton) in aggregate industrial output, compared to old industries and (ii) that the size of the industrial sector in the total economy was exaggerated. Since only a few new industrial sectors actually experienced a radical transformation and fast growth, the weightings of different industries will have an important impact on overall growth. Not knowing the exact relative size of the modern industries, authors made different assumptions, usually over-stating the actual weight of the new sectors. Another source of confusion over growth rates has to do with the familiar index problem. Using base year weights usually understates growth relative to an estimate based on end year weights. Today authors tend to stick to the Divisia index, which in a loose sense is an average of indices using base and end year weights. For example, using sectoral value-added proportions from 1770, overall industrial growth would be 1.6 per cent per year up to 1801, but using 1801 value-added shares, growth almost doubles to 3 per cent per year. The reason is, of course, that by 1801 the sectors that were relatively unimportant, but fast growing, in the late eighteenth century were increasing their share of industrial output. Attributing too large a share to a modern sector has the obvious effect of overstating growth.

Is it reasonable, then, in view of these radical revisions of growth rates, to speak about an industrial *revolution?* If we mean a quick and sudden change to higher per capita growth rates – a sharp upward turn in growth rates, as Ashton put it – the answer is *no.* Modern economic growth, say at levels around 1.5–2 per cent in per capita terms per year, prevailed in Britain from around the middle of the nineteenth century and only by the end of the century in the rest of industrializing Europe.

However, Joel Mokyr argues that the slow acceleration of growth concealed fundamental changes in the intellectual climate, which motivated his notion of an *industrial enlightenment* that flourished in that period. Europe was unique in having had more than a century of an emerging scientific culture of rational inquiry into the laws of nature. Nature could be understood by uninhibited systematic investigation, and what could be understood should be tamed and controlled. There are two elements worth stressing in this triumph of the scientific approach to nature and production. It was a pan-European movement, (meaning Europe and its later offshoots in North America), rather than an isolated British story. The steam engine was invented and widely diffused in Britain but, as we have said, relied on prior experiments conducted by scientists from all over Europe in the seventeenth century. The names of early (late eighteenth and early nineteenth century) contributors to the understanding of electricity also reveal a diversity of national backgrounds: Luigi Galvani (1737–98) and Alessandro Volta (1745–1827), Humphry Davy (1778–1829) and his disciple Michael Faraday (1791–1867), André-Marie Ampère (1775–1836), Hans-Christian Ørsted (1777–1851), who lived and worked in the Copenhagen building where the Ph.D. students of my Department now have their offices, and the German Georg Ohm (1789–1854). There were nationals of other European countries who were instrumental in increasing the understanding that opened up later industrial and commercial uses of electricity for lighting, telegraphic communication and electrical generators and motors. Early advances in chemistry are also attributable to scholars from all over Europe, such as the Swede Carl Wilhelm Scheele (1742–1786) and the Englishman Joseph Priestley (1733–1804), who independently discovered oxygen, and Antoine Lavoisier (1743–94), the unfortunate victim of an invention Europe could do without: the guillotine. In the second half of the nineteenth century chemistry was dominated by Germans educated and teaching in the expanding technical universities which supplied industry with professionals working in research departments. The costs of accessing the new knowledge fell as scientific societies were formed both as a forum for researchers to present new results and later to popularize and diffuse useful knowledge. Catalogues of useful inventions were edited, industrial exhibitions were organized, and the travel writers of the time reported on production methods and products used in other countries and propagated them at home if they were considered best or better practice. The nineteenth century was an age of improvement.

The industrial enlightenment was a *uniquely* European phenomenon (if we include European offshoots in North America), although some areas made no significant contributions, such as Eastern Europe and the Iberian Peninsula and its offshoots in Latin America. The drift towards the use of science in the control of nature for commercial purposes took place at a time when technological stagnation characterized the rest of the world. The Muslim golden age had come to an end in the twelfth century and China's self-chosen isolation led to stagnation in the Early Modern period. Europe was well prepared to be the unique location of sustained economic growth fuelled by new knowledge-based technologies. That the Industrial Revolution first occurred in Britain may be more accidental. Mokyr boldly asserts that had it not happened in Britain it would have happened somewhere else, but certainly in Europe, possibly with a delay of a decade or two. Behind this assertion is the assessment that Europe's unique institutional conditions for gainful accumulation of useful knowledge started its ascent to higher permanent growth.

The scientific societies formed before and during the Industrial Revolution were concerned with open access to knowledge and therefore offered prizes and tried to discourage innovators from seeking patents. A patent does of course increase access costs over its limited lifetime, but it nevertheless keeps the knowledge it protects in the public domain even if use of that knowledge is subject to paying the innovator a fee or royalty. However, patents were seldom if ever extended to abstract, theoretically ground-breaking discoveries, but only to commercially viable applications of knowledge. Nonetheless patent rights reveal a dilemma. From a social point of view, it would be advantageous for all useful knowledge to be freely available. The *tragedy of the commons* (see chapter 5, section 5), the risk of the resource being exhausted by use, does not apply to the commons of knowledge. However, it can plausibly be argued that the rate of invention of useful applications of knowledge would be lower in the absence of the incentive that patent rights offer. It has been debated, without conclusive results, whether patent rights were decisive in early industrializing innovations, say in the early nineteenth century. It seems that the gratification of fame and reputation was often sufficient, or so many an innovator maintained, but it is revealing that many of them were fighting for the proceeds of patent rights even at the end of the eighteenth century. In the second half of the

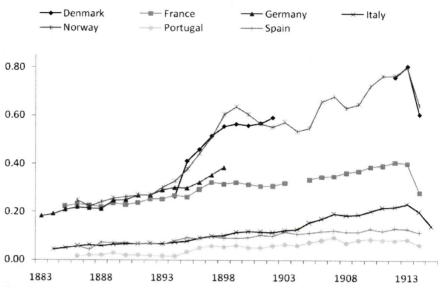

Figure 6.1   Patent applications per year in various European nations, 1860–1916. Per 1000 inhabitants. Source: WIPO statistics Database.

nineteenth century inventors rushed to the patent offices to file applications. The reason was that many ground-breaking innovations were developed simultaneously and independently, which in quite a few cases led to in long and bitter patent rights litigation. Thomas Edison (1847–1931) applied in 1877 to patent the 'speaking telephone': his patent was the number 474230 in the US patent office and at about that time several others made similar applications, including Alexander Graham Bell (1847–1922) in 1876.

Figure 6.1 shows substantial variations in the rate of patent applications across countries as well as a rising trend which is broken by the outbreak of the First World War. We noticed above that the Iberian Peninsula was remarkable for missing out on the Industrial Enlightenment and the nineteenth-century scientific breakthrough and this is again demonstrated by the low number of patent applications from Spain and Portugal. Scandinavian nations do well, on the other hand, even compared to France. Patent applications not only indicate the vitality of the scientific community in a nation but by implication indicate how good a society is at absorbing new knowledge produced elsewhere in the world. The wider implications of this insight will be discussed in Section 6.5 below.

Despite differences in levels of patent activities, there is a slow increase in all nations until the outbreak of the First World War. Wars kill not only people but patents as well.

The new era of sustained and higher economic growth has three characteristics with a profound impact on per capita growth. First, from the middle of the nineteenth century, science-based knowledge became a major factor in economic growth, and as a consequence total factor productivity increased. Secondly, the flow of inventions of new products and production processes stimulated investments, and capital per labourer increased, which led to an increase in labour productivity. Finally, increasingly sophisticated technologies and production processes increased the demand for education and human capital investment. New occupations emerged: engineers, teachers, accountants, university-trained scientists such as physicists and chemists. Science-based production technologies transformed old sectors such as metallurgy, and created new products and services relying on the taming of electricity and chemistry. The learning-by-doing process we know from the pre-industrial period remained, but science-based technology turned out to be much stronger in its effect on growth.

6.2 Science and entrepreneurship

An increased pace in the generation of new ideas and an increase in human and physical capital per employee are the major vehicles in the era of modern economic growth. Scientific truths are, however, seldom irrefutable and that certainly applies to early science. Still, it could direct inventors in the right direction. Quite a few nineteenth-century innovators had a poor formal training, but that did not preclude a scientific mind in the sense that they conducted endless trials and experiments and communicated results to critically minded fellows. Many innovators were more skilled and original as entrepreneurs than as researchers. Just two names suffice to illustrate that point. Alfred Nobel (1833–1896) is associated with the successful commercialization of dynamite, which after 1870 replaced gunpowder, a much less powerful explosive of Chinese origin. His major contribution was to make nitro-glycerine less hazardous by making its ignition safer in industrial use. Dynamite transformed the mining industry and helped the building of railways, tunnels and roads. Nobel's successful industrial pursuits generated the endowment for the Nobel Foundation and its prizes. Guglielmo Marconi (1874–1937), who was awarded the Nobel price for physics (in 1909), made wireless communication commercially successful and filed the first patent, although his theoretical and experimental work were anticipated by several researchers who failed to see its commercial potential.

The scientific foundation for new discoveries was often quite shaky until the mid-1850s. As the subsequent development of chemistry revealed, Lavoisier, Scheele and Priestley's discoveries rested on a flawed theory. This was not uncommon in the early development of scientific discovery. But accidental discoveries now attracted scientists searching for explanations. The preservation of food by canning under heat was increasingly used commercially from the beginning of the nineteenth century, but no one fully understood *why* food was successfully preserved until the work of Louis Pasteur (1822–1895) around 1860 on micro-organisms and microbes in the air. That sort of feedback from useful and accidental innovations to scientific advances was impossible or very rare in the pre-industrial era.

6.3 The impact of new knowledge: brains replace muscles

The new technologies emerging in the late eighteenth and in the nineteenth centuries developed production processes for known commodities such as paper and steel, but also opened up services and production processes for entirely new products. The basics of metallurgy and paper processing were and have remained quite simple. In paper making the cellulose from natural fibres has to be separated from other elements that negatively affect the quality and durability of the paper. This is done by mechanical and chemical processes; the latter became the dominant methods from the end of the nineteenth century. Mankind has used iron for millennia. Iron was originally made by heating iron ore with charcoal and blowing air over it, from which the word *blast* furnace stems. The iron generated this way will take up carbon, which makes the iron brittle, so-called pig iron or cast iron. In steelmaking you decarburize pig iron and add other metals to get the desired quality. Pig or cast iron is an input in steelmaking. Steel is more heat and impact-resistant than pig iron; it became the most important material in the new era and is now produced in hundreds of specific varieties or qualities. It can be hardened, say, for medical instruments or ball bearings, it forms the skeletons of high-rise buildings, and adding chromium turns it into stainless steel.

The single most important cluster of entirely *new* technologies in the nineteenth century centred on electricity, which affected a large number of old production processes and formed the basis for a large number of new products. Electricity was what is now called a general-purpose technology, which generated and still generates a flow of applications.

Instead of giving a detailed account of the development of each technology, we will discuss some general characteristics of technological change with examples from *old* (paper and steel) and *new* (electricity) technologies.

Which were the general characteristics? Technological progress (i) was resource saving, (ii) lessened the constraints of nature, in particular reliance on human and animal energy, (iii) improved the quality of commodities, (iv) developed new products and services, and (v) widened the resource base for industrial use.

(i)–(ii) Saving resources and lessening natural constraints

It is convenient to discuss the first two characteristics under one heading. Conserving the resources and delivering mankind from the constraints imposed by nature are the defining characteristics of technological progress and were not new in the nineteenth or twentieth century. What was new, however, was that these characteristics were working at an order of magnitude not known in history before. The Industrial Revolution was associated with worker protests by so-called Luddites, against the displacement of human labour by water or steam-powered spinning and weaving in the textile industry. It is certainly true that in a few formative decades from the 1760s a number of innovations greatly reduced the number of labour hours needed in spinning and weaving through the introduction of the spinning jenny (mid 1760s) and the mule (a watermill-powered spinning device), and varieties of mechanized weaving (the power loom). However, nineteenth-century inventions were not systematically just labour saving. The Oxford-based economic historian Bob Allen maintains, however, that in the formative years of the British industrial breakthrough a unique characteristic of Britain was the fact that it was a high-wage economy with cheap energy resources, that triggered off primarily labour-saving inventions. The hall of fame of textile industry inventors consists almost exclusively of Englishmen, such as Samuel Crompton (1753–1827), Thomas Highs (1718–1803) and James Hargreaves (1720–78), all of whom contributed to the labour-saving mechanization of spinning, and Edmund Cartwright (1743–1823), who pioneered mechanical weaving with the introduction of the power loom. The reputation of Richard Arkwright (1733–92) as an inventor is more tarnished. Karl Marx (1818–83), who inspired many a *social* engineer of socialist inclination, called him a 'thief of others' inventions', but Arkwright was the most successful entrepreneur and all the steps in textile production were mechanized in his factories. However, the most intriguing device was the Jacquard loom (1801) because it introduced pre-programmed control of the production process. The Frenchman Joseph-Marie Jacquard (1752–1834) built on designs by predecessors in eighteenth-century France. The Jacquard loom made it possible to weave complicated and refined patterns mechanically by having the weaving directed by punch cards. The punch card was the programme for the pattern and the technology was primarily labour-saving.

A resource-saving bias was typical of other sectors, however. Traditional steelmaking was extremely slow and consumed a lot of coal and man-hours. Two important technical breakthroughs in steelmaking made for mass-produced cheap steel, which saved both man-hours and coal: the Bessemer converter and the Siemens-Martin open hearth process. The Bessemer converter, named after Henry Bessemer (1813–98), blew cold air through molten pig iron to reduce impurities and decarburize the iron. The size of these converters increased over time and the duration of the steelmaking process was reduced to half an hour. However, in steelmaking much of the heat generated was lost. William Siemens (1823–83) designed and Emile Martin (1814–1915) perfected new processes, and the two, who did not collaborate, managed to agree to share the proceeds from the patent. It was a rare example of peaceful resolution of a conflict over intellectual property rights. The so-called Siemens-Martin process explicitly addressed the need to save fuel by reusing the hot gases to warm a brick chamber through which the fresh air needed for combustion was fed. The temperatures reached were extremely high, more than 1600 degrees centigrade. This method, duly improved over time, was important in steelmaking until the middle of the twentieth century, when more cost-effective methods were introduced (see below under (iv) for details).

The discovery and use of electricity well illustrates the saving of other resources as well as the softening of the constraints of nature. The electric motor, which was based on the principles of electromagnetism discovered by H. C. Ørsted and Michael Faraday, took a long time (until the 1890s to develop into a commercially useful device, for both home and industry. However, once developed the electric motor was superior to steam as a prime mover in industry because of the high proportion of electricity it converted to kinetic energy and its flexibility. However, the electric motor did not enter seriously into industrial use until the early twentieth century, when it loosened a location constraint imposed by earlier energy sources. A century earlier industrial location had been determined by the availability of water for the mills. Steam engines needed a critical size and cheap coal to be economically viable. Electric motors had none of these constraints. They can be purpose built to deliver widely different amounts of power, for anything from household fans to locomotives. Rather than having a central source of energy to which machines were linked by shafts, each machine could be driven by its own electric motor given an electricity grid. Electricity was produced initially by kinetic energy from steam engines and later by the more energy-saving steam turbine. In a sense, an electricity generator is the reverse of an electric motor. The steam turbine, invented in the late 1870s, proved to be a more efficient user of energy and is still the major producer of electricity from fossil fuels and nuclear energy. In the early years of 'the electrical age', the 1880s, electricity was generated locally for local use. The transmission of electricity over long distances involved large losses. Both production and consumption of electricity are most convenient at low voltages, but high voltage will reduce the losses in transmission. Transformers, which again used principles laid down by Michael Faraday, turned low-voltage electricity at the point of production into high voltage for transmission and then back to low voltage at the point of consumption. This stimulated the building of power plants, which exploited the scale economics of steam turbines. As geographical distance became less of a constraint the kinetic energy from flowing water driving turbines could be used to generate electricity which was then transmitted to far-away customers and across borders. Transformers were introduced in the 1890s. Long-distance electricity transmission technologies broke the link between the locations of production and consumption and gave a second lease of life to water and, more recently, wind power.

More generally the electrification of production processes in the twentieth century and the development of that other prime mover invented in the final decades of the nineteenth century, the internal combustion engine, replaced animate power supplied by the muscles of men and animals with inanimate power produced by fossil fuels like coal and oil. Brains replaced muscles.

(iii) Quality improvement (and quality differentiation)

Romantic critics of the industrial age, for example the Arts and Crafts movement in Britain, deplored the alleged vulgarity and cheapness of the machine-made commodities. It is true that luxury goods were not suited to the long standardized production runs that characterized mechanized production. However, the industrial age saw both quality improvements and quality differentiation. Sometimes quality differentiation is mistaken for a general fall in quality. But cheap low-quality products make perfect sense sometimes. The diffusion of cheap mass-circulation newspapers was made possible by the production of paper, a commodity which does not last long. Newspapers are not meant to last, except in the opinion of historians who deplore the bad state of newspapers in archives. Fortunately, most of theses sources are now available in electronic form.

The problem of quality improvement becomes significant when we measure the welfare gains from technological change. The *real wage* is the nominal wage deflated (divided) by a cost of living index. That index is supposed to trace the price changes in a bundle of goods of constant quality. Changes in the quality of a product are difficult to measure, however. This might generate a bias in the estimate of the true gains from technological change. Fast techno-logical progress in a specific sector relative to other sectors usually translates into a fall in the relative price of the commodities produced. However, if the quality of a product is improved we should control for that because in the case just referred to you pay less for an improved commodity. The problem is that the quality improvement of many products is difficult to assess pre-cisely. William Nordhaus, an economist at Yale University, has looked into an area in which it is possible to estimate the quality precisely, namely light. Light can be measured by lumen hours, but conventional price indices for light do not involve any serious quality control. The history of lighting is one of the many examples of the impact of the electrical age: electric light bulbs replaced a variety of illumination devices such as candles, gas lamps, kerosene and oil lamps. The perseverance of the light bulb as a major source of light to this very day is another example of the remarkable technological vitality of the late nineteenth century. Thomas Edison, the indefatigable American innovator, was one of many working on improved electric lighting; he was not the first to demonstrate incandescent light, although it was he who understood how to make economically efficient lighting systems. The first light bulb built on the principle of incandescent light was demonstrated in 1878 in England and ascribed to Joseph Wilson Swan (1828–1914). The subsequent technological refinement was directed towards improving the filament in the light bulb, i.e. the thread whose resistance generates the incandescent light. Initially, carbon-ized natural fibres were used by both Swan and Edison, but by the turn of the century metallic filaments dominated because of the efficiency gains in terms of lumen and the lifetime of the bulb. Conventional price indices for light tend to neglect these quality improvements, and according to Nordhaus that neglect seriously under-estimates the true fall in the price of light (lumen). According to his estimates, the true price of light fell in the order of between 3 and 4 per cent per year, relative to conventional measures of that price, between 1800 and 1990. The divergence between his quality-adjusted price assessments and the conventional assessment does not really begin until the middle of the nine-teenth century, however. Although light occupies only a small fraction of most household budgets the neglect of quality improvements makes for a signifi-cant under-estimation of the increase in real wages over time.

(iv) New products and production processes

The nineteenth century was unique in that an unprecedented number of inno-vations were made which in perfected form are still around and dominate our lives: mechanized textile production, electricity, electrically driven motors and household appliances (the first bread toaster was patented in 1909), electrical light, combustion engines and cars, wireless communication, the telephone, integrated production of paper, new materials (plastic) generated by advances in chemistry, reinforced concrete, high-quality steel and alloys.

The construction industry is interesting because it was initially unaffected by new technologies. However, from the middle of the nineteenth century the increased supply of cheap steel revolutionized building techniques, and these techniques remain dominant in the twenty-first century. In the early nineteenth century cast iron began to be used in bridges and buildings as well as for ornamental details. However, its tensile strength was insufficient and the expansion of the steel supply offered a better alternative. Steel can provide the skeleton in tall buildings, as the Eiffel Tower was supposed to demonstrate when it was built for the Industrial Exhibition in Paris in 1889. Steel became and remains the essential component of reinforced concrete (first patented in 1854) which became the dominant building material in the twentieth century. Concrete is a Roman invention, a mixture of cement, sand and water. Improved cement appeared in the early nineteenth century, but the great leap forward was *reinforced* concrete, in which a steel structure is placed within concrete. It combines the advantage of concrete (high scores in compression) with the high tensile strength of steel. Insufficiently reinforced concrete is very sensitive to shocks, for example earthquakes, as victims of corrupt builders repeatedly experience.

Even the only new prime mover invented in the twentieth century, the jet engine, has its roots in the nineteenth century. It is, after all, an application of the principles behind the internal combustion engine. In the four-stroke combustion engine, also called the Otto-cycle after the innovator Nicolaus Otto (1832–91), air or oxygen is mixed with fuel which is drawn into a cylinder, where it is compressed by the upward movement of a piston; the compressed gas explodes when ignited or by heat (in the Diesel variety of the combustion engine) and produces high pressure, which generates a thrust driving another piston. The early development of the combustion engine was dominated by German engineers, but the rationalization of the production process, which lowered the price so that cars became accessible to ordinary people, was initiated in the USA by Henry Ford (1863–1947). The first combustion engines were designed for industrial use as a more flexible alternative to steam engines. However, a remarkable saving of mass per unit of power produced reduced the size of the engine. A combustion engine was first used in motor cycles (1885) and for coaches (1886), which later developed into the car as we know it today. The automotive industry started to produce for the mass market in the USA in the 1920s, but its expansion in Europe was delayed by the Depression of the 1930s and the Second World War. However as early as 1900 the efficiency of motors had increased dramatically and their size had been reduced. The first combustion engine had an extremely high mass/power ratio, measured as weight-to-power generation, so that already by 1901 the state-of-the-art Mercedes engine already had a mass/power ratio only 3.5 per cent that of the first engine!

One new product that had a fundamental impact on agriculture was the industrial production of nitrates. Farmers have struggled with the problem of constraints on the supply of nitrogen since the dawn of civilization, as discussed in Chapter 3. Given the fact that we are surrounded by nitrogen, which constitutes about three-quarters of our atmosphere, it became a challenge for chemists in the late nineteenth century to find a fixation process whereby the nitrogen in such abundant supply could be used. Fritz Haber (1868–1934) finally succeeded in 1909 by using a catalyst to produce ammonia, which was transformed through oxidization to nitrates and nitrites. A precondition for the spectacular increase in agricultural yields in the twentieth century was thus created. This spectacular innovation not only made for the production of a new commodity, artificial fertilizers, but is a good case of what we shall discuss in the next section: a widening of the resource base.

(v) Widening the resource base

Papermaking underwent a process of mechanization that began when Nicolas Robert, a Frenchman, tried to design a continuous process from the 'wet' pulp start to the 'dry' paper end in the late eighteenth century. The process later refined became known as the Fourdrinier process after the British entrepreneurs who bought the rights. The increased demand for printing paper was hard to meet given the conventional sources of raw materials for paper pulp: rags, hemp and straw. Wood was in abundant supply but advances in chemistry were necessary to make it a suitable source of raw material. The early mechanical method of making paper pulp from wood, invented around 1850 and still in use, produced cheap but inferior-quality paper, which restricted its use. It soon became brittle and yellowed, as any visitor to newspaper archives will affirm. The chemical problem of making wood a suitable cheap source for paper pulp was not insurmountable. Paper pulp was produced by boiling the chipped and ground-up wood in sulphite or sulphate. The improved methods were directed at producing pure cellulose. Not surprisingly, in the 1870s the leading innovators were chemists and engineers from nations well supplied with wood: the United States, Germany and Sweden. The so-called sulphite method dominated at first but had its drawbacks, in that the acidity of the paper made it brittle in the long run. The sulphate process, producing so-called kraft paper (*kraft* is the Swedish and German word for strength, possibly a tribute to inventors of German and Swedish origin). Although the process produces a strong, cheap paper it is difficult to bleach. The environmental drawbacks of this method – water pollution – were not adequately addressed until the second half of the twentieth century or even later.

Although the Bessemer converter made mass production of cheap steel possible, it hit a resources constraint: it could not make use of the phosphorous-rich iron ores which were quite common on the continent. Henry Bessemer (1813–98) was British and his method, which was independently discovered in the USA by William Kelly (1811–98), worked well only with the types of iron ore available in Britain. The problem attracted metallurgists to experiment with methods that could be applied to phosphorous-rich iron ore. Two cousins, Sidney Gilchrist Thomas (1850–85) and Percy Carlyle Gilchrist (1851–1935), finally succeeded and took out patents at the end of the 1870s. Incidentally, the phosphorous reclaimed in the process as slag could be used as a fertilizer in agriculture.

6.4 The lasting impact of nineteenth-century discoveries and twentieth-century accomplishments

The most surprising element of late nineteenth-century scientific discoveries was their lasting impact on the twentieth century. The combustion engine was used in cars from the 1890s, but in 1900 the total number of cars worldwide did not exceed 10,000. Their breakthrough as a commodity for mass consumption did not come until after the Second World War in Europe. We can briefly mention innumerable other products which were conceived in the second half of the nineteenth century but were further developed in the twentieth century and became articles of mass consumption: the telephone, the gramophone and sound recording, cameras and movies, wireless communication including radio, chemical fertilizers which dramatically increased yields in twentieth-century agriculture, durable plastics, dynamite, viscose and the bicycle which attained its present design after decades of experimentation at the end of the nineteenth century. Steelmaking changed mainly by increased plant and furnace size. Open hearth furnaces (in the Siemens-Martin tradition) remained the dominant technology until the middle of the twentieth century, when what essentially is a more sophisticated Bessemer converter, the so-called basic oxygen furnace, replaced the open hearth. In Bessemer's original design, air was blown through the molten pig iron to decarburize it. Bessemer understood that it was better to use pure oxygen instead of air, but pure oxygen could not be produced at a reasonable cost in his time. The further development of Bessemer's intuition was due to work by a Swiss metallurgist, Durrer, in the 1940s. In industrial applications, this is called the Linz-Donawits method after two steel plant locations in Austria, but as the technology historian Vaclav Smil points out, it would be more appropriate to call it the Bessemer-Durrer method. Siemens also experimented with using electricity in metallurgy, and after further experimentation in the first half of the twentieth century these methods were generally applied, especially in the recycling of scrap for steelmaking.

By the beginning of the twentieth century, the centre of gravity of innovative processes had moved to the New World. The United States surpassed the leading economies in Europe in terms of income per head and the share of GDP spent on education and research. The USA's manufacturing sector had achieved a substantial productivity advantage by the second half of the nineteenth century. That lead was maintained partly because of the pioneering rationalization of production processes and partly because of the efforts devoted to innovative research and development. The rationalization of production, sometimes nicknamed 'Fordism' after Henry Ford the car manufacturer, was based on the principle of division of labour in which each worker did a limited number of tasks repeatedly. It could easily be applied to a conveyor-belt transmission of the product. In the Ford plants, the car chassis were moved by a wire driven by an electric motor. Car manufacturing introduced standardized products suitable for mass production. Almost 15 million so-called Model T-Fords were produced at an ever-falling price made possible by the reduction and standardization of the number of parts (under 100) to be fitted into the final product. American manufacturers exploited the advantage of a huge domestic market and could design mass production technologies. European industries did not have the same potential for economies of scale because domestic markets were smaller and consumer preferences across Europe were less homogenous.

Nathan Rosenberg made this point long ago and Stephen Broadberry, the University of Warwick economic historian, has developed the argument further. He contrasts American standardized mass production with European 'flexible and customized' production technology. The former used purpose-built machinery for long production runs, the latter skilled labour to meet customers' diversified needs. European managers studied American industrial technologies in the interwar period, but they were not widely transferred to European industries until after the Second World War, and in some nations this so-called scientific management was fiercely resisted by trade unions. An advanced division of labour enables further steps in automation by the introduction of numerically controlled machines. For example, a metal sheet can be cut into a specific shape automatically by programming the machine. Originally, this was done by simple programmes stored on punch cards, and the affinity to the Jacquard loom discussed above is obvious. With the development of microprocessors the next step towards full-scale, multitask machines – robots – became possible, but that is a post-1960 phenomenon. Still, it well illustrates the profound change in the use of humans in production. A robot welds and paints a car and human physical power is replaced by brainpower in designing the programmes directing the robot.

The most important general-purpose technology of the twentieth century (that is a technology that is useful in a large number of activities, sectors and industries), is electronic computing. The words 'computing' and 'computer' are becoming increasingly misleading, since a modern computer does all sorts of information processing and transmission by means of e-mail and the World Wide Web. Mechanical calculators were first designed in the seventeenth century in Europe and involved mathematicians and philosophers of the time such as Gottfried Leibniz (1646–1716) and Blaise Pascal (1623–1662). Commercially successful calculators, mostly used for addition, were developed in the 1870s and 1880s and production expanded quickly after 1890. The Swedish-trained engineer Willgodt Odhner (1845–1905) developed a string of calculators while working in Russia. His industry survived him but not the Russian Revolution in 1917. The company moved to Sweden, and the present author did some calculations for his early academic work on an Odhner calculator, which by then had adopted the Burroughs design. William Burroughs, another inventor-cum-entrepreneur based in the USA, made estimates of the labour productivity impact of simple adding machines, as they were sometimes called, and found that mechanical addition increased speed by a factor of six compared to manual calculation, that is the use of paper and pen. This is not a trivial increase – far from it – but it is dwarfed by the impressive improvement in performance of electronic computers. Such computers were developed simultaneously on both sides of the Atlantic in the 1940s, although American industry proved best at exploiting the commercial opportunities, including the development of the PC and simplified guidelines for programming and operating computers. The true cost reductions generated by the widespread use of modern computers are difficult to assess because they perform functions and services that mechanical calculators could not do. However, looking just at the cost savings of modern computers in doing calculations leads to truly astonishing results. William Nordhaus, the Yale economist, applied a method similar to that he used to assess the true fall in the price of light referred to above. He looked at a simple performance measure, computations per second, and estimated the increase in that performance relative to manual computation. He found that in constant 2006 prices the cost reduction was 7.3 times 10^{13}. As with the price of light, performance-based estimates tend to indicate that the true fall in the price of new products is under-estimated in conventional measurements of real output and real income. That means that conventional price indexes tend to have an upward bias in price change estimates. Since real output is measured by deflating output measured in nominal prices with a price index, the *GDP deflator**, the result will be that real output is under-estimated.

6.5 Technology transfer and catch-up

Knowledge, as noted earlier, has the particular characteristic of being a *non-rival good**, which means that it is not exhausted when it is used. Useful knowledge, once produced, is a 'free lunch' when access costs are low. Patent protection increases access costs but only temporarily. Your use of a non-rival good does not hinder others from using it. This makes knowledge profoundly different from the rival goods which surround us in the consumption and production spheres. Machinery – say a Jacquard loom – is a rival good, but the technology embedded in its design is a non-rival good.

Not only is knowledge a non-rival good but scientific knowledge is also described in terminology accessible to all in a particular field – say in mechanics, metallurgy or chemistry. That means that experiments can be replicated, tested and improved. Even if technologies were patented, they were in the public domain and could be improved. The telephone, for example, was not the product of one single inventor, but of several who contributed bits and pieces of the winning concept.

Knowledge is transformed into working technology by means of blueprints, which helps the rapid transfer of new ideas. By the end of the nineteenth century, most nations in Europe had people who followed and participated in research and development, *R&D**, as it is now called. Some nations were more advanced than others; but given the nature of ideas, we would expect differences in technological sophistication to disappear over time, at least among nations having institutions which favoured the search for, absorption and application of new technologies. The drift towards a scientific understanding of the world was, as pointed out above, a pan-European phenomenon. Europe can therefore be assumed to have had the necessary institutional requirements for technology transfer, although in varying degrees. These institutional requirements, what Moses Abramovitz called 'social capabilities', included that part of the public which was literate in matters scientific and technical;

a critical minimum level of education; a banking system which supported innovative entrepreneurs; and, of course, the general institutional characteristics of a modern economy as discussed in Chapter 5.

A comparison across nations of income per head at a given point in time is a reasonably accurate, although not perfect, indicator of the technological level, and technology transfer should therefore make it possible for less sophisticated economies to grow faster, to catch up, because they can benefit from the application of superior technologies invented in frontier technology economies. The larger the technology or knowledge gap vis-à-vis the leading economy, the more knowledge there is out there which can be transferred. This hypothesis suggests what is commonly known as beta convergence: relatively poor economies can be expected to grow faster than the more advanced economies once they get started. This has been known to several generations of economic historians. Less rich nations do have the *advantage of backwardness,* as suggested by the Russian-American economic historian Alexander Gerschenkron.

There are three distinct reasons for this phenomenon. The first is technology transfer as discussed above. The second reason operates on an aggregate level of an economy. The national product is the sum of the output of all sectors in the economy. Sectors tend to differ in terms of productivity, in that sectors dominated by large-scale firms are often more efficient than those with many small-scale firms. For example, metal manufacturing usually has higher labour productivity than small-scale retail businesses. Over time the least efficient sectors tend to be crowded out. For example, at the end of the nineteenth century the agricultural sector occupied between 30 and 75 per cent of the labour force in Europe, but that share has now dwindled to between 3 and 10 per cent. In the process agriculture has become a sector which compares well with industry in terms of labour productivity, but in most European nations labour productivity in agriculture was only half of that of the industrial sector a century ago. In a comparative perspective, the most advanced economies tend to have only small pockets of the old-style sectors while relatively poor economies initially harbour large traditional sectors. As a consequence the relatively poor economies will catch up with the most advanced simply by relocating labour and other resources from the traditional to the modern sectors. This is convergence by structural change. It is worth stressing that the structural effect is not only due to labour moving from less efficient to more efficient sectors. In that very process the less efficient sectors tend to increase their productivity levels because the inefficient units are squeezed out.

The third factor evoked in the context of convergence is more ambiguous and derives from insights in growth theory. The first generation of growth modelling, linked to Nobel laureate Robert Solow, predicted convergence in

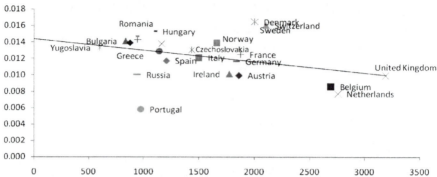

Figure 6.2 Annual rate of growth of GDP per capita 1870–1914 and GDP per head in 1870. Constant 1990 $. Source of Figures 6.2–6.7: Tables 1c and 3c in A. Maddison, *The World Economy: Historical Statistics*, (Paris: OECD, 2003). General note: some of the nations in the figures were not nation states in all periods and some that were have since been dissolved. Present or historical national boundaries have been used, as applicable.

a world of economies that were equal in all respects except the fact that some were initially poorer and had lower capital-to-labour ratios. These economies will typically save and invest more initially and enjoy higher growth rates. However, diminishing returns on capital will set in and backward economies will approach the income and growth of the leading economies. Subsequent developments in growth theory have however, made that expectation less deterministic. The actions of governments in providing R&D* spending may generate different growth paths and the assumption of diminishing returns has been questioned.

Over the forty years preceding the First World War most nations in Europe had a GDP per head growth of between 1 and 2 per cent per year, but growth rates slowed down for many of these nations in the interwar period. The twenty years after 1950 witnessed the fastest growth ever experienced in Europe – 3 to 5 per cent per year – but growth has since fallen back to 2 to 3 per cent per year. As a rule of thumb about half of the growth can be attributed to factor inputs such as education, capital and labour, and the other half to total factor productivity.

In Figures 6.2–6.4 we plot the growth performance of a number of European nations in three periods spanning about 100 years, 1870 to 1975. Annual percentage growth in per capita income, on the vertical axis, is plotted against initial income, GDP per capita in 1990 constant $, on the horizontal axis. The three periods are the first wave of European industrialization before the First World War , the World Wars and interwar period, and finally the so-called Golden Age of European growth, 1950–1973(5). What sort of pattern do we expect to discover? Since initially less developed economies have more scope for technology catch-up – after all they are poor because they do not use best-practice technologies – we should expect them to grow faster. Furthermore, less developed economies have less capital per labourer and there are therefore

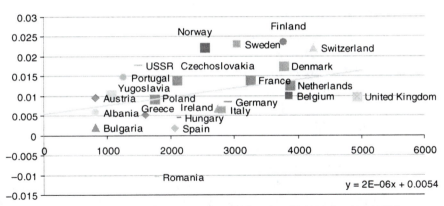

Figure 6.3   Annual rate of growth of GDP per capita 1914–50 and GDP per head in 1914. Constant 1990 $

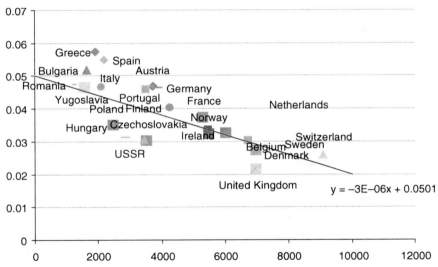

Figure 6.4   Annual rate of growth of GDP per capita 1950–75 and GDP per head in 1950. Constant 1990 $

better prospects for profitable investment, that is higher rates of return on capital. High rates of investment stimulate economic growth and it turns out that all the economies which converged on or overtook the UK had higher investment ratios. There is a fairly robust positive correlation across nations and periods between investments and the rate of total factor productivity. The most obvious explanation for that relationship is that investments are linked to the introduction of new technology. The less developed economies in Europe also had a larger traditional sector in services and agriculture and would therefore see more gains from structural relocation of the labour force from the traditional, low-productivity sector to the high-productivity modern sector.

All these factors suggest that there is a negative relationship between initial income and subsequent growth. This expectation is also met for two of the periods, the pre-First World War and post-Second World War periods. The straight downward sloping line is generated by a *linear regression**. Initially rich, the United Kingdom did not grow as fast as, for example, the less rich Scandinavian nations in the pre-First World War period, or as southern Europe in the post-Second World War era. But the World-Wars-and-interwar period was different. The regression suggests a positive relationship: the higher the initial GDP per head, the higher the growth rate of GDP per capita in the subsequent period. The difference between the World Wars/interwar period and the other two periods is explained by the fact that the 1914–50 period lacked the vital mechanisms for technology transfer, that is openness to trade, capital and people. In contrast, the 1870–1914 period was the first era of free trade in European history even though tariffs were not altogether absent. There was also international mobility of people, an era of mass migration, which meant mobility of brains and ideas. Finally, it was a period of unprecedented capital mobility, often linked to the import of capital goods, machinery and transport equipment, to the aspiring nations.

The years from 1950 to 1975 saw a reduction in trade restrictions inherited from the interwar period; and trade grew two to three percentage points faster than GDP growth. Increased trade enhances productivity levels because it forces domestic businesses to adjust, and those who do not adjust will not survive. The Golden Age was a period of massive American investment in Europe. Capital chased technology and vice versa.

In contrast, the two World Wars effectively closed borders. Economies traded less and nationalism fed suspicion of anything foreign. The interwar period had a brief prelude of international co-operation and openness to trade, but that soon gave way to trade restrictions and a revival of nationalism and parochial attitudes after the outbreak of the Great Depression in 1929. World trade fell drastically and intellectual exchange was restrained. The most important channel for knowledge transfer became the many talented scientists fleeing from the Nazi dictatorship. Given these conditions, a *positive* link between initial income and growth makes sense. Initially rich economies relied less on technology transfer because they had already established research departments in their largest firms as well as centres of research in universities. Furthermore, they had savings rates high enough to make the international capital market meltdown less of a problem for trade and investments. An important historical lesson emerges from the interwar experience: openness seems to be a particular advantage for poor nations.

The figures offer additional insights into under- and over-performance. The regression lines represent the expected growth in GDP per capita given a certain initial income. If a nation falls below that line, it is an under-performer; if it is located above it is an over-performer.

The UK (Britain) is clearly an under-performer from 1950 to 1975, whereas it performed as expected in 1870–1913. Growth was lower than for many other European economies during this first wave of industrialization in continental Europe, but as a technology leader Britain had less to gain from technology transfer from other European economies. For reasons explained above, American technologies were not easily adaptable; but Britain may also have been unwilling to absorb useful technologies and develop new. For the full 1870–1975 period, GDP per head grew at about 2 per cent per year in France, Germany and the Scandinavian nations, but at only about 1.2 per cent in the UK. Germany was performing as expected given its initial income in the first period and was an over-performer thereafter. Part of that over-performance was, however, caused by the self-inflicted low initial income in 1950, which was a consequence of the Second World War. Part of the so-called Wirtschaftswunder (economic miracle) was a reconstruction effect.

It is worth dwelling on the performance of initially poor European nations in the first period. Some of them did well, but not all managed to welcome the knowledge transfer. By and large those who did well had a high share of trade in their national income. It is worth noting that those parts of the Austro-Hungarian Empire which broke away from Austria after the First World War, Hungary and Czechoslovakia (both on the lower half of the income ladder), were over-performing before the War, but Austria was not. Greece, Ireland, Spain and Portugal also under-performed at that time. In fact their catch-up to the European average did not start until the Golden Age. In terms of initial income Ireland in 1870 was not very different from Sweden and Denmark, two over-performers, and they are all often lumped together in a category called the European periphery. Geographically that seems correct, but does it have an economic significance? We noted in Chapter 1 that proximity to similarity with core markets could stimulate trade and indirectly growth. Greece has an apparent problem here, being far away from the core economies in Europe. Portugal was clearly handicapped by having a laggard, Spain, as its closest trading partner and a slow-growing Britain as a major trading partner. Ireland shared the latter predicament, having historical ties with the UK.

The Scandinavian economies, on the other hand, had a dynamic Germany in their vicinity and traded a good deal with one another. The Scandinavian countries did better than expected in all the periods, and we might be tempted to ascribe that to the comparatively high quality of the educational system and a lively technological intelligentsia as witnessed by patent application statistics.

We have already noted the surprisingly active participation of these small nations in the development of useful knowledge, which revealed a high level of technical competence. Being small they were also the most open economies in all the periods, as measured by high trade/income ratios. (Trade promotes growth by directing resources from less to more efficient production units and sectors.) Their relatively good performance from 1914 to 1950 may also have to do with economic policy choices, particularly the early devaluations of over-valued currencies, which will be discussed in Chapter 10.

Greece, the Iberian nations and Ireland were conspicuously absent from the scientific breakthrough at the end of the nineteenth century. Ireland was, in fact, the last Western European nation to catch up with the technological leaders. Proximity to Britain may have been a mixed blessing in another respect, since many of Ireland's talented inhabitants headed there or to the USA. Ireland alone among European nations had negative population growth for most years until well into the Golden Age. Policy choices introduced in the 1930s seem to be a major factor explaining Ireland's poor growth performance, which continued well into the Golden Age. Despite political independence, Ireland pegged its currency to the British pound. Investments as a share of *national income** did not reach the European average until the 1970s, and the *protectionism* introduced in the Great Depression remained until the late 1950s, when the rest of Europe was already on its way to liberalizing trade. Successive governments also had an ambivalent attitude to foreign investment.

Using nation states as the frame of analysis can sometimes be misleading. For example, Spain was not uniformly backward. The northern part, particularly Catalonia, industrialized following a more typical European pattern, as did northern Italy. The growth performance of Eastern Europe, which housed the initially poorest nations of Europe, is difficult to generalize. In the Golden Age and under a socialist planning regime they under-performed, with Romania and Bulgaria as exceptions. Given its initial income, Russia (then within USSR borders and a socialist regime) did better than other economies only in 1914–50, a period of forced industrialization with extremely high investment growth.

Given the fact that knowledge is transferable, it is natural to look at institutional conditions when explaining differences in performance. Economies that under-performed initially tended to have a less developed educational system and a less advanced banking system. For example, the proportion of 5–14-year olds enrolled in schools in 1870 was almost 60 per cent in Sweden whereas it was just above 30 per cent in Italy and Ireland. However, a full understanding of differences in growth performance requires a little more detail. Let us first focus on Germany and Britain.

6.5.1 Why was Germany a late industrial nation … and why did it grow faster than Britain once it started to grow?

The short answer to this essential question is that Germany (particularly the Prussian areas) did not have the institutional preconditions for sustained economic development until well into the nineteenth century.

The institutional preconditions which were at hand in the first modern economies such as the Dutch Republic (the Netherlands) and Britain were efficiently functioning markets for goods and factors of production, that is labour, land and capital markets. Until land reforms were introduced (the so-called Stein–Hardenberg reforms imposed in 1807–21 after the humiliating defeat of Prussian forces by Napoleon), neither land nor labour markets worked properly. But these sweeping reforms introduced well-defined property rights in land and generated a more efficient labour market. The reforms freed labour from the control of landlords, but they also deprived working people of customary rights to common land. As a consequence, a new social division emerged with a landless proletariat seeking work in rural areas as well as in the growing cities. A class of farmers with ownership of land developed alongside the big estates, which relied on hired workers. The economic consequence of the reforms was an increase in labour productivity in agriculture. The elastic supply of labour changed the income distribution in favour of the property-owning classes, which stimulated savings and investment in industry.

Furthermore, the size of the market matters because an important element in productivity growth is gains from scale economies. Germany, as we now know it, did not emerge as a unified state until the 1870s. However, this nation-building was prepared by a long process of economic unification through currency and tariff reforms. Early nineteenth-century Germany was a geographical area composed of a multitude of small political units with different currencies and trade-inhibiting tariffs. However, the Prussian Customs Union (1818) triggered off subsequent economic integration culminating in the so-called *Zollverein* (1833), which gradually extended its geographical coverage over the next few decades. Alongside the stimulus to trade generated by the *Zollverein*, a *customs union**, came the simplification of the monetary arrangements leading to a common currency. So by the middle of the nineteenth century Germany – or what a little later became known as Germany – was ready for take-off into modern economic growth.

Once Germany got started, it performed better than Britain. Not only was Germany's growth in GDP per head higher than that of the UK, but it was also slightly higher over the 100 years from 1873 to 1973 than the growth rate of the new leading economy that emerged by the end of the nineteenth century, the United States. Germany's income per head relative to the UK was about 50 per cent in 1870 but increased to about 65 percent before the First World War. Because of the Second World War, Germany's relative position fell back to 60 per cent of the UK's in 1950, but by 1973 Germany had closed the income gap. This was due to exceptionally fast German growth and exceptionally slow growth in the UK. However, as far back as 1914 quite a few of the industrial sectors in Germany, including chemicals and metallurgy, had higher labour productivity than corresponding sectors in Britain, which kept its lead in financial services and retailing. Sweden also managed to catch up with British labour productivity levels in several manufacturing sectors by c.1910.

There were two periods of spectacular growth in Germany relative to the UK: 1870–1913 and 1950–73 periods, when German growth was approximately double that of the UK. In both periods, Germany started from a relatively low initial income. A substantial part of Germany's Golden Age catch-up was, however, a reconstruction effect after wartime destruction.

Is this the full story? No, because the UK was growing less rapidly than economies that were almost as rich or richer. Why did the UK not grow as fast as the United States, which overtook it as the leading economy by 1890, or as a number of continental European economies, for example France and Germany, did in the Golden Age period? We have to look elsewhere, to differences in investments in people, research and capital and in the institutional set up, if we want to understand Britain's growth pattern.

6.5.2 Human and capital investment

In terms of literacy and enrolment rates, that is the proportion of an age group attending different levels of education, the United States stand out as exceptional. There is an often-repeated claim that the British elite universities were not sufficiently attentive to teaching the hard sciences, which in the end may have retarded the growth of the British economy. It also seems that Germany had a superior system for training skilled labour. However, observations of this type are impressionistic and do not justify too strong conclusions.

Much of the discussion of Britain being unable to retain its leading position in terms of GDP per capita has focussed on the relatively low investment ratio (i.e. net investments as a share of GDP). By and large British domestic investments appear to have been exceptionally low, or about half the ratio in the USA, and substantially lower than in most industrializing European nations, until after the Second World War.

British investors have been said by a number of economic historians to be inadequately informed about domestic conditions, but others have noted that low investments may reflect only a shortage of high-yielding investment opportunities at home and a preference for foreign investments. However, institutions matter! Low domestic investments have been attributed to inadequate financial institutions unable to seek out promising investment opportunities. Britain's role as the world's principal banker in the later nineteenth century made the City of London rich in information on foreign investment opportunities, perhaps to the extent that inward investments were neglected. It is often argued that investors have what is called a *home bias*. That means that they do not diversify optimally between domestic and foreign assets. However, in the British case the argument has been reversed. The LSE economic historian William Kennedy, for example, argued that British financial institutions, unlike similar institutions on the continent, were not picking the 'right' investment objects, and were in fact missing a number of promising opportunities. In Germany, on the other hand, firms were serviced by specialist banks, often targeting particular sectors of industry and developing sophisticated knowledge about investment opportunities and the benefits of merging smaller firms into large units. The German (universal) banks operated as investment banks and have been credited with fostering the ability of German industry to form a strong presence in frontier technology.

A substantial part of British savings were in fact directed at foreign investments, reflecting, at least until the final quarter of the nineteenth century, the fact that profits were higher on foreign assets. It is worth noting that total domestic and foreign investments were not (much) lower than domestic investments in France or Germany as a share of GDP. The hypothesis that low British investment had to do with high capital endowment per labourer in Britain is not valid. In fact, the capital stock per employee was surprisingly small in the UK compared to the United States: about one third in 1913 and about 60 per cent of the US capital stock per employee in 1950. The reason for this difference has to do with a scarcity of labour in the formative period of American industrialization paving the way for capital-intensive and labour-saving capital equipment.

There are not only differences in the volume of investments but also in the sectoral direction. Much of British investment tended to remain in traditional sectors, which had a low growth potential because world trade in their products was growing only slowly. British export dominance was *not* in fast-growing high-tech industries such as cars and aircraft, electrical goods and agricultural equipment, but in industries such as textiles, soon to be under tough competition from low-wage producers. British industry suffered from an inability to diversify out of 'sunset' industries and out of markets that were growing slowly, that is the *Commonwealth** nations including the colonies. American and German industry, on the other hand, excelled in high-tech industries, which enjoyed fast-growing demand.

Although domestic British investments were exceptionally low pre-1914, after 1950 they converged on the European norm, although much behind Japan, which pioneered a high savings and investment regime later to be copied by other Asian economies such as Korea, Taiwan and more recently China.

6.5.3 Research and Development

We would expect a strong positive relationship between productivity growth and spending on *R&D**. The big American firms were the first to set up separate departments for applied research to develop new products and production processes, by the end of the nineteenth century. Since then spending on research has consistently been higher in the United States, securing it a safe lead in innovative industries. But Germany also emerged in the nineteenth century as a leading nation in pure and applied science, a role she safely held until Adolf Hitler chased away so many of Germany's brightest scientists. German universities have not regained their former glory since. In the early years after 1870, private research spending in Germany was probably stimulated by the fact that *cartels** were not prohibited as they were in Britain. It is known that firms that enjoy some protection from 'cutthroat' competition are more likely to spend on research. The reason is that *cartel* pricing enables firms to recover the outlay on research. The German *cartels* in steel, chemicals and electrical equipment may therefore have helped these industries to their early excellence by stimulating precisely targeted *R&D* spending. The latter is notoriously difficult to measure but it seems to converge among the leading industrial nations at the close of the twentieth century at around 3 per cent of GDP.

6.5.4 Industrial relations

Another factor that has been linked to the Anglo-German differences in economic performance is the state of industrial relations. In the past, trade unions in Britain were based on skills rather than industries. In any given industry workers were represented by a large number of unions, each one representing a specific skill (so-called 'multiple' unions). While econometric investigation cannot detect any negative impact of unions on productivity growth, there is a negative impact if workers are represented by 'multiple' unions. This can be explained by the fact that in a multiple-union context a particular union can acquire 'hold-up' power both in wage negotiations and in negotiations over the introduction of new technology. A union representing a key skill in a firm can gain much by fighting for its own interests at the expense of others. The implication is that Britain can be expected to adjust more slowly to new technology, resulting in a slower rate of total factor productivity growth. Indeed this expectation is supported by empirical data. Total factor productivity growth from 1950 to 1975 was only about a third of that level in Germany and France. Unlike those of Germany, trade unions in Britain did not co-operate closely with employers at either firm or national level. While trade unions in Germany and in Scandinavia were willing to trade the introduction of new technologies, sometimes labour-saving, for higher wages in the future, there was not much co-operative spirit in British industrial relations, and this probably delayed modernization. However, not only unions but also employers have been blamed for technological inertia. A paradoxical fact worth reflecting on is that the British-*owned* car industry was practically wiped out after 1950, whereas Britain has remained a major *producer* of Japanese cars in factories with different industrial relations, management and work practices.

Although Britain was at the top of the European income league in 1950, a number of economies in Europe, including Germany and France, overtook her in the Golden Age. A final contributory factor to that dismal growth record was the comparatively large nationalized steel and coal sectors, where total factor productivity was exceptionally low. However, by the close of the twentieth century Britain was striking back after a period of institutional reforms in the 1980s.

6.6 Convergence in the long run: three stories

When less rich economies introduce growth-promoting institutions and exploit best-practice technology borrowed from the leading economies, we can expect them to converge, at least in proportional terms, to the income levels of the leading economies. Has that pattern of convergence been discernible in Europe since the 1870s? The short answer is yes, but… It turns out that the pace and timing of that convergence vary and we shall now try to explain why some European economies started the convergence process in the late nineteenth century while others did not begin the process until after 1950.

Figures 6.5–6.7 track three trajectories in economic convergence, known as sigma convergence, that is convergence of (log) income per head in constant 1990 $ across nations. We measure log GDP per capita on the vertical axis and time on the horizontal axis. In Figure 6.5, American per capita GDP is compared to those of Argentina and Scandinavia. The growth pattern of Scandinavia is roughly similar to that of Germany and France except for the Great Depression of the 1930s, when the Scandinavian economies did quite well, relatively speaking. What we see is the persistence of the American lead, except (once again) during the 1930s. There is a convergence, but only in the Golden Age, after which the income differential remains stable but smaller in proportional terms than in 1870–1914. That the income gap just after the Second World War

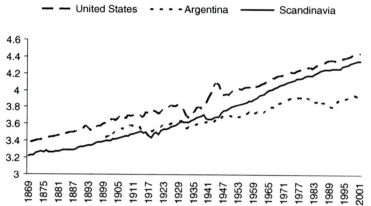

Figure 6.5   Log GDP per capita 1860–2000 in Argentina, Scandinavia and the USA. 1990 $. Source of Figures 6.2–6.7: Tables 1c and 3c in A. Maddison, *The World Economy: Historical Statistics*, (Paris: OECD, 2003). General note: some of the nations in the figures were not nation states in all periods and some that were have since been dissolved. Present or historical national boundaries have been used, as applicable.

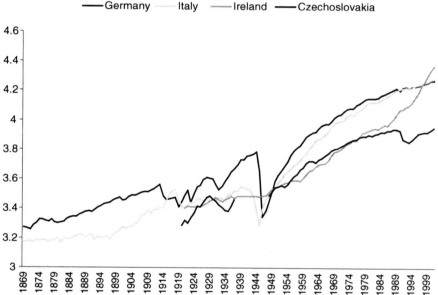

Figure 6.6   Log GDP per capita 1860–2000 in Germany, Ireland, Czechoslovakia and Italy. 1990 $. Source of Figures 6.2–6.7: Tables 1c and 3c in A. Maddison, *The World Economy: Historical Statistics*, (Paris: OECD, 2003). General note: some of the nations in the figures were not nation states in all periods and some that were have since been dissolved. Present or historical national boundaries have been used, as applicable.

is large represents a potential for Scandinavian catch-up, which was indeed exploited. America's lead is linked to its superiority in knowledge and technology generation. Argentina's growth trajectory tells a different and less

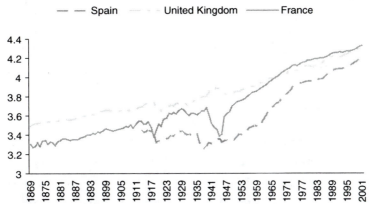

Figure 6.7   Log GDP per capita 1860–2000 in France, Spain and United Kingdom. 1990 $. Source of Figures 6.2–6.7: Tables 1c and 3c in A. Maddison, *The World Economy: Historical Statistics*, (Paris: OECD, 2003). General note: some of the nations in the figures were not nation states in all periods and some that were have since been dissolved. Present or historical national boundaries have been used, as applicable.

optimistic story. Until the Golden Age, its income level was roughly at par with Scandinavia's: slightly above it before the Great Depression and slightly below from then on. The income gaps with the USA and Europe increased, but do not cry for Argentina. Its dismal growth was of its own making. Like many primarily food and raw-material-producing nations, Argentina was severely hit by the Great Depression in the 1930s and embarked on an import substitution industrialization programme which initially boosted growth, but ultimately failed in the post-war period. A string of populist politicians in the second half of the twentieth century were willing to spend and please a public unwilling to pay taxes, which created foreign debts too large to manage without repeated defaults. Argentina's economic failure is largely a political failure.

In Figure 6.6 we follow an early catch-up industrializer, Germany, which became a leading new purveyor of technologies and products; Italy, a hesitant follower; and Ireland, a very late bloomer. Initially there is divergence in income per head; a first phase of convergence starts for Italy around 1900 with relatively fast growth. However, that advance is spoilt in the interwar period and by wartime destruction. Both Germany and Italy had spectacular growth in the first part of the Golden Age, partly due to the fact that they start from war-inflicted low income levels similar to those in 1914. The combined impact of reconstruction effects and the potential for technological catch-up stimulated high investment ratios in both nations. Since high investments are correlated with high total factor productivity, growth in both countries regained pre-Second-World War levels of income early in the 1950s. However, these high growth rates could not be sustained. The reason was that many of the gains from adopting

best-practice technology had already been exploited and the high rate of investments ultimately lowered returns on capital, which in turn slowed down
investment. Immediately after the Second World War both nations had growth
rates above their potential long-term growth, and they settled down to that
growth pattern. This is true of all nations that participated in the Golden Age
spurt. While long-term growth in GDP per head is from 2 to 2½ per cent per
year, Golden Age growth was often twice as high. Ireland's growth performance
has been hailed in recent years when Ireland had earned the nickname 'the Celtic
Tiger'. However, looking at the growth pattern, it turns out that it was more like
that of a Sleeping Bear in the Golden Age. Starting from a similar income level to
Italy's in 1950 it lagged behind until the late twentieth century. For all the merits
of being a Tiger economy, one must recognize the lost opportunities for growth
in the Golden Age which effectively denied the Irish people a standard of living
equal to that of Italians and Germans until around the year 2000. The sheltered
home market in Ireland made firms small and internationally uncompetitive,
according to the economic historians Cormac O'Gràda and Kevin O'Rourke.
None of the gains from scale economies could therefore be exploited. At the
risk of over-simplifying matters, it is worth noting that Ireland's catch-up did
not start until the country opened up to free trade at the end of the Golden Age.
The historical lesson seems to be that for small economies like Ireland and the
Scandinavians openness is a prerequisite for growth. Scandinavia learned that
lesson much earlier than Ireland. Czechoslovakia was one of the most advanced
of the economies that venturesd into socialist planning after 1945 and had a
growth potential. It traced Ireland's dismal performance until the middle of the
1970s, when the contradictions of socialist planning were starting to constrain
growth even more, as will be explored in Section 10.4 in Chapter 10.

A third distinct story appears in Figure 6.7 in which Britain (the UK) is
compared to France and Spain. Ignoring the wartime shocks to income in
France, it is possible to discern a long-term convergence of France on Britain.
In fact France overtook Britain by the end of the Golden Age. Again the spectacular growth immediately after the Second World War is worth dwelling
on. France regained its long-term trend – imagine a linear interpolation of
the income curve on the basis of past income – in less than five years. That
was possible despite the destruction of physical capital because the social
capital, the human capital and the institutions remained and made for a
quick return to normality. Spain differs from Italy in that there is no trace
of convergence until well into the Golden Age. It took eighty-eight years for
Spain to double income with the growth rate recorded from 1850 to 1950,
but only thirteen years with the observed growth rate in the Golden Age. The
Madrid-based economic historians Leandro Prados and Joan Rosés maintain

that the spurts of income growth in post-Second World War Spain have all been linked to fast total factor productivity, which is the best measure we have of the impact of technological progress and organizational change in the production process. The Civil War of the 1930s and the authoritarian nationalist government that subsequently ruled Spain ended the brief period of openness in the 1920s, and it was not until the economy opened up gradually in the Golden Age that the catch-up had visible effects. Another effect of the inward-looking and authoritarian policies was that inequality increased, and that trend was not broken until Spain opened up. Foreign trade and foreign investments were, as in other nations, bearers of new technologies. Technological progress is particularly important in agriculture for late starters since a high proportion of the labour force is tied up in low-income jobs. As late as 1950 Spain and Portugal had almost half their labour force in agriculture, as against 20 per cent in Sweden and five per cent in the UK. The labour-saving bias in agricultural development releases under-employed rural labour for industrial occupations and triggers off what we have called a structural convergence effect. The exodus of labour from low-productivity jobs in agriculture to manufacturing increases average labour productivity. That process is not possible without investment in both agriculture and industry. The time at which an economy starts to catch up is linked to the start of its agricultural transformation.

Summary

This chapter has focussed on the history and characteristics of modern technological progress and the particular nature of knowledge, that of being a non-rival good. Being non-rival, useful knowledge can be tranferred from technological leaders to laggards, given openness and basic social and educational capabilities in the receiving nations. Two important expectations were corroborated. Relatively poor European nations had above-average growth rates once they entered the phase of modern economic growth, and there was convergence of income levels in the long run. We also noted that late starters tended to grow faster the bigger the income and technology gap separating them from the leading economies. That is true for late starters like Ireland and former socialist economies like the Czech Republic, Russia and the Baltic states which, unusually, missed most of the gains from technological catch-up in the Golden Age. To some extent it was Cold War policies that denied the Socialist bloc access to superior technology, but, as will be seen in Chapter 10, it was mainly an effect of misdirected investment policies. The lesson for late starters is embarrassingly easy to state but difficult to learn: 'There is almost free access to better useful knowledge, but make sure you create the institutional set up to absorb that knowledge.'

Europe managed to close some of the income gap with the USA in the Golden Age, but since then it has remained constant. Why Europe has not continued to narrow the gap can be explained by a number of factors. Europeans on average work fewer hours per year and have slightly higher unemployment, which affects income per head. It also seems as if European *total factor productivity** has slowed down, which may reveal rigidities in the adoption of new technology.

Openness to trade and foreign investments correlate with the growth in income. By and large the growth in income per capita can be broken down into two factors of roughly equal strength: first the growth of human and physical capital; second, total factor productivity. In periods of exceptional catch-up with the leading economies, total factor productivity is the more important of the two factors.

European nations differed in the timing of their convergence spurts. Scandinavia, Germany and France had the institutional capacity to start industrialization and fast growth in the last third of the nineteenth century, while the process was more hesitant in Italy. The World Wars and the 1930s closed international capital markets and witnessed a breakdown in trade relationships as well as migratory flows. Thereby the economic forces that foster technology transfer and convergence ceased to operate. Nations that had not benefited from technology transfer and had weak scientific communities were not touched by convergence forces until the Golden Age. A nation like Czechoslovakia (see Figure 6.6), which had a sophisticated technological tradition before the Second World War, was in an institutional straitjacket imposed by Soviet-type planning and fell back relative to Western European economies until the breakdown of the communist bloc. The restoration of property rights, democracy, capital imports and markets has had spectacular effects on the former Soviet bloc economies, including Russia, which is a late twentieth-century demonstration of the forceful effects of institutional change.

Suggestions for further reading (see also suggestions under Chapter 10)

A very useful source of historical national accounts is available at Groningen University, search on http://www.ggdc.net/databases/hna.htm

Differences in American and European technology were explored by H. J. Habakkuk, *American and British Technology in the Nineteenth Century* (Cambridge University Press, 1962), and by N. Rosenberg: see the Introduction to *The American System of Manufactures* (Edinburgh University Press, 1969).

S. N. Broadberry has written extensively on productivity measurements and productivity comparisons. A good overview of his work is provided in *The Productivity Race: British Manufacturing in International Perspective, 1850–1990* (Cambridge University Press, 1997).

Joel Mokyr provides an innovative and influential view of technology and economic development. His ideas were first developed in The *Lever of Riches: Technological Creativity and Economic Progress* (New York: Oxford University Press, 1990). For a more recent elaboration consult *The Gifts of Athena: Historical Origins of the Knowledge Economy* (Princeton University Press, 2002).

An encyclopaedic survey of the technology of the nineteenth and twentieth centuries is provided by Vaclav Smil in *Creating the Twentieth Century: Technological Innovations of 1867–1914 and Their Lasting Impact* (Cambridge University Press, 2005) and *Transforming the Twentieth Century: Technical Innovations and Their Consequences* (Cambridge University Press, 2006).

The changes in consumer behaviour and market involvement preceding the Industrial Revolution are explored in Jan de Vries, *The Industrious Revolution: Consumer Behavior and the Household Economy 1650 to the Present* (Cambridge University Press, 2008).

N. F. R. Crafts has changed our view of the Industrial Revolution: see his *British Economic Growth during the Industrial Revolution* (Oxford: Clarendon Press, 1985).

R. C. Allen provides a new look at the same subject and suggests that one unique characteristic explaining the Industrial Revolution was the fact that Britain was a high-wage economy. See his *The British Industrial Revolution in Global Perspective* (Cambridge University Press, 2009).

The forces that generated convergence and rapid economic growth in the so-called Golden Age (1950–73) have been intensively discussed. A recent article which provides a representative list of references as well as new insights is Tamás Vonyö, 'Post-war reconstruction and the Golden Age of economic growth', *European Review of Economic History* 12(1) (2008), pp. 221–41.

A classic is A. Gerschenkron, *Economic Backwardness in Historical Perspective* (Cambridge, Mass.: Harvard University Press, 1962).

M. Abramovitz, 'Catching up, forging ahead and falling behind', *Journal of Economic History* 46(2) (1986), pp. 385–406, helped us start thinking about the conditions and mechanisms of catching up.

N. F. R. Crafts and G. Toniolo edited a very useful collection of country-specific studies with a well-considered introduction in *Economic Growth in Europe since 1945* (Cambridge University Press, 1996). Additional insight on Spain is offered in L. Prados de la Escosura and J. Roses, 'The sources of long-run growth in Spain, 1850–2000', CEPR Discussion Paper 6189, 2007 and forthcoming in *Journal of Economic History* 69(4) (2009).

7 Money, credit and banking

7.1 The origins of money

We have learned that one major cause of productivity increase in pre-industrial economies is the gains from division of labour resulting from occupational diversification in an economy where regions and nations exploit their *comparative advantages**. But these gains cannot be reaped without exchange between increasingly specialized producers. Money, as a means of exchange, developed alongside the occupational and regional division of labour. The first money, some five or six thousand years ago, did not consist of stamped coins, but rather of standardized ingots of metal which were generally accepted as a means of payment. The Chinese and Greek civilizations introduced coins which were stamped like a modern coin. To understand the advantages of money it is worth looking at its historical antecedent and alternative. Direct bilateral exchange of one commodity for another, so-called barter, requires *coincidence of wants** between trading partners. It means that if you want to exchange a pair of shoes for wheat you have to find someone who has wheat and wants a pair of shoes. The matching process necessary to detect coincidence of wants will be very time-consuming, and time matters because it is scarce and has alternative uses. Barter will not only be associated with high search costs, but will also reduce the volume of trade to below its potential level because trade must be balanced. However, the volumes participants want to trade need not balance and in those cases the 'minimum' trader will determine the volume of trade. For example, a weaver might find a baker willing to exchange bread for cloth at an agreed price, but the weaver might not be willing to buy as much bread as the baker wants to sell. After all, bread is more perishable than cloth and is typically bought daily in small quantities. The volume traded when relying on bilateral balanced trade will thus, in this particular example, be constrained by the cloth maker, the 'minimum' trader.

The price pattern in a barter economy is not very transparent because prices are not expressed in a single unit of account, say the euro: the price of wheat will be expressed in iron, salt, cloth etc. The price of a loaf of bread might be 15 grammes of iron or 5 centimetres of cloth or 110 grammes of salt. The price is the number of units of various goods bread is exchanged for.

The evolution of money is a fine illustration of how societies invent and develop instruments and institutions that minimize transaction costs and risk, with the consequence that trade and specialization are stimulated. More specifically, the invention of money solves the problem of non-coincidence of wants, and we can imagine that money might develop spontaneously, as in the following example. Consider a case of non-coincidence of wants as in Figure 7.1, which features four producers, Ms Baker, Mr Farmer, Mr Smith and Ms Brewer. The problem arises when Mr Farmer needs to sell all his wheat to Mr Smith in order to get a plough. Mr Smith does not want wheat for his own consumption, but rather bread and beer. Knowing that Ms Baker demands wheat he accepts wheat as a *means of payment* – one of the three functions of money. He does not intend to consume the wheat, but he is not nervous about accepting it because he knows that it can be stored for up to about three years. Wheat thus assumes the second function of a *store of value*, meaning that Mr Smith can wait until he needs beer and bread before he uses the wheat for purchases. Ms Brewer has beer to sell and wants bread, but Ms Baker is not interested in beer. However, by exchanging beer for wheat with Mr Smith, Ms Brewer gets the wheat she can exchange for bread. Implicitly wheat has also been used as a *unit of account*, the third function of money, because in the exchanges performed the plough, the bread and the beer have been priced in terms of wheat. For example, one loaf of bread may cost 0.2 kg of wheat while one litre of beer is priced at 0.5 kg of wheat. Wheat as money is not entirely

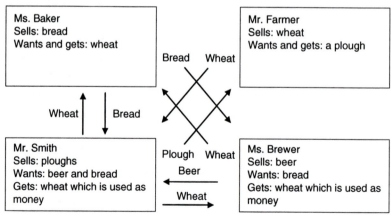

Figure 7.1   Spontaneous evolution of wheat as money when there is no coincidence of wants

hypothetical. Grain was widely used as money, for example in Ancient Egypt, and later on if there was a shortage of coins.

Throughout most of history money can be characterized as *commodity money*, which means that money has been made of commodities which have alternative, often ornamental, uses and an *intrinsic* value*, such as gold and silver or pearls and shells. A sheet of silver was useful as a means of payment since it could be weighted and clipped to an appropriate weight and value for the transaction in progress. When transactions become frequent it is practical to develop standardized denominations, although for a long time standardized coins continued to be clipped into smaller pieces if that helped to perform a transaction.

Any commodity can in principle be used as money, but some commodities are better than others. We can exclude perishable commodities and commodities that are subject to high price volatility because they cannot serve as a suitable store of value. The store-of-value function of money addresses the problem that a seller of a good, say cloth, might not want to buy anything at the moment of selling but wishes to postpone the purchase of, say, wool, to next month or next year. In Europe, commodity money has historically been made of precious metals such as gold and silver, and sometimes copper. To be widely accepted as a means of payment, money must be easy to recognize because it must serve in daily transactions among strangers. Furthermore, the chosen commodity needs to have a high value-to-weight ratio because otherwise it could not easily be stored or carried to and from the market place. This is an important characteristic, which first eliminated copper as a monetary metal (except for small denominations and tokens) and favoured silver and gold. Pre-industrial mint technologies were fairly primitive, which made it easy to counterfeit money. Not until the nineteenth century did technologies develop counterfeit-proof coins. Coins with an *intrinsic value* equal or close to their official denomination or face value (so called full-bodied coins) precluded counterfeiters from reaping sizeable profits. If counterfeiters tried to reduce the silver or gold content or the fineness of the metals it would soon be detected. At major markets, there were moneychangers who specialized in assaying the fineness of coins in circulation.

7.2 The revival of the monetary system in Europe: coins and bills of exchange

With the decline of the Roman Empire, Europe lost an orderly monetary system. Trade was reduced also for other reasons and coins from the more vigorous Byzantine and Arab civilizations circulated alongside old Roman coins. In the absence of ordinary coins, other commodities such as salt or grain could be used as money substitutes in order to evade the costs and constraints imposed by simple barter. The revival came with the Carolingian Empire, which introduced the principle of a hierarchy of denominations that had a lasting impact on European monies and survived in Britain into the 1970s, when the decimal system was introduced. A pound of silver was divided into 240 pennies (*denarii*), each containing approximately 1.7g of silver, and later a dozen pennies were called a shilling or *sou* (*solidus*); 20 shillings consequently made a pound (libra). The penny was for a long time the only coin struck, however. A sheet of silver with a weight of 1.7g would buy as many goods as one Carolingian penny. But the mint levied a fee when it was striking coins, often around 5 to 10 per cent of the face value of the coin, a so-called *seigniorage** fee. That fee covered the actual minting cost but was also a way to raise income for the government. However, governments found it tempting to fund expenditure by debasing the coin, that is by lowering the gold or silver fineness of the coin. In the end, however, that practice created trouble because it would drive good money, that is full-bodied coins, out of circulation and eventually start an inflationary process.

The period of centralized minting did not survive the Carolingian Empire, and very soon cities and monasteries assumed the right to mint coins and the silver content varied a great deal across regions. Money of different origins and denominations circulated all around Europe, giving moneychangers the job of assessing the exchange rate which converged to the ratios of the metal content of the coins. As time passed, new denominations were minted which were multiples of the penny. A persistent problem was the occasional shortage of small-denomination coins; it was not adequately solved until the nineteenth century when small *tokens**, i.e. coins without an *intrinsic value*, were made convertible at fixed rates to higher denomination and full-bodied coins. However, there are many historical examples of tokens emerging spontaneously for use in small daily purchases.

Money is most useful in local spot exchange of commodities. International or inter-regional trade required a more sophisticated means of payment because carrying specie, that is gold or silver coins, from trading post to trading post was both dangerous (due to the risk of theft) and cumbersome. In the course of the medieval and early modern periods, a series of financial innovations minimized the use of commodity money as a means of payment but at the same time kept money as a store of value and a unit of account. These innovations also introduced credit. Exporters might need payment at the time of shipping the goods while the importer wanted to defer the payment until the goods had arrived and could be inspected and sold. The time that elapsed in intra-European trade between the Mediterranean ports and, say, London or Bruges, could be several months. The instrument that gained acceptance and widespread use from the thirteenth or fourteenth century, and dominated international payments until the early twentieth century, was the bill of exchange, which minimized the actual transfer of coins or bullion between trading parties. The bill of exchange is essentially a promise from the debtor to pay the creditor at a specified point in the future.

The essential impact of bills of exchange was to permit the flow of goods while still minimizing the costly and risky business of shipping precious metal money. Institutions developed so that debts and credits could be offset between accounts held by merchants through simple bookkeeping transfers in the ledgers of banks. These operations depended on moneychangers and banks having opened up for deposits and clearing between different account-holders.

The early development of the bill of exchange was initiated by Italian merchant bankers, and it spread throughout Europe thanks to Italian migration to the major ports along Europe's Atlantic coast. The Hanseatic League, which operated out of Germany in the Baltic and north-west Europe, only later learned about the use of the bill of exchange. Although initially emerging as an instrument facilitating trade, the bill of exchange over time increasingly became a financial credit instrument and a substitute for money. It was also widely used for 'inland' transactions, that is, the currency exchange element disappeared when the bill circulated within, say, England.

Since the bill is essentially an obligation for a debtor to pay the creditor a given sum at a given future date, it can be a very risky instrument. What if the debtor defaults on his promise to pay? Most trading cities had legal procedures to force debtors to honour their obligations. The use of branch offices and correspondents of identical ethnic origin was a way of minimizing the risk of default in the settlement of debts. A correspondent of Genovese extraction in Antwerp who cheated on Genoa could be penalized more effectively because his ties with his home town would be cut and his reputation, together with that of his family, would be destroyed. With the diffusion of the bill of exchange, attempts were made to make it less risky and more easily transferable from person to person, like modern notes. There were, however, a number of legal hurdles involved in increasing the transferability or negotiability of a bill, which were sorted out during the fifteenth and sixteenth centuries. Each person who took part in the chain of transfers of a bill had to be responsible for ensuring that the promise to pay the debt was honoured when the bill matured. As a consequence, a bill could be used in a chain of commercial transactions and it also became a liquid asset for many banks, because it could be re-sold if the bank needed cash. Deposit banks accumulated liabilities to their depositors, but held only part of the deposits as reserves and invested the remainder in profitable assets or loans to the public. That was the birth of the practice of modern commercial banking, the so-called *fractional reserve bank**, which was established in Italy in the fourteenth century and spread to other commercial centres in Europe. However, the history of early banking was one of recurrent bankruptcies, because banks tended to hold too small a share of their deposits as reserves and because banking involves the monitoring of borrowers whose commercial success is difficult to assess. Banks were therefore vulnerable to so-called bank *runs,* when people demanded their deposits in cash because of rumours of insolvency. In cities, that had sophisticated financial structures, such as Venice and Amsterdam, authorities might react by prohibiting fractional reserve banking entirely for longer or shorter periods and setting up public clearing banks.

This practice was in general use in the Low Countries in the later sixteenth century. At about the same time the discounting of bills was introduced in Antwerp. Discounting a bill means that a financial intermediary buys the bill at a discount before it matures. Discounting soon became a lively activity, and when Antwerp financiers were driven to London by religious persecution in the late sixteenth century, this brain drain contributed to the dissemination of new financial instruments and practices.

In the sixteenth and seventeenth centuries financial innovation centred around cities like Amsterdam, Antwerp, Bruges and, later, London. However, authorities were at times suspicious of private financial institutions because of bankruptcies during the sixteenth-century 'bullion famine', and leading commercial centres (Venice, Barcelona, Hamburg, Amsterdam) established public deposit banks which were required to hold adequate reserves or retrain from fractional reserve banking. The Amsterdamsche Wisselbank, established in 1609, was one of the most successful, and performed clearing bank functions, that is mutual offsetting of debts and claims among a large number of account-holders involved in international trade. The bank built up a good reputation thanks to which most major companies involved in foreign trade around Europe opened accounts there, making this the most important bank in seventeenth-century Europe.

A lively bill market became an important factor in the development of the deposit banking system, since banks needed safe, interest-bearing liquid assets. By the end of the nineteenth century the development of information technology and the international banking system with branch offices changed the role of the bill, first in domestic and later in international trade. Banks, some of which had international reach, managed international payments and provided traders and firms with overdraft facilities. Gradually the bill of exchange lost its pre-eminence as a means of payment and credit.

7.3 Usury and interest rates in the long run

Banks charge borrowers interest and pay it to depositors. However, interest was long under critical scrutiny from both Church and political authorities. Early Christian thought looked on any positive interest rate as usury and as such incompatible with Christian faith. The Church subsequently adopted a more flexible stance when trade and economic activity increased the demand for and use of credit. A reasonable interpretation of the usury prohibition is that it was directed against creditors who exploited people in need, permitting lenders to charge high interest rates, often above 50 and sometimes above 100 per cent on a yearly basis. Political authorities therefore supported the foundation of public pawnshops which charged much lower interest rates. These pawnshops, the *montes pietatis* as they were called in Italy, also had a philanthropic aim and were widespread in medieval Italy but were also found in north-west Europe from the late Middle Ages. Pawnshops did not make commercial loans and were mainly used by the common people for short-term credit to ease temporary economic hardship. The Church interpreted the interest rate as a payment for the costs the pawnbroker incurred for storage of the commodities which the borrowers deposited in the pawnshop. Not all types of interest were considered as usury in late medieval scholastic discourse. A borrower who was not paying back the loan could be charged a fee for not honouring the letter of the loan contract. Sometimes that fee was agreed on in advance, which seems to make it another word for interest. More importantly, the *opportunity cost** of money lent became a legitimate ground for an interest rate. If a borrower had an alternative profitable use for the money lent, then the lender was actually taking a loss when lending for which he ought to be compensated. Not all theologians agreed, but by the sixteenth century, a much greater tolerance of loans at interest was gaining ground in theological debate, which also had an effect on secular usury legislation. This was not linked to the Reformation because different currents of Reform were as divided on the issue as Catholics. However, Reformed churches retreated from the role of arbiter and accepted that secular authorities should be given the role of regulating interest rates. It is unclear what effect, if any, prohibition of usury had on interest-rate levels. It may in fact have driven borrowers into the hands of loan sharks or lenders who were not Christians and therefore not restrained by usury laws. It may also have driven up interest rates by constraining lending, since there was great uncertainty about what actually constituted usury on the one hand, and a legitimate interest rate on the other. Over time, interest rates have tended to decline. Commercial loans often had interest rates in the range of 10–20 per cent in the twelfth to fourteenth centuries, but they fell to single-digit levels thereafter, down to 5 per cent or lower in the eighteenth and nineteenth centuries. This implies that *real interest rates** were as low in the nineteenth as in the twentieth century.

7.4 The emergence of paper money

The next decisive step in the evolution of an efficient means of payment was the emergence of notes, that is paper money, which were easier to carry around than coins for cash transactions and cheaper to produce. The *intrinsic value* of paper money is insignificant and notes are therefore not commodity money. In a way, the banknote is a 'mutation' of the bill of exchange which reduced the risk and transaction costs involved in making the bill transferable and negotiable by written endorsements. The banknote had obvious advantages over the bill of exchange because it did not require the chain of liability created by the assignment process necessary to make the bill transferable. What mattered now was only the reputation of the bank that issued the note. If the public trusted the bank they accepted the note as a means of payment. The first two centuries of paper money kept a link to commodity money in that notes could be converted, on demand, to full-bodied coins. Since the first note-issuing banks were profit-maximizing and the average customer did not have full information on their solvency, banks were forbidden in many nations to issue notes with low denominations. The reason was the suspicion that they had a tendency to over-issue such notes in the belief that they were rarely redeemed for specie, that is full-bodied coins. The entitlement to exchange notes for gold or gold coins did not disappear until the interwar period of the twentieth century, by which time the private note-issuing banks had been replaced by public central banks with a monopoly on the issue of notes.

Initially paper money developed spontaneously. If a merchant deposited gold or coins with a goldsmith or moneychanger the receipt could be used as a means of payment, so that receipts could go from hand to hand as long as the public trusted the issuer of the receipt. This can be seen as a non-standardized form of banknote, and such receipts circulated long before standardized notes gained widespread acceptance in the eighteenth century. These receipts were pieces of paper which were redeemable, that is convertible to gold or full-bodied coins. To accept them meant one had confidence that the institution that had issued the receipt would honour its promise to convert paper to gold. We see here the origin of *fiat** or *fiduciary money*; *fiduccia* is Italian for 'trust'. The first bank-note was issued by the Swedish bank Stockholms Banco, led by the banker Johan Palmstruch, who not surprisingly was of Dutch origin. The diffusion of finan-cial as well as industrial innovations was fostered by migration. Stockholms Banco was a deposit bank which also lent money to the public. The loans and deposit receipts were issued in banknotes, which were claims on the bank. The banknotes were standardized like modern paper notes and were preferred to the heavy copper plates used in Sweden as a means of payment at the time. The plates were simply too heavy to handle and this called for an alternative means of pay-ment. However, the public lost confidence in the bank's ability to honour all its outstanding liabilities, and a run on the bank ended its short history (1657–68). Instead, England became the pioneer in developing note-issuing banks during the 1690s and into the eighteenth century. Banks in London, and later in the cen-tury throughout England and Scotland, offered deposit facilities, discounting, clearing and note-issuing: most notably through the Bank of England, founded in 1694, but also through a number of local banks. Note-issuing banks practised *fractional reserve banking*: the deposits they held as reserves were only a fraction of their total note issue. Thereby banks contributed to the monetization of the economy as they increased the money supply, i.e. the sum of currency (notes and coins) and deposits in the economy. There is a virtuous circle in the devel-opment of banknotes in the sense that the more people use notes the greater will be the advantages of using them, since they reduce costs: it is very much like using one language rather than many in a conversation. Note issuing by banks spread to the continent but at an uneven speed in the early to middle nineteenth century. However, by the end of the century the state and its central bank had monopolized the issuing of notes in most European nations.

The general drift in the monetary system has been towards economizing on the use of commodity money, making payments through transfers between accounts in banks, and using bills and notes. But when notes were introduced in the eighteenth and nineteenth centuries they were convertible to full-bodied money. Paper money became increasingly popular during the nineteenth century, but there were great national differences. There are numerous histor-ical examples of private note-issuing banks failing to honour their obligations in the eighteenth and nineteenth centuries, which fostered public suspicion and delayed the introduction of *fiat money*. France had a strong preference for payments in specie well into the nineteenth century perhaps because of previous traumatic experience with paper notes issued by the state, whereas paper money dominated transactions in Sweden as far back as the middle of the nineteenth century.

Non-convertible paper money, that is *fiat money*, was used for short periods during crises but it only emerged in an orderly fashion after the final break-up of the international gold standard in the 1930s. At that time note-issuing by private for-profit banks had disappeared. Why did it take so long for the modern paper note to get accepted? After all, pure paper money represents a considerable social saving. First, the production cost of paper money is a fraction of that of full-bodied coins; second, holding large gold reserves, as central banks did, means having reserves which do not yield a positive interest rate. Rondo Cameron, an economic historian, conducted a thought experiment which showed that had France's gold reserves been used to import capital goods, this would have had a significant positive effect by increasing the growth rate of the late nineteenth-century French economy.

The reason for the slow acceptance of *fiat money* is that it requires trust on the part of the public that the issuers will not be tempted to issue too many notes, which would fuel inflation and erode the purchasing power of money. Convertibility of banknotes to specie was an assurance to the public that paper was as good as gold. In the eighteenth and nineteenth centuries, when private banks were issuing their own notes, a bank which was not prudent enough would see its notes fall in value relative to their face value. Those defending free banking, that is a system without a central bank, believed that non-prudent banks would be abandoned by their customers and that would eventually discipline all banks. If banks managed to improve the collective reputation of the banking system it would be like a *public good** and there would be a *free rider problem**. A single bank might be tempted to exploit the good reputation of the banking system and break the unwritten rules of conservative risk-taking. In the world of finance, the default of one bank will have a contagious effect on the entire banking system, as witnessed by the recurrent financial crises in the history of banking. The reason is that customers, the depositors, do not have the information that banks have about their condition. It is therefore difficult to judge whether a problem which is fully revealed in one bank is an isolated phenomenon or a sign of a general distress, and depositors will therefore withdraw their money as a precautionary move. It was therefore in the interest of (almost) all banks to establish some supervisory agency, together with a *lender of last resort** mechanism to prevent defaults and the contagious effects of defaults. Such an agency could, at least in principle, be set up by member banks. However, the impartiality of a member-led supervisory agency was difficult to accomplish since members were also competitors. If one bank was threatened with bankruptcy, competitors would not necessarily rush to rescue it. The lender of last resort mechanism was also difficult to handle by a union of banks if they were *all* threatened by financial stress.

The *raison d'être* of central banks is thus to contain a particular set of market failures which can lead to banking panics, not unknown anywhere in Europe. Quite a few of the central banks formed in the second half of the nineteenth century were transformed private banks, including the Bank of England and the Banque de France, which subsequently scaled down their profit-making commercial activities. The transition to central banks with a note-issuing monopoly was in some cases linked to specific crisis in the private banking system, as in Italy at the close of the nineteenth century – but not in all, for example Sweden, where a strict regulatory regime seems to have permitted private note-issuing to work quite well, although a note-issuing monopoly was granted to the central bank at about the same time as in Italy, perhaps just following the European pattern. As it turned out, no regulatory scheme seems to be able to eradicate financial crises, although the effects may be mitigated. The reason lies at the heart of *fractional reserve banking**. Banks promise to honour depositors at the fixed nominal value of their deposits. However, a bank's assets, its loan portfolio, is subject to unforeseen changes in value. Therefore, banks need a *lender of last resort**.

However, the public had every reason to be suspicious about central banks as well. If a government exerted control over its central bank, as most did initially, there was a risk that the government would ask the bank to lend freely to the government. In the end, that would fuel inflation and increase mistrust of paper money. The gold standard imposed a constraint on money supply because it was supposed to be constrained by gold reserves. An inflationary monetary policy would therefore lead to a loss of gold from the central bank because it would drive down the value of the domestic currency and force the central bank to sell domestic assets to the public, that is to decrease the money supply. (See Chapter 10 for a full discussion.) But when the link to gold was finally abandoned after the demise of the re-established gold standard in the interwar years, the problem arose of how to constrain the monetary authorities from embracing inflationary policies. Two major changes contributed to public acceptance of *fiat money*: accountable government and an independent central bank.

Before the breakthrough of full parliamentary democracy in most of Europe in the early twentieth century, governments were only partly accountable to the public. Assuming public fear of high inflation we would expect accountable governments to refrain from funding their spending by loans from the central bank, whereas undemocratic governments need have no such fears. However, that is not always true. Weak governments such as those in France and Germany immediately after the First World War were forced to please the electorate by public spending, but were unable to raise sufficient revenues from taxes. At that time the pre-war gold standard was not operating and there were no weak constraints on money supply as discussed in Chapter 9. After the monetary reforms of the mid-1920s, nations with an inflationary history granted national banks greater independence and/or restricted government involvement in central bank policy. In nations where governments continued to have more say over monetary policy, such as the UK and Sweden, the inflationary experience of the 1970s and 1980s had a similar effect in that central banks were granted independence from government direction in the early 1990s and established a publicly known inflation rate as their goal. As long as inflation is low the public have come to accept paper money. But when inflation soars there will be a flight to stable foreign currencies and to commodities. There is a compelling logic in that behaviour: money is used in transactions to buy goods, and as long as the purchasing power for goods is reasonably stable paper money is practical.

7.5 What do banks do?

When banks started to take deposits and offer loans to the public, i.e. to practise *fractional reserve banking*, they clearly entered a new phase by increasing the money supply in addition to facilitating trade by providing foreign exchange and clearing services between accounts. In the nineteenth century banks expanded their role as intermediaries between savers and borrowers. What is the rationale for such an intermediary? There is a straightforward answer to that question: it lowers transaction costs and risks for both savers and borrowers. Box 7.1 highlights the major problems faced by savers and borrowers and the way banks act as intermediaries.

Box 7.1 What banks do		
Savers' problem	What banks do	Investors' and borrowers' problem
Costly to assess investors	Banks exploit economies of scale when processing information about firms' solvency	Firms face cash constraints High cost of finding lenders
Risky not to diversify saving	Banks hold diversified asset portfolios	Firms need not rely on a multitude of lenders
Savers want liquid assets	Banks have reserves to meet savers' liquidity demands	Firms need long-term commitment for investment in fixed capital
Asymmetric information Savers do not have access to borrowers' private information	Banks practise delegated monitoring of firms by either relationship banking or short-term credit to penalize poorly performing borrowers	Firms exploit private information in their own interests

For savers it is time-consuming and difficult to collect and assess information on a vide variety of potential investment projects. It is necessary to assess a large number of projects and hedge against the risk of putting all one's savings in a single project. Furthermore, it is difficult for anybody, but especially for a non-specialist, to discover if borrowers as investors are exploiting the fact that they are better informed about the prospects of an investment project by concealing the true risks. There is what is called an information asymmetry, which investors can use to their advantage if it is not properly monitored. But it is practically impossible for small to medium-sized savers to monitor investors. There is need for an intermediary. Banks thrive by exploiting economies of scale and gains from specialization in collecting and analysing information about borrowers. Furthermore, savers want their assets to be liquid, that is they prefer to be able to convert their deposits to money at short notice. Borrowers, who typically will be investors in fixed capital, e.g. land, buildings and machinery, need a long-term commitment from their creditors because of the illiquidity of their investments. Banks learn how to transform short-term liabilities (deposits) into long-term assets (loans) by holding appropriate liquid reserves which can be used to service depositors when they occasionally and on short notice want to withdraw money. Banks which have built a good reputation seldom if ever become victims of bank runs, that is a situation when all or nearly all depositors withdraw their deposits.

Investors also have an information problem in finding willing long-term lenders outside the circle of close associates, family and friends, who were a major source of lending in the early phase of economic revival in Europe, and continued to be so well into the initial phase of industrialization. But as the size of firms increased the need for external finance mounted. Early modern banks mainly serviced trade with short-term credit, but by the nineteenth century industry was becoming an increasingly important client. However, in return for long-term credit, banks needed to monitor the performance of borrowers in the depositors' and their own interests. Banks do that by a mix of supervision and penalties imposed on borrowers who do not perform adequately.

Why does this system of monitoring and intermediation break down in bank runs? The heart of the matter is this. Banks accept deposits and promise a positive return, an interest rate, and the right for depositors to reclaim the deposit at a fixed nominal value. Banks also manage a portfolio of assets: they offer fixed nominal value loans to borrowers, but the underlying asset has an uncertain future value. Inevitably, banks occasionally miscalculate because it is inherently difficult to assess the future value of an asset. This will trigger off a chain of events: borrowers cannot pay back their loans, depositors fear for their deposits and run to rescue them, banks have liquidity constraints and will fail in the absence of a *lender of last resort*, a central bank. Some of these runs are unjustified by fundamentals, but depositors are victims of another information asymmetry: they do not know what the bankers do about the bank and if they are loss-averse they will secure their deposits as soon as possible.

Box 7.2   The anatomy of financial crises

The history of financial crises is as long as the history of banking. Roughly speaking, such crises take the form of either a liquidity crisis or a crisis of solvency, but either can easily spill over to the other. A liquidity crisis stems from the very nature of *fractional reserve banking*. Banks occasionally under-estimate the volume of liquidity needed to meet customers' need for cash. A liquidity crisis can develop into a bank run that involves even solvent banks because of the contagion of customers panicking and withdrawing their deposits at an unforeseen rate. Over the course of history liquidity crises have been contained by the development of the central banks as *lenders of last resort*. That means that central banks lend freely to the banking system (the so-called Bagehot's rule) until the public has regained confidence in the banking system. The introduction of deposit insurance, which evolved mainly in the second half of the twentieth century, has also contained the impact of liquidity crises because customers know that their deposits are safe even if the bank fails.

Crises of solvency have historically been more difficult to contain and tend to have a severe impact on income and growth. They usually appear after a period of excessive risk-taking linked to low interest rates and/or rising asset prices, so-called financial bubbles. When the bubble bursts equity and/or house prices fall by 25 or even up to 50 per cent. These crises are also linked to an inherent characteristic of banking, the difficulty of revealing the true risk and value of the assets typically held by banks. Excessive risk-taking involves non-diversification of assets, for example if banks hold a large fraction of their total assets in specific industries that can be hit by a shock. An initial decline in the value of assets is easily aggravated because financial institutions can be forced to stage 'fire-sales' to raise cash, futher pushing down the value of the assets. A large proportion of assets turn out to be what are now being called 'toxic assets', i.e. assets no one wants to touch, or more precisely, to buy. The ultimate solution for insolvency has been for the state to nationalize the failing banks. Since the value of the toxic assets has often been driven down to very low levels there is a chance that nationalized banks can sell them off at higher prices at a later date, when markets have regained confidence. An oft-cited example of a successful nationalization and later privatization is that of Swedish banks in the 1990s. Although the cost of bailing out a number of banks was very large initially, the re-privatization recouped most of it. However, the macroeconomic cost, in terms of a sharp fall in output, was significant. The Swedish case was fairly typical, leading to a sharp rise in unemployment, and had a long duration from trough to peak, about five years.

7.6   The impact of banks on economic growth

The impact of banks on economic growth operates through three mechanisms: the impact on the savings ratio; the impact on the efficiency of the use to which savings are channelled; and the effect of increased monetization of the economy. Monetization is linked to the effect of *fractional reserve banks* that issue banknotes to create money, that is to increase the money supply.

There are good reasons as well as evidence that the spread of banks outside the metropolitan areas actually increased the savings ratio, that is savings as a share of *national income**. We do not have adequate data on savings in the pre-industrial period, but we suspect that the savings ratio rarely rose above 5 per cent of *national income*. In the second half of the nineteenth century, savings increased considerably and varied between 10 to 20 per cent of *national income*. Banks were essential to mobilize savings because they increased the *opportunity cost** of hoarding. Households make choices about present and future consumption, that is savings. If the transaction costs and risks of decisions about savings are reduced, savings will become more attractive, and hence they will increase and consumption will fall as a proportion of household income. In the absence of banks there may not be any viable alternative to savings apart from the consumption of durable 'store of value' goods, such as gold and silver. But hoards of gold and silver in the public coffers represented a lost opportunity. Had the equivalent money been deposited in banks, it could have been put at the disposal of investors. Furthermore, there is a strong link between domestic savings and domestic investments and hence economic growth. Direct and systematic evidence of the economic effect of the growth of banking is scanty for the early modern period. However, the Vanderbilt-based economic historian P. Rousseau looked into the impact of the monetization of the Dutch economy on the activity of the trading companies and found a strong link in the seventeenth and eighteenth centuries. Cash constraints were serious impediments to investment. More importantly, Rousseau found that monetization (measured by the Bank of England's deposits and liabilities, mainly circulating banknotes) had a strong impact on industrial production from 1730 to 1850, that is during a good part of the Industrial Revolution. A 1 per cent increase in monetization was estimated to lead to a 2 per cent increase in industrial output after five years. These findings indicate the importance of mobilizing savings and activating the process of money creation by banks.

Citizens of small to moderate means were initially reluctant to trust banks. Bank failures were not infrequent in the late eighteenth and early nineteenth century. The savings banks that developed all over Europe in the early nineteenth century (an early starter was Hamburg in 1778) were meant to provide ordinary citizens with safe deposits, and by implication make them familiar with bank practices. Philanthropists and local governments were often involved in the early phase of their development, seeking to promote self-help for the common people in old age and spells of hardship. But given the fragility of trust, savings banks initially had to pursue a very conservative asset strategy. In some countries, they did not lend to the public at all but invested only in secure government debt. In the later nineteenth century, the constraints on lending were relaxed although the types of collateral accepted were restricted. Real estate and land were considered secure collateral, but other institutions, often with the help and guidance of the state, had developed which were granting loans with land as security. This was of particular importance in the nineteenth century when land reforms enabled a growing class of farmers to borrow for land improvement or to consolidate their holdings, which tended to increase productivity. Savings banks were originally designed for, and in fact attracted, low and middle-income earners, who otherwise might not have saved at all. Despite the care savings banks showed in evading risky investments, they played an important role in providing finance for infrastructure investments, and over time they developed an asset strategy not very different from other banks. The other element in nineteenth-century banking development is the emergence of the joint-stock bank, which relied less on depositors' money and more on investors' capital. These banks were not constrained by depositors' preferences for liquidity and were urged by their owners to adopt a less conservative loan strategy in order to increase returns to the owners. Typically these banks were involved in the financing of commerce and industry to a higher extent than the savings banks. Through the twentieth century the differences between these two types of banks diminished, however. Joint-stock banks built nationwide branch offices and attracted deposits, often in competition with the savings banks. However, some joint-stock banks developed in another direction and became pure investment banks, servicing industrial firms and helping in mergers and acquisitions.

Banks specialize in gathering information about borrowers' solvency and the viability and profitability of investment projects (see Box 7.1). In so doing, they typically set up strict criteria which must be fulfilled before a loan is granted. However, there is an asymmetry of information in that a borrower, say an entrepreneur, may know more than the bank manager about the true nature of the firm that the entrepreneur is setting up or runs. This asymmetry is a source of potential cheating on the part of the borrower. Therefore, banks must also regularly monitor their borrowers and be able to penalize them if they do not live up to the expectations on which they were granted loans. It is plausible that when an institution specializes in information-gathering and monitoring, borrowers' savings will be used more efficiently than if savers invest individually, unmediated by financial institutions. There is empirical confirmation from cross-border studies in the second half of the twentieth century that *bank depth* (meaning, more or less, the volume of financial intermediation in the economy) is positively linked to investment and productivity growth when other relevant factors that affect growth have been controlled for. But the same results apply to *stock market depth*. And it makes sense: bank managers aim to select the most promising technologies and they monitor firms, but in the stock market a large number of unco-ordinated individual traders and investment fund managers do the same job. While European nations developed both stock markets and banking systems in the nineteenth century, the relative importance of these two types of financial institutions differed. The legal framework for the incorporation of firms may be of significance here because it affected the ease with which they could raise capital from sources other than banks. In the early nineteenth century only Britain had a well-developed banking system, consisting of a wide network of country banks and a strong centre in London. It provided mostly short-term credit to industry and commerce bill discounting and deposit banking. The rest of Europe had a financial system which was not at all adequate for the tasks ahead. Neither stock markets nor banks were particularly well developed. There is an argument, developed by one of the pioneers in economic history, Alexander Gerschenkron (1904–78), that this backwardness in continental Europe prompted banks to play a more active role in fostering industrial development by establishing close links between themselves and industry. It is true that by the middle of the nineteenth century the banking structure evolving particularly in France and Germany was in many ways different from the British model, and quite a few will argue that the continental European variety was better at picking the best firms and developed better means of coping with the asymmetric information and *agency problems** inherent in the bank–borrower relationship. The heart of the matter is how good banks were at doing their monitoring job, and there is a well-developed although controversial argument that Victorian Britain (*c.* 1850–1900) failed as witnessed by comparatively low growth, at least partly because of the failure of financial intermediaries to direct savings towards the most profitable investment opportunities in industry. Banks were unable or unwilling to provide industry with the necessary finance, which slowed down industrial progress, according to this argument. William Kennedy, an economist who worked at the London School of Economics, showed that British merchant bankers were risk-averse, invested in lower-yielding assets, and thereby made life hard for evolving, but more risky, technologies. Britain's pre-eminent role in international finance was a hindrance rather than a help, because a much too high proportion of savings was invested in overseas assets. On the continent, on the other hand, banks were more inclined to develop close and long-lasting ties with industry and to take risks in investing in new technologies; they also secured some influence by participating on the boards of these companies. British banks excelled in commercial banking, which included the discounting of bills and the provision of short-term credit, for example as overdrafts, deposits and clearing. This has earned the British system the name *transaction banking*. The system developing in France and Germany had the commercial banking functions but then added a number of other services, such as investment banking and mortgages for houses. Since these banks embraced a wide variety of activities they have been termed *universal banks.* Some but not all universal banks preferred to take a long-term stake or provide varieties of corporate finance to particular firms: banks typically followed a firm from its start to its maturity. This approach has earned the name of *relationship banking*, as opposed to transaction banking of the British variety, which did not strive for long-term relationships between banks and firms. The relationship banking promoted by German banks has in some accounts been given a prominent role in Germany's rapid catch-up in the last third of the nineteenth century. And this line of argument is in some sense the reverse of the argument that British transaction banking neglected firms at the technological frontier and slowed down growth in the UK.

This view has been revised in recent research, however. Relationship banking is supposed to diminish the problem of asymmetric information and constrain cheating by borrowers by establishing a relationship of trust between entrepreneurs and banks. Long-term relationships also save on the costs of gathering information about firms, in that information is not lost as happens in short-term relationships between banks and firms. Relationship banking was formerly also believed to ease the cash constraint which transaction-type banks imposed on their customers, but the historical record does not altogether support that conclusion. Furthermore, British banks seem to have been able to overcome this disadvantage of the lack of a long-term relationship between bank and industry by establishing highly efficient routines for scrutinizing borrowers. Furthermore, the short-term nature of British lending has been exaggerated. It is true that British banks relied more on deposits than, say, German universal banks, which forced British banks to hold more liquid assets, i.e. short-term credit. But short-term loans were routinely rolled over to the next period, effectively making them less short-term than they appear at first sight. The discussion of the advantages of relationship banking also neglects the risks for the banking systems of having too close ties with industry. British banks were less likely to default when industry was in recession compared to continental banks heavily involved in large firms and often concentrating their lending on particular sectors of industry, such as steel or electrical engineering: there are a number of examples from nations with relationship banking of bank failures during industrial downturns. In France, banks partly retreated from relationship banking and long-term investment in industry as a consequence of the dangers inherent in that model. In Sweden, lawmakers intervened to limit the banks' exposure to industrial distress by regulating their involvement in industrial finance. More recently, when the financial crises starting in 2008 imperilled the banking system worldwide new demands for separation of commercial and investment banking were heard.

Was relationship-type banking more efficient in securing good performance in firms and channelling savings to the best use, and was this model therefore better at promoting economic growth? These are the big questions, and as always with big questions, there are no conclusive answers. The question boils down to whether the asset portfolios of relationship banks had higher yields than those of transaction-type banks, and there is some evidence that British banks held assets which were not optimal at the end of the nineteenth century. Hence we cannot exclude the hypothesis that Victorian Britain's relative failure – that is its not growing as fast as major continental economies – had at least something to do with its banking system.

7.7 Banks versus stock markets

Stock markets, which mainly traded government debt and shares in trading companies until industry, bank, and transport securities were introduced in the later nineteenth century, fulfil similar functions to banks, but by other means. They enable savers to diversify risk and provide an instrument, that is equity, shares or stocks, which is liquid for savers but a long-term commitment for borrowers. Thousands of shareholders exert control over firms by buying or selling stocks with no intermediary other than the stock market. Stock-market traders exert control by *exit* or *entry*, whereas bank managers monitoring firms *voice* their concerns and penalize borrowers if necessary. The information needed and the costs involved in obtaining information about firms have precluded the vast majority of the public from investing directly in the stock market. While almost all households had bank accounts by, say, 1950, fewer than 10 per cent owned stocks. *Mutual funds**, which invest in a portfolio of stocks, can thrive because they exploit economies of scale in gathering information which individual savers cannot. An increasing share of total savings was also diverted to mutual funds, especially in the last third of the twentieth century. However, buying shares in mutual funds is less attractive to risk-averse savers because mutual funds cannot promise a positive return on shares, nor can they guarantee the nominal value of the original deposit. Therefore, total savings will be higher with a combination of bank and mutual funds compared to a state where only one (either one) of these alternatives is available. Stock markets in Europe developed as modern banking emerged in the second half of the nineteenth century, which suggests that stock markets and banks are complementary rather than rivals. But why did banking reach a sophisticated level of development before stock exchanges did? The simple answer is that banks and stock markets deal with different assets. Stock markets trade marketable assets, that is stocks in firms large enough to bother issuing them, while banks deal with non-marketed assets.

Banks extend loans to firms against collateral in non-marketed assets such as buildings, inventories and machinery. Because these assets are non-marketed, their value is difficult to assess, which motivates the hands-on monitoring of borrowers by banks. Before the middle of the nineteenth century, very few firms could offer marketable assets and that favoured bank financing. The shares traded in pre-nineteenth-century stock markets were typically those of large trading companies, rarely industrial firms.

Within Europe the relative importance of banks and stock markets in providing finance and the monitoring of firms differed markedly by the second half of the nineteenth century and some of these differences remain today. German banks took an early lead in supplying firms with credit and exert control, which they still do. The reverse is true for the UK. The co-existence of rival institutions fulfilling the same functions is puzzling. One explanation is *path dependence** based on the argument developed by Alexander Gerschenkron, who suggested that large banks in Germany were particularly well suited to provide finance to industry at a crucial formative moment and that they subsequently stifled the development of the stock market. According to this argument, initial conditions determined which of the rival solutions would dominate. A supplementary explanation suggests that any combination of the two institutional solutions is better than just one, because there are different sources of potential inefficiencies in both bank and market monitoring of firms. Banks often fail, with serious negative consequences for borrowers and lenders alike. Stock markets, on the other hand, function even in periods of widespread banking crises, which make them an essential complement to banks.

In a perfect stock market, all available information regarding a firm is expressed in the price of a stock. However, markets are not perfectly efficient. Stocks can be over-priced or under-priced – not permanently, but over sufficiently long periods to harm the efficient monitoring of firms. It is particularly difficult and costly to assess the fundamental value of firms using new technologies and/or developing new products. However, there is no way a stock-market investor can keep the information she collects about a profitable investment project private. Let us assume that such an investor uses resources to investigate a firm and finds that its stock is under-priced (or over-priced). When that investor starts buying (selling) the stock to earn a capital gain, the new information will be revealed by her trading and others will follow the lead and bid up (or depress) the price. This implies that stock markets do not sufficiently reward those who research the fundamentals of firms, which will lead to under-investment in information gathering. Historical stock-market bubbles confirm this argument. Excessive price movements unrelated to fundamentals typically occur for stocks in new industries where there is a need to invest heavily in the collection and processing of information. Insufficient information can lead to herd behaviour. When investors are not able to assess information properly, they follow the behaviour of other investors, believing that the first mover's behaviour is based on solid knowledge.

Banks that develop long-run relationships with firms are better placed to keep their information private and thus invest more in research to explore the fundamentals of firms, which may improve the efficiency of investments. However, relationship banking can also generate inefficiencies. If a bank has inside information about a firm and owns much of its debt, this will give the bank market power, which can be used to secure a larger share of the profits of the firm. In conclusion, an economy in which firms are neither totally dependent on banks nor totally dependent on stock markets may be the best solution. History has acknowledged this by permitting both not only to survive but to thrive.

Summary

The historical development of monetary instruments and financial intermediaries indicates substantial social savings over time. Recurrent and costly banking crises are nonetheless dwarfed by the gains from a sophisticated financial system. The evolution of commodity money into paper money is a striking example. Financial intermediaries, such as banks, took a long time to develop the trust needed for the public to use them and thereby contributed to an increase in the savings ratio. The history of banking is a dramatic one, with recurrent failures. However, the long-term trend has been a reduction of the risks in using the services provided by banks. The discussion is summarized in Figure 7.2. At a given point in time, the prevailing technology and institutions can be represented by combinations of cost and risk levels associated with different means of payment. In the figure we associate some stylized facts with three different epochs: the early modern period (c.1600), the middle of the nineteenth century, and the present. Over time, institutions and technology have reduced both costs and risks with payment systems. In around 1600, full-bodied coins were the least risky of alternative means of payment (upper left in the graph), but also the most costly, since coins are difficult to assay and, from a social point of view, costly to produce. Transaction costs were also high because coins were heavy. In the eighteenth century, £100 in silver coins weighed about 15 kg. There was also a risk in using coins because of the circulation of counterfeits. Not until the nineteenth century was mint technology

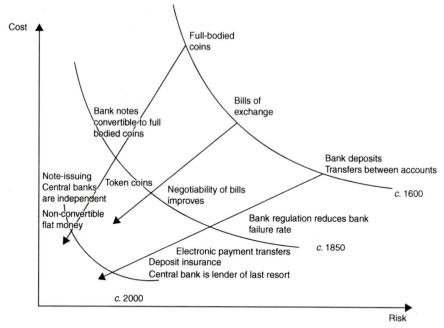

Figure 7.2   Payment systems reduce cost and risk over time. The graph is a free elaboration of A.N. Berger *et al.* 'A framework for analysing efficiency, risks, costs and innovations in payments systems', *Journal of Money, Credit and Banking* 28 (1996), pp. 696–732.

with steam-powered stamping sufficiently advanced to make counterfeit-proof coins. The introduction of paper money came late, in fact after some 10,000 years of commodity money, and relies on public trust in money-issuing institutions. The independence of central banks is a vital precondition and it represents a social saving of some importance.

Bills of exchange were initially a lot less costly to use as a means of payment than full-bodied coins, but the risk of debtor default made the bill more risky. Payments by transfers in the ledgers of deposit banks were even less costly, but banks were unstable institutions and the bankruptcy risk was real. Over time both the costs and the risks of using banks for deposits and payment services declined. Bank regulation reduced the failure rate and increasingly the national banks took on the role of *lender of last resort* in a financial crisis. The so-called Bagehot's rule, which prompts the central bank to lend freely at higher interest rates in a financial crisis, was formulated in the middle of the nineteenth century, but was not consistently practised until 100 years later. Subsequent innovations, which reduced risks for depositors, include deposit insurance, which emerged after the Great Depression. The reason why we see alternative means of payment at a given point in time has to do with the fact that the preferred choice of payment in local trade, say coins or notes, is not suitable for international trade, where bills of exchange and clearing operations in deposit banks are preferable. In small transactions, currency is appropriate and practical, but large transactions typically involve the intermediation of banks. Bank deposits that can be used for transfers and the clearing of accounts have become less costly and more rapid. It is simply a bookkeeping operation where by payment consists of a transfer from one account to another account; in the nineteenth century this would be made using the telegraph rather than the postal system.

Although the bill of exchange has now ceased to be used as a means of payment, both transaction costs and risk were reduced as it developed. Most importantly, it became an easily transferable payment instrument, and a safer one, because the transfer process became one of collective responsibility for eventual payment.

The successive inward shifts of the curves in Figure 7.2 are associated with a dramatic increase in monetization or liquidity measured in terms of the money supply (currency, that is notes and coins in circulation and deposits in banks) as a share of GDP. Today that ratio is around 70 per cent, whereas around 1850 it varied more across nations; but an average of 30 per cent is plausible, increasing from 5 to 10 per cent in the pre-industrial era, although it would be higher in an economy with a sophisticated banking system like Britain.

Appendix: The bill of exchange further explored

The bill of exchange originally involved four parties in a unidirectional trade flow.

Imagine a silk importer in Antwerp, Mr van der Wee, importing silk from Genoa. To pay for goods exported by the Genoa silk trader, Mr Federico, van der Wee buys a bill from his local merchant banker in Antwerp, Mr van der Woude. The latter is the drawer of the bill and van der Wee the drawee. This is the first step in the operation (see Figure 7.3). The bill is paid in the local currency, but states the amount of money in Genoese currency that the silk exporter Federico, the so-called payee, is to receive: step 2. When the bill arrives in Genoa, Federico presents the bill to a local merchant banker, Mr Toniolo, the accepter or payer, who pays Federico: step 3. In this process actual money transfers are strictly local but goods – silk – have moved from Genoa to Antwerp. Payments of money have been executed from drawee to drawer in Antwerp and from accepter to payee in Genoa.

But the accepter in Genoa, merchant banker Toniolo, has extended a short-term credit to merchant banker van der Woude in Antwerp. The bill of

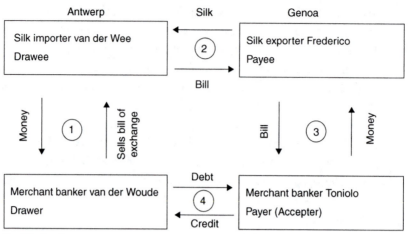

Figure 7.3   The bill of exchange

exchange was an instrument of short-term credit. When the bill matures, merchant banker van der Woude must settle his debt to Genoa banker Toniolo. However, in most cases that debt will not be settled by a money transfer from Antwerp to Genoa because both parties are probably involved in international trade and the Genoese merchant banker's claim on Antwerp can be offset by van der Woude's claim on Genoa, provided both parties have accounts in Genoese banks.

In the case described in Figure 7.3 an importer is the drawee, but the bill of exchange was flexible enough as a means of payment and credit to reverse the order. An importer needing money could assume the role of drawer and sell the bill to a local financier. Bills were typically instruments of short-term credit, say two or three or up to six months.

Suggestions for further reading

An excellent survey of the evolution of British banking, with a comparative perspective on Europe, is S. Quinn, 'Money, finance and capital markets', in R. Floud and P. Johnson (eds.), *The Cambridge Economic History of Modern Britain*, Vol. 1 (Cambridge University Press, 2004), pp. 147–74.

Y. Cassis (ed.), *Finance and Financiers in European History 1880–1960* (Cambridge University Press, 1992). Of particular interest is a chapter by Richard Tilly on German banking.

M. Collins and M. Baker, *Commercial Banks and Industrial Finance in England and Wales, 1860–1913* (Oxford University Press, 2003) provides a balanced overview of the merits and shortcomings of British banking.

C. Fohlin, *Finance Capitalism and Germany's Rise to Industrial Power* (Cambridge University Press, 2007) challenges the conventional view of German banking. Fohlin provides a re-interpretation of the role of German banks in industrialization while downplaying the unique role of relationship banking.

T. Guinnane has written with insight on German and European banking and corporate structure; see e.g. 'Delegated monitors, large and small: Germany's banking system 1800–1914', *Journal of Economic Literature* 40 (2002), pp. 73–124.

A classic is A. Gerschenkron, *Economic Backwardness in Historical Perspective* (Cambridge. Mass.: Harvard University Press, 1962).

W. Kennedy, *Industry Structure, Capital Markets and the Origin of British Economic Decline* (Cambridge University Press, 1987). An analysis which argues that UK banks failed to modernize British industry.

R. Levine, 'Financial development and economic growth: views and agenda', *Journal of Economic Literature* 35 (1997), pp. 688–726. A concise summary of the theoretical literature on banks and financial intermediaries.

L. Neal, *The Rise of Financial Capitalism: International Capital Markets in the Age of Reason* (Cambridge University Press, 1990). A pioneering quantitative study of the first phase of international capital markets.

P. L. Rousseau, 'Historical perspectives on financial development and economic growth', *Federal Reserve Bank of St. Louis Review* (2003), pp. 81–106. A rare attempt to give econometric significance to the role of banks in early growth.

A. Teichova *et al.* (eds.), *Banking, Trade and Industry: Europe, America and Asia from the Thirteenth to the Twentieth Century* (Cambridge University Press, 1997). Chapters by Herman van der Wee and Håkan Lindgren are of particular interest.

On the evolution of central banking see C. Goodhart, *The Evolution of Central Banks* (Cambridge, Mass.: MIT Press, 1991).

8 Trade, tariffs and growth

Karl Gunnar Persson and Paul Sharp

8.1 The comparative advantage argument for free trade and its consequences

David Ricardo (1772–1823) put forward the idea that countries trade in order to profit from their *comparative advantages**. In his model, countries differ only in the productivity of their labour when producing different goods, and a country that is relatively efficient at producing something should export it. So, for example, England should export cloth to Portugal and import wine. An important implication of this theory is that countries should trade even if they do not have an *absolute advantage* in the production of goods: it is not whether a country is better at producing something than another that decides whether or not it should export it, but whether it is relatively better in comparison with other goods. The argument relates to the concept of *opportunity costs** and is the same idea as we met in Chapters 2 and 4 as one of the bases of pre-industrial growth. When population or the "extent of the market" expands, specialization is possible. Trade allows the "extent of the market" to cross international borders and countries to specialize.

The concept of comparative advantage is often considered to be one of the most difficult to grasp in economics, but to understand it is crucial. In short, producing a good diverts labour from producing other goods, which are thus lost (the opportunity cost). Of course, in the absence of trade it is necessary to produce all goods, and this is unavoidable. However, if there is trade it is best for a country to focus on the goods it produces relatively well, because by so doing it can produce most. The extra output can then be traded for the goods it is relatively poor at producing, which will enhance the level of consumer welfare. A numerical example is given in the appendix to this chapter.

Ricardo's theory was further developed in the early twentieth century by the two Swedish economists Eli Heckscher and Bertil Ohlin, giving rise to the Heckscher–Ohlin theorem. This states that comparative advantage is based on the relative abundance of factors of production, rather than on differences in labour productivity. Countries will have a comparative advantage in products produced using factors which they are relatively abundant in. So, for example, a capital-abundant country will export capital-intensive goods, such as industrial products (and import others), whereas land-abundant countries will export land-intensive goods, such as agricultural produce. Heckscher and Ohlin's model gave rise to a number of important results: the *Rybczynski theorem*, the *Stolper–Samuelson theorem* and the *factor–price equalization theorem*, all of which are explained below.

Probably the most important result of the Heckscher–Ohlin model is the factor–price equalization theorem, which states that free trade will make factor and commodity prices converge, although this has found little empirical support as far as wages are concerned. This relates to the discussion on globalization and market integration in Chapter 12. The Rybczynski theorem states that when the amount of one factor of production increases, the production of goods produced intensively using that factor will also increase. This can be observed in history during, for example, times of mass migration: when the supply of labour increases due to immigration or population growth there will be a tendency for countries to produce more labour-intensive goods, such as industrial products. Another example is the growth in the supply of land due to the westward extension of the frontier in nineteenth-century America. The United States then became a world leader in the production and export of agricultural goods, which use land intensively.

The Stolper–Samuelson theorem is important for understanding why, despite the gains from trade due to the exploitation of comparative advantages, countries often restrict trade, for example through tariffs. This theorem states that the relative prices of factors are driven by the relative prices of output goods. Since opening to trade will have an impact on commodity prices, it will also impact on the relative prices of factors, for example by increasing the return on capital relative to labour. History teaches us that this has been a cause of strife *within* nations, since it implies that there are winners and losers when a country opens up to trade and thus different groups will support different trade policies. The price of a country's export goods will increase along with trade, while the price of the goods it imports will fall. Suppose a country's comparative advantage lies in capital goods, which it will then export as opposed to land–intensive agricultural goods, which it will import. This means that the people who own resources employed intensively in the production of export goods – the capitalists – will win and the landed interests (the landed aristocracy or farmers, for example) will lose. Trade policy is thus a source of conflict within countries.

It can also be a source of conflict *between* countries, since countries protecting their agriculture, for example, are hurting those countries that have a comparative advantage in agricultural produce. If these countries retaliate by protecting themselves against imports of industrial goods, world trade will decline and all countries will lose. For this reason, *protectionism* is often considered to be a *zero sum game*: each country's gain or loss is balanced by other countries' losses or gains.

8.2 Trade patterns in history: the difference between nineteenth and twentieth-century trade

Heckscher and Ohlin drew inspiration from their observations of the pattern of nineteenth-century international trade. This was largely *inter*-sectoral, that is goods from different sectors and industries were traded between countries. So, for example, in the late nineteenth century well over 80 per cent of the UK's exports were manufactures, and well over 80 per cent of her imports were primary products. In north-west Europe the situation was rather more balanced, with about 50 per cent to each. Elsewhere, exports were often dominated by primary products, and imports by manufactures. Even in the USA in 1913, for example, nearly 75 per cent of imports were primary products.

The USA and Canada, and many countries which make up today's developing world, exported raw materials and food and imported machinery and other manufactured goods from the European core and the UK in particular. This was completely in line with the predictions of the Heckscher–Ohlin model: the USA was a land-abundant country, giving it a comparative advantage in agriculture. Although the USA also imported primary products, these were from areas that could exploit their own comparative advantages, such as tropical zones with an advantage of climate.

The USA and Canada did not, however, import a particularly high proportion of manufactured goods in comparison with less developed areas: just about one third of total imports. This shows that it was not just comparative advantages that determined trade patterns. Trade policy mattered as well: both countries protected their manufacturing and became increasingly self-sufficient in industrial goods. As will be demonstrated below, if *economies of scale** occur (i.e. the cost of producing one additional unit of the good in question falls as output increases) *at the level of the industry* it can provide a reason for protection.

Although trade in the nineteenth century seems to have followed the theory of Heckscher and Ohlin, from the twentieth century this started to change.

Trade became increasingly *intra*sectoral – that is, countries exported similar goods to those they imported. In fact, trade with other industrial countries accounted for over one third of industrial countries' trade in the 1950s, and this increased to half by the end of the twentieth century. These countries were producing similar goods. This may initially seem surprising: why should countries import goods they can produce just as well at home? However, a moment's reflection would reveal that this happens all the time. Sweden exports cars, for example, but also imports them. Denmark both imports and exports pharmaceuticals.

One reason for this is that trade need not be based on comparative advantage if there are economies of scale. Economies of scale *at the level of the firm* result in imperfect competition. Since firms have a scale advantage, larger firms will be more efficient. The model of *monopolistic competition* describes how this environment will lead to a number of firms producing differentiated goods, each firm having a monopoly in terms of the specific good it produces; but monopoly profits are competed away as additional firms, each supplying different varieties of the product, enter the market. The larger this market for the products, the more and larger firms can be supported. Free trade thus offers both cheaper goods and more variety. Consumers love variety, and welcome the range of products that international trade brings.

In fact, the vast majority of world trade (even including that of many less developed countries) is now in industrial products. The *income elasticity** of demand for industrial goods is larger than for agricultural produce, and this has meant that as incomes have increased around the world, there has been a general shift towards industrial goods in world production and trade.

Does all this mean that the Heckscher–Ohlin model is no longer relevant? No, for various reasons. Most importantly, trade between the industrialized and the less developed countries is still primarily inter-sectoral. For example, consider the trade between Germany and China. Germany is richly endowed with skilled labour, whereas China has a relative abundance of unskilled labour. The result is that Germany exports high-tech machinery to China, and China exports (for example) textiles and less sophisticated mass-produced consumer electronics to Germany. Another point to take into account concerns our definition of intra-sectoral trade. Going back to our earlier example, although Denmark both imports and exports pharmaceutical products, Danish medicines are specialized in certain areas, such as insulin and antibiotics, which reflects the comparative (skill) advantages Denmark enjoys in relation to the production of these sorts of medicines. Aggregation of statistics into broad categories can thus mask trade based on comparative advantage.

8.3 Trade policy and growth

Although trade has long been considered the 'handmaiden of growth', traditional trade theory does not postulate any such relationship, simply because it does not discuss growth rates at all. However, as discussed above, trade does imply a one-off welfare improvement, since, with the advent of trade, previously inefficiently allocated resources will become more efficiently used thanks to international specialization and production will increase.

Trade also has an impact on economic growth through technological change: put simply, since technological knowledge is embedded in capital equipment, trade enables this knowledge to travel across borders, thus aiding growth in the recipient country. First-generation growth theory (the Solow model) fails to capture this simply because technology is assumed to be exogenous. This is not the case in endogenous or 'new growth theory', however: it considers knowledge to be *non-rival**, i.e. one person's use of it does not detract from another's use. This means that if one country learns of a new technology from another, that does not take the technology away from the original country. Thus, by spreading technological knowhow, trade fosters growth.

There are some caveats, however. New growth theory also links technological change to spending on research and development. Since spending by firms is linked to the expected returns on this investment, highly competitive environments can actually imply *less* spending on *R&D**, since any competitive advantage such firms receive as a result of their new technology will be eroded as their competitors take advantage of its non-exclusiveness. To the extent that international trade fosters competition it may, therefore, have a negative impact on technological progress and hence on growth. Of course, a large number of institutions, such as patent law, have been established to ensure that firms have an incentive to invest in *R&D* even in a competitive environment. However, these laws can be difficult to enforce internationally.

The possibility of gains from protecting industry implies that the impact of trade policy depends not just on how much you protect, but on what is protected. Here the consequences of trade policy become rather ambiguous. For example, if protection has a bias towards agricultural products, it may make capital goods cheaper in relative terms, and thus stimulate investment. However, it has also been argued that if tariffs help manufacturing output relative to agriculture, they can speed up the relocation of labour from lower-productivity agriculture to higher-productivity manufacturing. This would result in higher growth rates as labour reserves in agriculture move into industry. This would clearly pull in the opposite direction, since it is not possible to favour agriculture and industry at the same time!

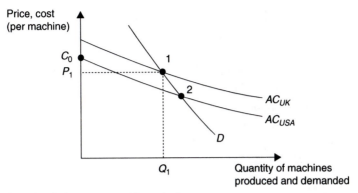

Figure 8.1   The infant-industry argument for protection.

The most important argument for protection is so-called *infant-industry protection*: and this relates to the story of nineteenth-century American protection of industry as discussed in the previous section. If technological progress is aided by learning-by-doing and dynamic economies of scale, this might justify *protectionism*. The idea is illustrated in Figure 8.1.

Imagine a situation at point 1 where the UK is the established producer of machines and is producing quantity Q_1, at which point demand, D, is satisfied at a given level of average costs. The cost of producing each unit of production (shown by the AC curve) falls with the level of production. This can be due to learning-by-doing, which implies that it becomes cheaper to produce machinery with experience; or to economies of scale, which mean that it is cheaper to produce large volumes. At this level of production the UK's average cost per unit of production is equal to P_1, which is also the price at which it is able to sell each machine. Although the USA's average cost curve is lower than the UK's, when America starts producing it cannot offer a price below C_0, and the nascent industry will be outcompeted by the UK. Imagine, however, that the USA decides to protect its industry while it gets established. As output expands, average costs will fall, until eventually the USA is able to outcompete the UK, protection is no longer necessary, and quantities and prices are at point 2.

This argument seems compelling, but there are several problems with it. In practice it is difficult to determine which industries have potential. Protecting incorrectly will simply create an industry dependent on government support, and it may be politically difficult ever to remove the protection. Moreover, simply offering the protection may lead to industries becoming less competitive, since they may adjust to a protected environment and never reach the level of competitiveness necessary for its removal. The advantages of removing protection in an environment where there are economies of scale are sometimes referred to as *dynamic gains* from trade. In fact, the infant-industry argument really depends on there being market failures, because industries that have true potential will attract private investors who are prepared to borrow in the short term to secure a long-term gain. These market failures may be substantial, however, especially in emerging countries where investors are uncertain of their returns, and thus may not be prepared to invest.

All in all, trade theory is rather ambivalent about the impact of trade on growth. Economic historians can help us understand the connection, however, by looking at the historical experience of the world in various trade regimes, and through more formal empirical investigations of the relationship.

8.4 Lessons from history

8.4.1 From mercantilism to free trade

Ricardo's theory of trade based on comparative advantage drew much inspiration from his observation of the functioning of the Corn Laws, which regulated the import of grain into Britain until they were famously repealed after a long popular campaign in 1846. This set the precedent for a wave of trade liberalization in the second half of the nineteenth century and brought about the first era of free trade, from about 1850 to 1875. Some economic historians (such as John Nye) have disputed that Britain led this movement to free trade, but there is evidence from research into the Corn Laws and the important wheat trade that tariffs were falling in Britain even before 1846.

Agriculture was not the only industry protected. Governments were heavily dependent on tariff income, which typically constituted between 10 and 50 per cent of total state income before the free trade era, and remained high in the USA during the nineteenth century. During the mercantilist era in the seventeenth and eighteenth centuries, tariffs were also used to promote or protect home industry. Mercantilist policy aimed at building up the international reserves needed in a risky environment where international conflicts were endemic – partly because of trade conflicts. Mercantilists believed that tariffs and subsidies to home industry would generate a *current account** surplus by promoting exports at the expense of imports. However, this was only the case as long as other countries did not retaliate, which of course they did.

The mercantilist era was, however, not a period of stagnant growth in trade. This was the time of European expansion overseas, and the mercantilist empires engendered a considerable growth of trade between Europe and the rest of the world. Recent work suggests that trade grew at an average of over one per cent per annum from the sixteenth to the eighteenth centuries and that this trade was associated with higher rates of growth in the imperial powers. This trade was, however, normally in *non-rival** goods: European countries imported, for example, sugar and cotton from the colonies, which they could not easily produce at home. Britain was heavily reliant on American markets during the Industrial Revolution, at a time when European countries were protecting their own emerging manufacturing. Britain's military successes over her rivals may therefore have helped ensure the continuance of the Industrial Revolution by guaranteeing markets for its expanding industries. Nevertheless, world trade only really took off with the dismantling of mercantilist trade barriers.

Although a critique of mercantilist policies emerged amongst French and British liberals by the end of the eighteenth century, it took some time for protectionist barriers to be torn down. This relates to the Stolper–Samuelson theorem explained above. There were conflicting interests involved: for example, the movement to repeal the Corn Laws pitted the owners of the scarce resource, land, against industrialists and trade unions, who argued that the laws increased wage costs in manufacturing and/or lowered real wages.

It is often the case that losing interests can have an impact on trade policy disproportionate to their size. For example, agriculture today is still heavily protected in Europe through the European Union's Common Agricultural Policy, resulting in higher prices for European consumers, even though farmers are a very small proportion of the total population. The reason is that small groups can be badly hit by trade liberalization (in the end, they may lose their jobs), whereas everybody else is only marginally affected by the potential fall in prices. Farmers thus become organized and lobby government to ensure high prices, and everyone else has a relatively small incentive to campaign for the opposite.

The Corn Laws and other protectionist measures in the UK and Europe were repealed, however, bringing both winners and losers. That this was possible reflected a changing balance of political power in favour of the growing urban classes at the expense of the traditional landed elite. The impact was softened due to the consequent increase in trade, which automatically increased state revenue above spending plans, so governments could reconcile a moderate increase in spending with falling tariffs.

The years 1850–75 saw the first free trade era in Europe, with tariffs reduced on both agricultural and industrial goods. The Anglo-French or Cobden–Chevalier Treaty of 1860 marked a milestone with its use of the Most Favoured Nation (MFN) clause, which is still a cornerstone of free trade policy. The MFN principle states that if two nations, A and B, extend MFN status to each other, then any further concessions in terms of lower tariffs that A extends to third

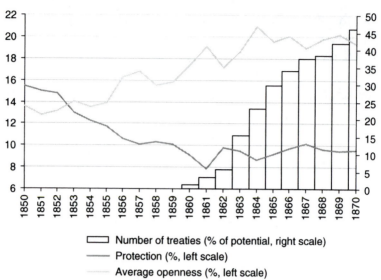

☐ Number of treaties (% of potential, right scale)

⋯⋯ Protection (%, left scale)

⋯⋯ Average openness (%, left scale)

Figure 8.2   The first free-trade era in Europe. *Source*: O. Accominotti and M. Flandreau, 'Bilateral treaties and the most-favoured-nation clause', *World Politics* 60(2) (2008), pp. 147–88.

nations will automatically be extended to B. Bilateral trade negotiations can thus have multilateral consequences.

Figure 8.2 illustrates the movement to free trade after 1850 for a sample of the most important European trading nations. 'Protection' is measured as the ratio of custom revenues to total imports and 'openness' is the ratio of imports to GDP. Also illustrated is the number of bilateral treaties signed as a percentage of the potential total.

Although Britain remained a free trader until the interwar period, other European nations, despite initially also reducing tariffs, eventually reversed their policies in the last two decades of the nineteenth century. Cheap grain imports from the USA, in particular, caused landowners to campaign for agricultural protection. In some countries there was a more general reaction to free trade, such as in Germany, where the so-called 'iron and rye' alliance gave protection to industry and agriculture alike. Protectionists in Germany and the USA invoked the infant-industry argument for protection. Despite this, however, customs income as a percentage of the value of imports remained lower than before 1850, and did not exceed 10 per cent even for Germany and France.

New World nations such as the USA did not share the movement to free trade. The American case is interesting, because in contrast to Europe, landowners were the owners of the more abundant resource, and thus in favour of free trade. Due to labour scarcity, on the other hand, urban wages were quite high and manufacturing interests therefore wanted protection from cheap imports.

The United States was and remained highly protectionist for several reasons. It became protectionist early on because of the need for government revenue and as part of a deliberate protectionist policy to help domestic industry. Tariff rates thus increased after independence, and although they declined in the middle of the nineteenth century, the Civil War of the early 1860s increased the need for revenue to finance the war effort and tariffs increased again. After the war, tariffs remained high because the victorious northern states, with their emerging industries supplying the home market, were more inclined towards protection than the export-oriented southern cotton and tobacco producers.

8.4.2 The disintegration of international trade in the interwar period

Turning to the twentieth century, the interwar period has generally been interpreted as a prime example of the negative effects of restrictive trade policies on growth. Even before the First World War, there was growing protectionist sentiment around the world, although some nations, such as the UK, Denmark and the Netherlands remained free traders until after the war.

During the war, most countries reduced food tariffs, but free trade only lasted until the 1920s, after which countries became more and more protectionist; but it was the outbreak of the Great Depression in the 1930s that saw the most radical departure from free trade and almost a return to mercantilist thinking, in the sense that countries attempted to protect and promote home industry at the expense of foreign competitors. The Great Depression itself had a large impact on trade volumes, and this was enhanced by the escalating 'war' of reciprocal trade restrictions in response especially to American trade policy. In 1930, the United States passed the infamous Smoot–Hawley Act, increasing tariffs considerably. In this environment, any country pursuing an independent free trade policy would be very unlikely to experience a beneficial impact on growth. The interwar years saw a departure from the trend of rapidly increasing world trade.

Not only did world trade fall in real terms, but so did the ratio of exports to GDP for almost all nations. In fact, trade/income ratios did not recover their pre-1913 rates until the 1960s. This is especially remarkable, since from 1850 trade had been growing by one or two percentage points above the annual growth in income per head.

The reason for the fragmentation of the established trade regime was simple. The Great Depression decreased American demand for imports, and in the absence of international liquidity other nations also curbed their imports because export earnings fell. This initial negative shock to trade volumes triggered a fall in prices, in particular for food and raw materials, and the combination of the fall in prices and in traded volumes meant falling export revenues.

The fall in prices differed among nations. Food and raw material producers were hardest hit because export prices fell more than the prices of their imports. Many of these countries had inadequate international reserves, so when export earnings fell, they needed to borrow on the international capital market. However, the main sources of loans, the American financial institutions, were no longer willing to lend. Unable to borrow to finance their imports, countries saw protection as the fastest way to restore balance on the *current account**. (As discussed in Chapter 9, another alternative was to increase competitiveness by leaving the gold standard and allowing their currencies to depreciate, but most countries were hesitant to do this until the UK took the lead in 1931.)

The end result was that the world divided itself into trade blocs. The British *Commonwealth** established preferential treatment among its members, which led to an expansion of internal trade at the expense of external trade. Germany introduced a system of administrative regulation of trade on a bilateral basis. Lacking sufficient international reserves, Germany rationed them for use in trade with Western Europe and the USA. For countries in Eastern and Central Europe, they were able to force acceptance of payments in the non-convertible 'aski' mark. This created a forced balance of trade, because Romania, for example, received payment for exports in aski marks which could only be used to buy imported goods from Germany.

8.4.3 The restoration of the free-trade regime after the Second World War

After the Second World War, countries recognized the dangers of trade wars, and saw that if it had been possible to co-ordinate the removal of trade restrictions, then the impact of the Depression might have been mitigated since trade liberalization would not have been reliant on very risky unilateral efforts. Work started before the end of the war on an international framework for solving trade disputes and negotiating tariff reductions. Progress was not as fast as it had been after 1850, largely because many countries had *current account** constraints, and a quick opening up of the extremely protected economies was not a priority.

Tariff reductions were, however, agreed in the first so-called GATT (General Agreement on Tariffs and Trade) round in Geneva in 1947. Over the years an increasing number of nations joined the GATT negotiations, and a major breakthrough came during the prosperous 1960s with the 'Kennedy' Round. Alongside this, there was the creation of customs unions such as the European Economic Community (later the EU), which opened up trade within the union, producing an increase in internal trade at the cost of erecting tariff barriers against the outside.

Agriculture was explicitly left out of the GATT negotiations, and the European Union (through the Common Agricultural Policy) and the United States have continued to protect their agriculture heavily, at the expense of many poorer countries which are largely dependent on agriculture. This has tended to sour trade relations, and reform is still controversial. Other industries, such as manufacturing, however, have seen a reduction in tariff rates to levels comparable to those of the first free trade era in the nineteenth century. Moreover, starting in 1987, the Uruguay Round established a formal international body, the World Trade Organization (WTO), which now has 153 members (compared to just twenty-three 'contracting parties' for the first GATT agreement). Trade-generating tariff reductions have been agreed, and discussions have started on agricultural trade and intellectual property rights.

Since 1986 tariffs on goods have fallen from a world average of 26 per cent to just 8.8 per cent in 2007, the decline being especially marked in developing countries, from a much higher initial level. Trade has grown more than twice as fast on average as world output, and developing countries have almost doubled their share of world exports, to 37 per cent in 2007. The latest WTO 'Doha' Round, launched in 2001, has, however, recently broken down due to disputes over agricultural subsidies in the EU and USA. Moreover, the 2008/9 financial crisis sent trade volumes and commodity prices plummeting, and at the time of writing there is a concern that countries may again be about to reach into their protectionist toolboxes as they did in the 1930s.

8.4.4 Empirical investigations

Empirical investigations of the relationship between tariffs and growth meet some difficulties. In particular, it is difficult to find an adequate measure for protection. The most common approach is to measure a nation's trade policy by its tariff revenue divided by the value of its dutiable imports. This is a very unsatisfactory indicator, however, as a simple example will illustrate.

Imagine a country which imposes a 20 per cent *ad valorem* tariff on all commodities. This will be given a 20 per cent value for protection. Another allows free imports of all goods, but imposes a 50 per cent *ad valorem* tariff on wine. This will be considered to have a value of 50 per cent for protection, and be considered more protectionist! Clearly that does not seem reasonable.

In fact, the difficulties go even further. Suppose that in the country with the high wine tariffs everyone takes to drinking beer instead of wine (as happened in Britain). In the extreme case, the country will stop importing wine altogether and will then be calculated to have a zero level of protection. So any country imposing prohibitive tariffs will be judged relatively open!

Nevertheless, attempts have been made to test the relationship between trade policy and growth. Early empirical research into the period of free trade in the nineteenth century, such as that of Bairoch, did not find evidence for free trade being good for growth; but his analysis is now considered too crude to be of value. More recently, however, a much more sophisticated analysis has been performed by O'Rourke for ten rich countries which seems to confirm Bairoch's results. This is not surprising. Germany and the United States were two of the most successful economies of the late nineteenth century, but were heavily protectionist. Free-trading Britain, on the other hand, was losing ground.

Clemens and Williamson have applied O'Rourke's approach to a larger sample of thirty-five countries, including some poorer European nations and some from Asia and Latin America. They find that the correlation was indeed positive for the rich countries, but negative for the poorer ones. So *protectionism** was no use in the countries where it did not foster industrialization. This suggests that, as discussed in the previous section, it may be the structure of protection which matters, rather than protection itself. This point was taken up by Lehmann and O'Rourke in preliminary work. For the period 1875–1913 and a small set of countries they found industrial tariffs to correlate positively with growth, but possibly some evidence that agricultural tariffs were negatively related to growth. They therefore argued that the overall positive tariff–growth relation found previously was not spurious and was probably due to the growth-promoting benefits of protecting industry. Clearly, however, this literature is still producing results that call for a consistent explanation.

For the twentieth century, a number of studies seem to show a strong positive relationship between trade policy and growth. An important contribution was that of Sachs and Warner, who investigated the relationship between growth and an index of openness. Based on a large sample of countries for the period 1970–89, they find that growth related negatively to an attitude of being 'closed.'

Although their methodology has been criticized, a recent study by Estevadeordal and Taylor, which answers some of the critiques of previous attempts, seems to find support for their results. They look at the relationship between growth and openness during what they call the 'Great Liberalization' from the 1970s to the present day. In a similar way to Lehmann and O'Rourke, they stress the importance of considering in which goods trade is being liberalized. However, their results are rather different from those found for the nineteenth century. They find that liberalization of trade in capital and intermediate goods leads to faster growth, but that this is not so clear for other goods. This might suggest again that there was a difference between the nineteenth and twentieth-century experiences. However, their sample of countries is considerably larger, and more generally they enjoy the benefits of working with much more detailed and relevant data than those available for the earlier period, so their results are in no way directly comparable. In general, it seems, the debate about the relationship between protection or openness and growth seems far from being resolved.

Summary

Box 8.1 summarizes the European trade regimes.

Box 8.1 The European trade regimes				
	Before 1850	1850–1913	1920–39	After 1945
Nature of trade	Non-rival goods	Inter-sectoral	Transition	Intra-sectoral
Trade policy	Mercantilist	Movement to free trade	Return to protectionism	Return to free trade (except agriculture)
Trade growth experience	Slow	High	Stagnation	High
Trade/income ratio	Low	High	Low	High

Trade theory is ambiguous about the impact of *protectionism** on growth. There are clearly gains from trade by way of specialization and technology transfer. Nevertheless, in the short run some degree of protection may be useful. Empirical studies have largely confirmed this latter point, although it is important to protect the correct industries, if protection is not to be counterproductive. Historical experience suggests that a little protection is not bad for growth, and may even be helpful, but extreme protection is disastrous. So, as in everything, moderation is the key.

Appendix: Comparative advantage

We can consider Ricardo's original example. Imagine a world in which there are just two countries, Portugal and England, and two goods, cloth and wine. There is one input, labour, which is free to move between cloth and wine production within either country, but not between them.

We will assume that Portugal is more efficient in both cloth and wine production, i.e. she has an absolute advantage in the production of both. More specifically, 100 English labourers are required to produce one unit of cloth, but only ninety Portuguese. For wine, 120 English labourers are required to produce one unit of wine, but only eighty Portuguese.

Although England is disadvantaged in the production of both, we can show that she has a comparative advantage in cloth, and ought to specialize in the production of this, given trade. Assume that England forsakes the production of one unit of wine and diverts those resources into cloth production. She would then be able to produce 120/100 = 1.2 extra units of cloth. That is precisely the opportunity cost of producing wine: for every unit of wine production, England sacrifices 1.2 units of cloth. England thus has a comparative advantage in cloth production. We can perform the equivalent exercise for Portugal to demonstrate that she has a comparative advantage in wine. For each unit of cloth sacrificed, she can produce 90/80 = 1.13 extra units of wine. It is then clear that world production, and thus welfare, will be maximized when the two countries specialize in what they are best at producing: wine for Portugal, and cloth for England.

For mutually beneficial trade to occur, however, prices must adjust. In a state of autarchy (i.e. with no trade), prices are determined by the relative cost of producing each good. This means that the price of wine in terms of cloth will be 1.2 in England, and 100/120 = 0.83 in Portugal. With trade, the price of cloth will decline relative to Portugal's autarchy price, while the price of wine will decline in England. Ricardo assumed the new price to be 1, implying that Portugal now gets one unit of cloth for every unit of wine, as against 0.88 before trade, and England now only has to pay 1 unit of cloth for a unit of wine, as opposed to 1.2 before trade. Wine has become less expensive in England, where it is imported, and more valuable in Portugal, from where it is exported, thus bringing gains to both countries.

Suggestions for further reading

P. R. Krugman and M. Obstfeld, *International Economics: Theory and Policy*. (London: Pearson Education, Inc., 2008) is an excellent textbook introduction to trade theory.

The following are economic histories of trade and trade policy:

J. Foreman-Peck, *A History of the World Economy: International Economic Relations Since 1850* (London: Harvester Wheatsheaf, 1995); A. G. Kenwood and A. L. Lougheed, *The Growth of the International Economy, 1820–2000* (London: Routledge, 1999).

R. Findlay and K. O'Rourke, *Power and Plenty: Trade, War, and the World Economy in the Second Millennium* (Princeton University Press, 2007), covers a much longer period of time, and provides a truly global perspective on the history of trade.

The following also provide histories of the time before the nineteenth century:

K. O'Rourke and J. G. Williamson, 'After Columbus: Explaining the Global Trade Boom 1500–1800', *Journal of Economic History* 62 (2002), pp. 417–456.

K.G. Persson, *Grain Markets in Europe 1500–1900, Integration and Deregulation* (Cambridge University Press, 1999).

For a more modern perspective, see: E. Helpman, 'The Structure of Foreign Trade', *The Journal of Economic Perspectives* 13(2) (1999), pp. 121–44.

J. Nye and D. Irwin have long been intellectual adversaries as regards the history of trade liberalization in the nineteenth century:

D. Irwin, *Against the Tide* (Princeton University Press, 1988).

J. Nye, *War, Wine, and Taxes: The Political Economy of Anglo-French Trade, 1689–1900* (Princeton University Press, 2007).

P. R. Sharp, '1846 and All That: The Rise and Fall of British Wheat Protection in the Nineteenth Century', Department of Economics, University of Copenhagen Discussion Paper 06–14, 2006, attempts to shed some light on the working of one part of the liberalization story: the movement towards free trade in grain in Britain.

There are numerous studies on the relationship between trade policy and growth. See:

D. Acemoglu, S. Johnson and J. A. Robinson, 'The Rise of Europe: Atlantic Trade, Institutional Change and Economic Growth', *American Economic Review* 95 (2005), pp. 546–79.

P. Bairoch, 'Free trade and European Economic Development in the Nineteenth Century', *European Economic Review* 3(3) (1972), pp. 211–45.

M. A. Clemens and J. G. Williamson, 'Why did the Tariff–Growth Correlation Change after 1950?' *Journal of Economic Growth* 9 (2004), pp. 5–46.

A. Estevadeordal and A. M. Taylor, 'Is the Washington Consensus dead? Growth, Openness, and the Great Liberalization, 1970s–2000s'. NBER Working Paper 14264, 2008.

I.B. Kravis, 'Trade as a Handmaiden of Growth: Similarities Between the Nineteenth and Twentieth Centuries', *The Economic Journal* 80 (320), (1970), pp. 850–72.

S. Lehmann and K. H. O'Rourke, *The Structure of Protection and Growth in the Late 19th Century.* Institute for International Integration Studies Discussion Paper No. 269, 2008.

K. H. O'Rourke, 'Tariffs and Growth in the Late Nineteenth Century', *Economic Journal* 110(463) (2000), pp. 456–83.

F. Rodriguez and D. Rodrik, 'Trade Policy and Economic Growth: A Skeptic's Guide to the Cross-National Evidence'. NBER Working Paper 7081, 1999.

J. D. Sachs and A. Warner, 'Economic Reform and the Process of Global Integration', *Brookings Papers on Economic Activity* 1 (1995), pp. 1–118.

9 International monetary regimes in history

Karl Gunnar Persson and Paul Sharp

9.1 Why is an international monetary system necessary?

In Chapter 7, we discussed why money is important for economies: without it, all trade is based on barter and is limited due to the need for *coincidence of wants**. The same is true on an international scale. Normally, although occasional international experiments, such as the euro, have proved exceptions to this rule, countries do not share currencies. Nevertheless, they must be able to convert their currencies if trade is not to be restricted to barter. Hence the need for an international monetary system.

In fact, without such a system, trade will normally be restricted to *balanced bilateral trade*. Suppose, for example, that Denmark wishes to import 10 billion kroners' worth of goods from Norway. It is important that the countries are able to barter, i.e. that Norway actually desires goods from Denmark in return. Even if this is the case, it might be that Norway only desires 5 billion kroners' worth of goods from Denmark. In the absence of an international monetary system it is impossible for Norway to lend the difference to Denmark, i.e. there are no channels for international credit, and Denmark's imports are therefore restricted to 5 billion kroner. Trade is thus hampered, and countries are disadvantaged, because they cannot fully realize the gains from trade and specialization discussed in the previous chapter.

There are additional advantages to an international monetary system. These can best be understood by considering the well-known *national income** accounting identity (as seen from the demand side) below:

$$national\ production = consumption + investment + \\ government\ consumption + net\ exports$$

This simply states that production, or aggregate supply, in an economy must be equal to aggregate demand, because national saving is defined by the difference between income (production) and consumption, i.e.

$$savings = production - consumption - government\ consumption$$

Thus *net exports = savings – investment.* This is an identity and must hold for every economy.

A *current account** deficit (negative net exports) implies that the country is borrowing from the rest of the world to finance investment, whereas a current account surplus implies that it is investing abroad. The desirability of this depends on whether investments are more profitable at home or abroad. Clearly, however, if there is no international monetary system, and trade is balanced, then net exports are equal to zero, and domestic investment is constrained by domestic saving.

Without a functional international monetary system, then, trade is restricted and foreign investment is impossible. History provides solid historical support for this: during periods when international monetary systems have functioned poorly, trade volumes and foreign investment have suffered.

9.2 How do policymakers choose the international monetary regime?

Historically, it was believed that *commodity currencies* and *fixed exchange rates* were essential to a functional international monetary regime. In fact, the former implies the latter. Commodity money is fixed in value relative to some particular commodity, usually a precious metal such as gold or silver. This had the implication that currencies based on the same commodity, such as gold, were fixed in value in relation to each other. For example, if country A fixed its currency at 1 unit per ounce of gold, and country B fixed its currency at 2 units per ounce of gold, then the exchange rate must be fixed at 2 units of B's currency for 1 unit of A's (in practice, small variations in the exchange rate were possible, but this will be discussed below).

Today, however, *floating exchange rates* dominate: for example the five major world currencies – the US dollar, the European Union's euro, the Japanese yen, the British pound and the Swiss franc – are all floating against each other. In the late twentieth century, there was a move to *fiat** currencies (where the value depends solely on the order, *fiat,* of the government), and the automatic link between currencies broke down. The reason for the dominance of floating exchange rates in today's world is the changing priorities of policymakers and a more general recognition that they are not the evil it was once supposed.

Fixed exchange rates provide some advantages (given crucially that the fixed exchange rate is credible and sustainable – more on that later), because international traders are not subjected to unexpected changes in exchange rates and do not need to factor this uncertainty into the price they demand for their goods. Fixed exchange rates also have disadvantages, however, in that monetary policy, i.e. the use of the interest rate to regulate demand in the economy, becomes unavailable.

The interest rate is a useful macroeconomic tool. Lowering it increases the range of profitable investments in the economy and will stimulate investment and thus increase aggregate demand and hence production. Under a fixed exchange rate regime, however, monetary policy is geared towards ensuring that the currency maintains some fixed value against other currencies or (equivalently in the case of a world based on commodity currencies) a certain commodity, usually gold. If the central bank lowers interest rates, investors will sell the domestic currency and buy higher-yielding foreign assets. If demand for the domestic currency is lowered, its value will tend to depreciate against other currencies, something which is not allowed in a fixed exchange rate system. Monetary policy is thus restricted.

Or is it? This argument depends crucially on the role of *arbitrage*. Speculators respond to the lower return to domestic capital by moving assets out of the country and thus impacting on the exchange rate. If *capital controls* are in place, however, this is impossible. By limiting the movement of capital between countries, capital controls can free up monetary policy even in a fixed exchange rate system. Capital flows are, however, related to trade flows as described above. Thus, capital controls may be unattractive in the sense that they limit trade.

From the argument above, however, it is clear that fixed exchange rates can only be combined with monetary autonomy at the expense of unrestricted capital mobility. Fixed exchange rates and unrestricted capital mobility, on the other hand, involve the sacrifice of monetary autonomy. It follows, therefore, that unrestricted capital mobility can only be combined with monetary autonomy at the expense of a fixed exchange rate regime. This problem has been described by Obstfeld and Taylor as the 'open economy trilemma', and is illustrated in Figure 9.1. It is only possible to pick two policy goals.

Which two macroeconomic goals are chosen, i.e. which monetary regime, is a political decision and is influenced by the (often conflicting) macroeconomic policy goals of policymakers. They will have aims relating to a range of issues, including maximum employment, price level stability, balanced trade and others. The choice of monetary regime impacts on all of these. As in trade policy, different groups prioritize these goals differently and favour different regimes. In fact, the choice of international monetary regime is still contentious today, as witnessed by the ongoing debate in Denmark (a country which still fixes its currency) as to whether to join the European Union's common currency, the euro. A *monetary union* is the extreme form of a fixed exchange rate, where exchange rates are abolished altogether.

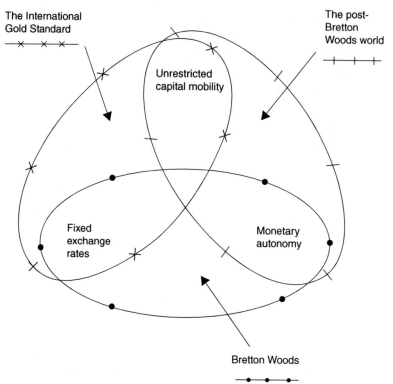

Figure 9.1   The (Obstfeld–Taylor) open economy trilemma: pick two policy goals, only two but any two. Adapted from M. Obstfeld and A. Taylor, *Global Capital Markets: Integration, Crisis and Growth* (Cambridge University Press, 2004), pp. 29–41.

   In fact, it is impossible to understand contemporary debates about monetary policy without reference to the historical experience. It turns out that the trilemma in Figure 9.1 is a convenient way to understand the history of international monetary regimes. From the second half of the nineteenth century until the First World War, the *International Gold Standard* fixed exchange rates and permitted unrestricted capital mobility at the expense of monetary autonomy. When political and social changes meant that monetary policy became important the system collapsed and, after the Second World War, the *Bretton Woods System* fixed currencies against the American dollar but permitted monetary policy at the expense of restricting capital mobility. When the growth of world trade and other pressures meant that restricting capital mobility was no longer possible, the Bretton Woods System collapsed, and the modern world of floating exchange rates emerged, permitting both unrestricted capital mobility and monetary autonomy. On a more local or regional level, however, the picture is rather more nuanced, since some countries do still fix their currencies. Worldwide fixed exchange rate systems, however, are a thing of the past.

9.3 International monetary regimes in history

9.3.1 The International Gold Standard *c.* 1870–1914

The history of international monetary systems can be seen as a gradual realization that fixed exchange rates are not necessary, although a political attachment to them remains in and between certain countries. In a sense, fixed exchange rates emerged by accident. Gold had been used as money (a medium of exchange, unit of account and store of value) since ancient times. When countries began to fix their currencies against gold in a more institutionalized way in the nineteenth century, their currencies automatically became fixed against each other, as described above.

The gold standard as an institution, however, has its origins in Britain's Resumption Act of 1819, which both resumed (after the Napoleonic Wars) and institutionalized the practice of exchanging currency notes for gold on demand at a fixed rate. Simultaneously, restrictions on the export of gold were repealed. These were the institutional building blocks of what was to become known as the gold standard.

The gold standard did not emerge overnight, however. Previously, countries had often practiced bimetallism, whereby both gold and silver formed the basis of the monetary supply, the logic being that gold was too valuable to be practically divisible into units small enough to be suitable for smaller purchases. Britain led the way in basing her currency on gold alone, however, and her success and emergence as the leading economic power led other countries to gradually follow her lead, although the United States, for example, was bimetallic until 1873, when silver was demonetarized, and pressure for a return to bimetallism remained until the late nineteenth century.

The history of the emergence of the gold standard shows that it is politics as well as economics that determines monetary policy. Emerging states, such as the United States and Germany, were quick to form their own monetary unions. A more general spirit of internationalism in the globalized world of the late nineteenth century (see Chapter 12) led to attempts at international monetary union, with the Scandinavian Monetary Union from 1875 and the Latin Monetary Union (LMU) from 1865 among a large number of European countries, including France, Belgium, Italy, Switzerland, Spain and others.

Although strong trade and financial links between members was an important reason for the move towards monetary union, much more important was the French quest for political and economic power. France saw the LMU as the nucleus of an international – perhaps global – system based on the franc and Paris. One consequence of this was that the LMU was based on a bimetallic standard, rather than the gold standard favoured by Britain. The economic rivalry between France and Britain was to play a large role in the debate over international monetary systems.

In practice, despite their political significance, monetary unions are not particularly economically important in a world of fixed exchange rates, and by the 1870s, almost all countries were basing their currencies on gold. In the previous section we touched on the fact that this implied fixed exchange rates. This was due to the 'rules of the game' of the gold standard, which were not based on any formal institutional structure, but rather on the law and practice of individual countries.

The most important of these rules were as follows:

1. The currency should be freely convertible to gold at a set price or *mint parity*.
2. There should be no barriers to the flow of capital, i.e. gold, between countries.
3. Money should be convertible on request to gold, and thus backed by gold reserves.

Box 9.1 Example: why was the gold standard a fixed exchange rate system?

- US mint parity: $20.646/ounce.
- UK mint parity: £4.252/ounce.
- Exchange rate must be 20.646/4.252 = $4.856/£
- Reason: any other exchange rate gives possibility of *arbitrage*.
- E.g. use rules 1–3 to see that e.g. $ 1/£ gives possibility of:
    1. Presenting £1 to Bank of England to get 1/4.252 = 0.23 ounces of gold.
    2. Presenting gold to US Treasury to get 0.23*$ 20.646 = $ 4.85
    3. Exchanging dollars on foreign exchange market for £ 4.85!
    4. Flow of gold to US leading to increase in $ supply, decrease in £ supply:

The £ strengthens on the foreign exchange market.

In reality, however, small deviations in the exchange rate, or 'gold points', were possible due to the transport and transaction costs involved in shipping gold. Since shipping gold between countries and continents is not costless, arbitrage will only take place as long as the gains from it outweigh the costs. Exchange rates thus fluctuate within bands, which depend on the cost of transporting gold.

Governments under the gold standard took on the whole a *laissez faire* (hands off) attitude towards economic policy. In part, this was justified by theory. In 1752, Hume described the *price – specie-flow mechanism* (*specie* being a word for precious metal), whereby the gold standard should automatically ensure *balance of payments** equilibrium. He imagined a situation whereby gold was flowing into Britain from abroad, thus causing British prices to rise in relation to those abroad. As the British demand for foreign goods increased and demand for British goods decreased, gold would start flowing abroad again, and equilibrium would be restored. Although in reality trade normally used paper money rather than gold, this made no difference since money supply was linked to gold reserves. If Britain was enjoying a trade surplus, traders would accumulate an excess of foreign currency. They would present this to foreign banks for gold, which would then flow into Britain and be exchanged for British currency by British banks. The money supply and the price level in Britain would thus increase, restoring equilibrium in the same way as before.

In practice, however, central banks were more worried about gold losses than gold gains. Central banks often practised *sterilization** of gold inflows, thus preventing them from entering the money supply, in direct contravention of the rules of the game. This enabled them to build up excess gold reserves, without affecting the money supply. The Bank of England, for example, used an active interest rate policy to stem anticipated gold losses. Its reason for so doing was that if the pound weakened, investors would withdraw bank deposits, convert pounds to gold and export it. This could give rise to a liquidity crisis whereby depositors abandoned banks and so threatened the banking system. If gold was flowing abroad, the Bank of England ought to have reduced the money supply by selling domestic assets, but instead it lent freely to banks at higher interest rates, thus increasing the money supply.

Nevertheless, despite these deviations from the rules of the game, the gold standard lasted many decades. The reasons for this are often summarized as *commitment, confidence* and *symmetry*. Commitment implied that deviations from the gold standard would be followed by a return to the original parity. Confidence implied that people believed that exchange rates would remain fixed, so all speculation went in the direction of maintaining the fixed exchange rates. Symmetry implied that no one country had an overwhelming influence on price levels. In fact, all national price levels were dictated by gold demand and supply. So, for example, when gold became scarce towards the end of the nineteenth century, price levels decreased (deflation), but when a new method was found for extracting gold from ore, prices increased with the new supply.

This latter property was to have important political consequences. Although the gold standard ensured price stability over longer periods, for shorter periods there were uniform rates of inflation or deflation across countries. High inflation and deflation can cause economic distress, but governments generally turned a blind eye – something they were able to do in a time when economic policy did not focus on domestic objectives, such as combating unemployment. An exception which proves the rule is the American political unrest during the period of deflation at the end of the nineteenth century, when a return to bimetallism was campaigned for. The USA was noticeably more democratic than many other countries, and thus domestic issues played a larger role in political debate.

9.3.2 The interwar years

The interwar years were to see the end of the gold standard, for both political and economic reasons. During the First World War, the gold standard was suspended, and government expenditure was financed by expanding the monetary supply by issuing bonds and in the extreme case by printing money. After the war, some governments financed reconstruction by printing even more money. This led to inflation, sometimes on a massive scale. For example, German hyperinflation reached the staggering heights of 3.25 million per cent per *month*.

Governments around the world looked back on the pre-war years as a golden age, and prioritized a return to gold. The United States emerged relatively unscathed by the war, and returned to the gold standard in 1919. According to the rules of the game, all countries should have returned to gold at the original parities, but wartime inflation meant that this would require deflation, to an unrealistic extent in some countries.

Deflation can be painful for economies, because wages do not normally fall, so labour becomes relatively expensive and output declines. This had been acceptable before the war, but now the spread of democracy, socialism and powerful trade unions meant that governments could no longer act in this way. Thus, although some countries returned to gold at the pre-war parity, for example the UK in 1925, other countries, such as France, which returned at 20 per cent of the pre-war parity, were more pragmatic. The UK was in a somewhat special situation, since prior to the war she had played a central role in administering the gold standard system through the Bank of England, and by returning to gold at the original parity, the government wished to restore confidence in the gold standard and in its ability to manage the system. This required considerable deflation, however, and unemployment soared.

By 1929 the US was trying to slow its overheated economy through monetary contraction, and France was ending an inflationary period with a return to gold. Both France and the US were *sterilizing* gold inflows and absorbing the world's gold, to the extent that they ended holding 70 per cent of global supply. This meant that other countries were forced to restrict their money supply. This worldwide monetary contraction and the Wall Street Crash of 1929 led to the Great Depression of the 1930s. The Great Depression had a worldwide impact owing to the Wall Street crash, unemployment and bank failures. Eichengreen has demonstrated that the gold standard played a large part in prolonging and worsening the Depression. Bank failures worsened because countries refused to provide liquidity because they needed to protect their gold reserves. Many countries that had previously been forced to rely on American loans were forced to introduce currency controls, as described in the previous chapter. The widespread use of capital and currency controls, in addition to very low capital mobility, led to an actual decline in world trade in the 1930s.

In 1931 the UK could not stem the outflow of gold and left the gold standard. Other countries soon followed, including the USA in 1933. This proved to be a blessing in disguise. Nations leaving gold early devalued to about 60 per cent of their 1929 exchange rate and recovered faster from the Great Depression. Early devaluation meant that the economies were released from the fetters of an over-valued currency. Industry improved its market share both locally and abroad. Devaluation also implied an increase in inflation, which reduced *product wages*, that is the wage cost relative to the price of the product, and *real interest rates**, because nominal wages were constant while devaluation permitted producers to increase prices. Finally, monetary policy was no longer subject to the defence of the fixed exchange rate and could be used to boost the growth of the economy. Countries, such as the UK, which left the gold standard early, enjoyed a faster recovery than countries like France, which did not. France was the last major country to leave in 1936. For several years, and again largely for political reasons, she tried to form a small club of countries still basing their currencies on gold. This stubborn adherence to gold caused them to miss the revival of the international economy in the mid-1930s.

The international gold standard relied on fixed exchange rates and free capital mobility, and thus could not survive in a world where monetary policy became crucially important. It died, along with the related Latin and Scandinavian Monetary Unions, which had been practically non-operational anyway for some years. The desire for fixed exchange rates and monetary unions did not die with it, however.

9.3.3 The Bretton Woods System

The reaction to the Great Depression was disastrous. *Protectionism** increased, restrictions were imposed on capital flows and countries generally became more autarkic. World trade declined, fascism emerged, and the progress of the nineteenth century was put back almost to square one.

In July 1944, forty-four countries signed the Articles of Agreement of the International Monetary Fund (IMF) in the American east coast resort village of Bretton Woods. The British representative, John Maynard Keynes, wanted a much more flexible system than the traditional gold standard. He and others hoped to design a system whereby exchange rates could be fixed and monetary policy applied without trade restrictions being necessary.

Their belief in fixed exchange rates was paradoxically the result of the inter-war experience, and the feeling that floating exchange rates had been a cause of instability and harmful to trade. They thus designed the *Bretton Woods System* as a *dollar exchange standard*:

- The dollar was fixed against the price of gold: $ 35 an ounce.
- Member countries held reserves in gold or dollar assets, with the right to sell dollars to the US Federal Reserve for gold at the official price. These reserves were to guard against short-term swings in exchange rates, without a link to the monetary supply as they had had under the gold standard.
- All currencies were fixed in value against the dollar, giving N–1 exchange rates.

This implied that all but one of the member countries were responsible for maintaining the exchange rate, with the USA simply responsible for maintaining the dollar price of gold. Ostensibly, then, the Bretton Woods System was very similar to the gold standard system. The crucial difference concerned the freedom of countries to use monetary policy.

This implied, according to the trilemma, that capital movements must be restricted. This was done by requiring convertibility of currencies only on the *current account** (for goods and services) and *not* on the financial account (for financial assets). The interwar experience had led to the belief that private capital movements and speculation led to instability. Moreover, the Bretton Woods System aimed to ensure *flexibility* for countries that were experiencing current account deficits. This implied two things. First, that the IMF would control a pool of gold and currencies from member countries which it could lend to members that were experiencing current account deficits, but where contractionary policy would cause unemployment. Members that borrowed from the IMF would be supervised by the IMF.

Second, parities were adjustable. If the balance of payments was in 'fundamental disequilibrium' (which, crucially, was not defined), countries could devalue against the dollar if they suffered permanent adverse international shifts in the demand for their products. For example, although inflation was actually fairly uniform under the Bretton Woods System, the UK had higher underlying inflation than other countries in most years, but was able to devalue rather than have to deflate.

This flexibility was, however, to be one of the causes of instability of the Bretton Woods System. Although capital mobility was restricted, speculators found ways around this by borrowing from abroad, by delaying payment for goods, or lending by forwarding money in advance: 'leads' and 'lags'. Speculative pressures were thus able to emerge, because if countries had large and persistent current account deficits, they might be suspected of being in 'fundamental disequilibrium'. This prompted destabilizing speculation: the opposite of what had happened with the pre-First World War gold standard. The UK devalued in 1967, and France in 1957, 1958 and 1969.

The downfall of the Bretton Woods System was its asymmetry. Although currencies could be devalued against the dollar, this option was not of course available for the *Nth* currency, the dollar itself. Moreover, whilst all countries were required in normal times to use monetary policy to tie their currencies to the dollar, only the USA had the freedom to set its interest rate and use monetary policy. This was acceptable as long as all countries were prepared to follow American monetary policy and for their inflation to follow that of America.

However, in the 1960s Democratic administrations expanded welfare spending and got involved in the Vietnam War. This led to budget deficits and expansionary monetary policy, and inflation doubled. European governments had other inflation targets, but were forced to import American monetary policy. The German solution was to re-value: in 1961 and 1969. However, the USA did have one commitment, and that was to preserve the dollar price of gold. With the dollar becoming more and more over-valued, this eventually was unsustainable, and America devalued against gold in 1971. As inflation continued, gold convertibility was abandoned in 1973, destroying what remained of the credibility of the Bretton Woods System, which then fell apart.

The Bretton Woods System thus lacked commitment, confidence and symmetry. The possibility of combining monetary freedom with fixed exchange rates depended crucially on the ability to avoid destabilizing speculation. When capital controls failed, the lack of confidence in the Bretton Woods System meant that it could not survive. Unlike the gold standard, traders had no confidence in the commitment of central bankers to the fixed exchange rates, and the dominance of the dollar meant that when the USA was no longer prepared to work for the system, it soon collapsed.

9.3.4 The world of floating exchange rates

Floating exchange rates thus emerged by accident. They were initially seen as a temporary measure, although at the time of writing no new worldwide fixed exchange rate system seems likely. One of the reasons for this is that in the

1960s theorists such as Robert Mundell had shown that fixed exchange rate regimes that were very diverse in their membership had little chance of surviving, because economic shocks were asymmetric and political preferences differed across countries. Moreover, when Bretton Woods was abandoned, price levels quickly diverged to an even greater extent, with prices doubling in Germany and Japan over twenty years, but quadrupling in the USA – this made the return to a fixed exchange rate regime even more unlikely. Even more importantly, countries soon lost interest in an international fixed exchange rate system, since floating exchange rates turned out to be compatible with free capital flows and trade.

Typically, the new exchange rate orders that developed after the disintegration of Bretton Woods were regional rather than truly international: for example, the European Monetary System (EMS) in operation in the 1980s and early 1990s. However, even at a regional level the stability of a European system was difficult to maintain without defections and frequent exchange rate adjustments. In the EMS Germany was the conductor of monetary policy very much as the USA was in Bretton Woods, but with widely differing results. Many countries, including Denmark and France, pegged their currencies to the German mark, because Germany had a reputation for low inflation. But as a consequence they had to obey the monetary policy of Germany, which they believed was the only way of curbing inflationary domestic expectations. The belief that a link to gold was necessary to curb inflation was disproved by the European experience in the last decades of the twentieth and the first of the twenty-first century.

Despite several defections from the EMS over the years, with the last major crises in 1992, the EU had been working on tighter monetary co-operation, a monetary union, since the late 1980s, which eventually materialized as the euro bloc in 2002. It was a surprising move given the crisis-prone EMS. A monetary union deprives domestic governments of monetary autonomy, and the independent European Central Bank has adopted an explicit inflation target. The monetary union addresses the problem that the Bretton Woods System faced – that members were not committed to fixed exchange rates in the long run. Whether it can withstand the strains posed by severe shocks will depend on an ability to co-ordinate fiscal policy. So far this co-ordination has mainly aimed at setting ceilings on public debt and borrowing, and even that has not been easy to accomplish. It is not obvious that the euro members constitute an optimal currency union; but it might turn Europe into one, provided it survives the crises ahead.

There seems to be one important lesson to be learned from the history of monetary unions. Political motives have normally been primary when forming such a union. The Latin Monetary Union was in many ways based on the political ambitions of one country, France, but also on a foundation of political solidarity, as was the Scandinavian Monetary Union. In both cases, the foundation of co-operation upon which the union was built had been severely tested before the First World War, but the war itself was the final nail in the coffin. Other, less traumatic, events could surely have had a similar effect, however. In both cases, when the monetary union was threatened, there was no central institutional structure to fall back on. The supranational dimension, which plays a key role in the modern European monetary union (and which evolved into a unified state in the case of Germany), had no early twentieth-century equivalent.

Summary

Box 9.2 is a summary of the world experience under different exchange rate systems.

Box 9.2 Exchange rate systems						
	1870–1913	1919–30	1931–9	1950–73	1975–2000	2000–9
Exchange rate regime	Fixed	Floating to fixed	Managed float	Fixed in the short run but adjustable in the long run	Mixed: floating or currency bloc pegged to German mark	Mixed: floating or currency union (euro)
International capital flows	High	High	Low	Low	Increasing to high	High
Interest rate differentials	Low	High but falling	High	High	Falling to low	Low
Nominal exchange rate adjustments	No	N/A	Yes	Yes	Yes	N/A
Convertibility of currencies	Yes	Yes	Limited. Currency controls	Convertible currencies for trade transactions	Yes	Yes
Inflation rates	Uniform	Large national differences		Significant national differences until 1992/4	Uniform after 1994	

The history of international monetary regimes is one of a gradual realization that fixed exchange rates are not necessary for a functional world economy. Moreover, with the rise of the importance of domestic policy goals and an independent monetary policy, they became more and more difficult to enforce.

In short, without some sort of supranational authority to enforce them, in modern times fixed exchange rates are made to be broken.

Suggestions for further reading

For a textbook introduction to international monetary theory, see P. R. Krugman and M. Obstfeld, *International Economics: Theory and Policy* (London: Pearson Education, Inc., 2008).

Among histories of international money:

B. Eichengreen, *Globalizing Capital: A History of the International Monetary System* (Princeton University Press, 2008).

R. I. McKinnon, *The Rules of the Game: International Money and Exchange Rates* (Cambridge Mass.: MIT Press, 1996), which provides one of the classic accounts of the workings of the various international currency regimes; and M. Obstfeld and A. M. Taylor, *Global Capital Markets: Integration, Crisis, and Growth* (Cambridge University Press, 2004).

There are many books on the gold standard. One of the best is B. Eichengreen, *Golden Fetters: The Gold Standard and the Great Depression, 1919–1939* (Oxford University Press, 1995).

This is a modern classic. Eichengreen was one of the first to suggest that adherence to the gold standard was the reason for the severity of the Great Depression. Traditional accounts, such as that of Nurkse, had reached the opposite conclusion: R. Nurkse, *International Currency Experience* (Geneva: League of Nations, 1944).

M. D. Bordo, *The Gold Standard and Related Regimes* (Cambridge University Press, 1999), is another excellent account of the workings of the gold standard.

The N – 1 problem of the Bretton Woods System is described by P. de Grauwe, *International Money* (Oxford University Press, 1996).

W. F. V. Vanthoor, *European Monetary Union since 1848* (Cheltenham: Edward Elgar, 1996), gives a colourful account of the history of European monetary unions up to the introduction of the euro.

10 The era of political economy: from the minimal state to the Welfare State in the twentieth century

10.1 Economy and politics at the close of the nineteenth century

In the last third of the nineteenth century, a number of Western European economies started to catch up with Britain (see Chapter 6), and participated in a phase of modern economic growth. It was an era of the minimal state. Government expenditure, central as well as local, as a share of GDP was around 10 per cent and most public expenditure was consumed by the military, law and order and civil administration. Public education, state-funded health and assistance to the poor and elderly amounted to less than half of government expenditure. The role of the state was to set the rules of the game, i.e. to enact laws and regulation for industry and trade, which might include legislation about maximum hours of work and safety standards for industrial workers. Poor relief actually stagnated in the nineteenth century and did not surpass 1 per cent of GDP until democracy gave the poor more say. In some nations, unemployment insurance was introduced with the help of the state, but trade unions were instrumental in setting them up. State subsidies were resisted in other nations on liberal grounds. A liberal consensus emerged, although attitudes to free trade differed when the losers from trade liberalization triggered off a protectionist backlash in the 1880s. However, the role of government was limited.

Money supply was left to the banking system and ultimately to central banks when they were granted a monopoly on note issuance. Macroeconomic management by using deliberate changes in *taxation** and expenditure to influence the business cycle had not been heard of. The first use of the word *macroeconomics* stems from the early 1940s. An economic orthodoxy which viewed the economy as a self-regulating entity dominated the minds of the ruling elite. It was thought that shocks to the economy could be absorbed through changes in prices and wages and would therefore have no real effects even in the short to medium term. The alleged automatic equilibrating mechanism of the gold standard, described in Chapter 9, can be seen as representing the harmony of the liberal order. State intervention should be kept to a minimum. Even if the franchise had been extended to a larger proportion of the male population, the voice of the people was still of no great importance to governments.

The First World War changed all that. Established trade routes were disrupted, the gold standard was suspended and after fifty years during which inflation rates had been practically identical over most of Europe, price levels now diverged dramatically. Full parliamentary democracy was introduced, except in those nations that drifted to right or left-wing authoritarian rule. Trade unions strengthened and social-democrat parties gained a wide electoral base. There was a desire for change, but the inertia of the past was strong among economists and economic policymakers across the political spectrum.

10.2 The long farewell to economic orthodoxy: the response to the Great Depression

The strength of the forces of economic orthodoxy was most obvious in the choice of monetary order in the interwar period. With the suspension of the gold standard, most European currencies were in a free-floating exchange rate system immediately after the First World War. Exchange rates adjusted to reflect widely differing inflation histories during the war. *Purchasing power parity** was restored, but *nominal exchange rates** differed greatly from pre-war rates. The liberal conviction that prices were (or should be) flexible nurtured the idea that a return to pre-war nominal exchange rates and gold parities was desirable, possible and (potentially) rapid. Even if a return to pre-war gold parities could lead, initially, to domestic currencies being over-valued against those currencies opting for a less doctrinaire resolution of the exchange rate choice, the downward flexibility of prices and wages was supposed to restore the purchasing power parity of the currency. That was the dominating conviction in Scandinavia and Britain even if there were dissenting voices, for example that of John Maynard Keynes, whose thinking finally helped to break down the orthodoxy in the 1930s. In the economies where inflation had been practically uncontrolled, such as France, the magnitude of the nominal price and wage-level adjustment necessary to restore competitiveness at pre-war gold parity was simply too large to be conceivable, and consequently a more pragmatic solution was found, namely to return to gold but at a lower parity. As it turned out, the different exchange rate choices did affect countries' ability to resist the economic shock that was in the making: the Great Depression that began in 1929. The nations which were under the spell of orthodoxy, the

Scandinavians and Britain, found themselves at a competitive disadvantage relative to economies like France. Had the equilibrating mechanism of the gold standard worked swiftly and painlessly the excessively high price and wage levels might have adjusted so as to restore competitiveness. Nothing of the sort happened, however, and international reserves flowed from economies with current account deficits to France and the USA. New political forces made deflationary policies less likely: trade unions were not willing to negotiate wage cuts even when faced with mounting unemployment, and pricing of industrial goods had become less flexible as firms increased in size and imposed their own prices. Over the short lifespan of the interwar gold standard very little nominal price or wage-level adjustment occurred, and therefore the initial imbalances remained at the outbreak of the Great Depression in 1929.

The Great Depression was the first truly international growth disaster. It originated in the USA and spread to the rest of the world. The severity of the depression was to a large extent caused by policy errors or the absence of adequate policy responses. The origin of the Depression was a large negative shock to consumption and investment following a period of stock-market excesses. When the stock-market bubble burst in 1929 it shattered business confidence and reduced wealth, consumption and investment, which aggravated the crisis. The banking system went into a deep decline. The drop in consumption was, however, only partly linked to the destruction of wealth on the stock markets, in Wall Street and the rest of the world. Industrial output declined sharply, though food production in real terms was only marginally affected. Food and primary product prices fell dramatically, depriving raw material producers of export income to pay for industrial imports from Europe once the USA ceased to lend internationally in 1930. America brought in protectionist policies and the rest of the world followed suit. Between 1929 and 1933 world trade fell to a third of its value at 1929 prices. Nominal interest rates were very low, but deflation kept *real interest rates* * high enough to prevent a recovery of investment. The public had lost confidence in the banking system and governments did not do enough to restore that confidence, which deprived the banks of their money-creating function.

Circumstance rather than conviction forced Britain off the gold standard in 1931. Scandinavia and several other nations immediately followed Britain and devalued their over-valued currencies. This was the first important move towards a reconsideration of received wisdom in economic management, even though it was not fully understood at the time. Monetary policy had formerly served as the instrument by which the exchange rate was defended. Having abandoned gold, monetary policy was no longer constrained by 'golden fetters', a term ascribed to Keynes. The response in terms of economic recovery was almost instantaneous. The recovery is fairly easy to explain. The Great Depression was associated with a fall in prices while nominal wages remained at their pre-crisis level. As a consequence real wages and product wages (wage costs divided by the price of an industry's product) increased, which worsened profitability and threatened companies' survival. The devaluation stopped the deflation and turned it into a mild inflation, which reduced product wages because the high unemployment made it impossible to negotiate higher nominal wages. Inflation also reduced *real interest rates**, which stimulated investment. Domestic industry got a competitive edge in the home market because imported goods became relatively more expensive, while export market penetration was eased by falling prices of exports relative to the prices charged by local producers on foreign markets. Britain's recovery was slow, but the Scandinavian economies did reasonably well in the 1930s because of their early break with orthodox exchange rate policies. But the economic re-orientation was incomplete. Although there was an intense and innovative debate among economists from Cambridge, Mass. to Cambridge, UK to Stockholm, which eventually laid the ground for modern macroeconomics, the new ideas had few practical implications for the management of the Depression in the 1930s. In fact, quite a few governments reacted to falling tax revenues as people were laid off by increasing taxes, thereby worsening the crisis. The idea that fiscal policy should be used actively to influence employment and growth was still too radical for policymakers, although monetary policy was less constrained when the gold standard was abandoned. Budget discipline and the notion that the balance of government revenue and expenditure should be respected were not seriously challenged. In fact quite a number of nations pursued a *pro-cyclical economic policy** rather than a neutral or counter-cyclical one.

Continental Europe remained a bastion of economic orthodoxy with effects that ranged from dismal economic performance (France) to political disaster (Germany). France fared relatively well during the first year of the Great Depression because she had adequate international reserves to withstand the shock to export earnings. France remained a stubborn defender of the gold standard, in fact she was the last major economy to leave it, as late as 1936. Remaining on gold forced deflation and stagnation on France, although those who had jobs experienced a significant increase in real wages, whereas real wages stagnated or fell in the devaluing nations. The adjustment to the French exchange rate in 1936 was too close to the outbreak of the Second World War to generate a recovery.

Germany entered the interwar period humiliated by a military defeat and with weak short-lived governments, whose reckless spending exploded into hyperinflation in the early 1920s. Once stabilized, the currency joined the gold standard and enjoyed the immediate confidence of international, mainly American, investors. The Reparation payments that Germany had to pay to the victorious nations of the First World War were more than offset by the inflow of foreign capital. However, the combined burden of servicing the mounting foreign debt and the Reparation payments became a serious constraint on economic policy when the Great Depression shocked export earnings. To reduce the current account deficit the German government introduced austerity measures, which reduced economic activity and imports but sent unemployment up to levels similar to those in the USA, some 25 per cent of the labour force in the early 1930s. An already unstable political situation went from bad to worse. In 1928, Adolf Hitler's party (the NSDAP) got less than 5 per cent of the votes, but five years later more than 40 per cent of the electorate voted for him, even if that election was not a fair one. The link between economic decline and the political rise of Nazism was obvious as demonstrated in Figure 10.1.

Why did economic policymakers not change course? A strong current of German historiography argues that the state of the economy, combined with Germany's commitment to the gold standard and the Reparations payments, gave her no chance to act differently. An expansionary monetary policy would have driven down interest rates and frightened away capital. However, in the summer of 1931, a couple of months before Britain abandoned the gold standard, Germany introduced capital controls. This was in itself a violation of the

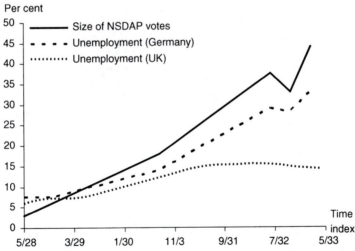

Figure 10.1   Unemployment paves the way for Adolf Hitler. Sources: Christian Stögbauer, 'The radicalisation of the german electorate: swinging to the right and the left in the twilight of the Weimar Republic,' *European Review of Economic History* 5 (2001), pp. 251–80; B. R. Mitchell, *International Historical Statistics*, 4th edn (London: Macmillan, 2003).

unwritten rules of the gold standard, but it gave Germany the chance to follow an independent monetary policy once she had the means to curb destabilizing currency movements. She did not use that option. It is difficult to understand why she did not take the next step, that is to follow Britain off gold and devalue, having already introduced currency controls. Had Germany followed Britain, the recovery experienced by the devaluing nations would have occurred in Germany as well. In 1932, Reparation payments were suspended and there were signs of a fragile recovery. From the middle to the end of 1932 there was a slight decline in both unemployment and the Nazi vote (see Figure 10.1). However, that recovery was too weak to prevent the ascent of Hitler. The crucial period stretched from the summer of 1931 to the summer of 1932. Britain and Scandinavia had opened up to an alternative policy in 1931; the USA followed, belatedly, in 1933. Although a new president, Franklin D. Roosevelt, determined to combat the depression, was elected in November 1932, he was not inaugurated until March 1933, by which time Hitler was already in power.

Britain was also spared some of the disastrous effects of the depression. As shown in Figure 10.1, unemployment never reached German levels and the increase came to a halt after the 1931 devaluation. Had unemployment not been allowed to continue increasing in Germany in 1931 and 1932, we might have had a history without the atrocities of the Nazi regime and Hitler might have been forced to return to his origins, to the political fringe.

Box 10.1 Growth disasters and the Great Depression

The Great Depression was not the greatest output shock to European economies over the last 150 years. Only in Germany did GDP decline as much as in the USA, from peak (1929) to trough (1933) or by more than 25 per cent. In the rest of Europe the decline was around 10 per cent although consumption declined less than GDP, by about half of the percentage decline in output. In depressions it is mainly investment and consumption of durables which are affected. Investment declines because there is spare capacity in industry and because the real debt of investors has increased and made them a bad risk for banks. Since depressions are associated with deflation, real interest rates are high enough to discourage investment. A fragile banking system usually turns away from excessive risk taking and becomes extremely cautious when it is teetering on the brink of insolvency. The great growth disasters in Europe were associated with the World Wars and/or adjustment after these wars. Large drops in output such as the Great Depression are almost always linked to stock-market crashes and banking crises. However, only one in four stock-market crashes generates a depression, although severe banking crises usually have a strong negative impact on output. A decline of one euro in stock-market wealth is estimated to produce a decline in consumption of about 5–10 cents.

10.3 Successes and failures of macroeconomic management in the second half of the twentieth century: from full employment to inflation targeting

The macroeconomic doctrines which were originally labelled 'Keynesian' were the result of work by a large number of economists from the 1930s onwards.

Although Keynes' ideas are commonly associated with spending financed by government debt – deficit spending – this is a superficial description. Deficit spending occurs routinely in periods of war or in preparation for war, as was the case in Germany after Hitler's rise to power. Keynesians showed more precisely that an increase in government spending worked, that it was legitimate and gave precision to the 'larger-than-spending' effect of government outlay on *national income,* by applying the *multiplier** theory. Keynesian models advocated not only stimulating the economy in an unemployment crisis but also reducing activity (e.g., say, by reducing government spending) if demand was hitting production capacity. The fast promulgation of Keynesian ideas is worth noting. Eleven years after the publication of Keynes' *General Theory* in 1936, and one year after Keynes' death, the first textbook of 'Keynesian' ideas was published. As a contrast, it took about fifty years before the Ricardian idea of comparative advantage was popularized in the nineteenth century. Over the years, Keynesian economics has adjusted to criticism of a theoretical nature and to the experience of policy mistakes. It is now thriving under the brand name 'New Keynesian' and is the dominant inspiration for economic policy-makers, true to its original conviction that economic fluctuations are manageable through fiscal and monetary policy. Those who opposed active economic policy intervention to smooth economic fluctuations lost influence in economics departments and ministries in the 1940s and 1950s, but re-surfaced in the 1970s and 1980s, a period of slow growth, high unemployment and inflation for most European economies. This so-called New Classical critique was based on the belief that economic fluctuations stemmed mainly from technological shocks, and that competitive markets could and should be left to work out the necessary adjustments. The real effects of economic policy intervention were questioned, despite the clear empirical evidence that changes in demand really affected output and that changes in interest rates had effects on GDP. Why do economists quarrel about these fundamental relationships?

It all goes back to questions about the nature of real-life economies. Are markets competitive or characterized by monopolistic competition? Are prices and wages fully flexible, or are they rigid in the medium and short run as Keynesians, New and Old, would argue? The contribution of the New Keynesians was to work out more precisely why prices and wages were not fully flexible. The reason why this matters is that if the market structure is one of monopolistic competition then firms have (some) price-making power and can operate with prices above marginal costs. An increase in demand can therefore be met by an increase in output rather than by increasing prices. Since price adjustments entail costs (so-called menu costs), they are not made continuously but are staggered. Prices, in other words, take time to adjust. If prices are not fully flexible then the central bank can influence, in particular, the *real interest rate**, which is what matters for investors. However, Keynesians have admitted that they previously neglected the problems of inflation when firms and trade unions anticipated government demand management. As a consequence a lot more attention is now paid to containing the inflationary expectations of macroeconomic policies. Furthermore, the political economy of demand management tended to make politicians more willing to increase spending in difficult times than to raise taxes in good times. As a consequence most European economies built up a considerable public debt in the 1970s and 1980s. However, the Keynesian lesson has not been forgotten. The reaction to the 2008/9 financial crisis contrasts favourably with the inaction during the Great Depression eighty years earlier. Much more was done to prevent the banking system from collapsing, and very few disputed the need for vigorous debt-financed increases in government spending.

A broad outline of macroeconomic policies would stress that the optimistic belief in combating fluctuations by fine-tuning policy and economic outcomes, as tried in the 1950s–1980s, has given way to a policy of bridging major shocks, but also to an acceptance of unemployment levels not tolerated in the 1950s and 1960s.

Keynesian principles were not universally accepted immediately after the Second World War, and when they were, fiscal policy was not used consistently over the business cycle. The politics of demand management makes it easier to combat unemployment by reducing tax or increasing spending than by cooling off an economy with spending cuts. Germany was initially reluctant to embrace the full-employment principle and France, true to her traditions of state intervention, experimented with a more comprehensive indicative planning. It was mostly co-ordination by rhetorical gestures than hands-on socialist-type planning. Elsewhere, the rallying cry for the new macroeconomic management in the immediate post-war world became 'full employment', which was interpreted as unemployment levels well under 5 per cent. Average unemployment in Europe was also quite low in the 1950s and 1960s, about a third of the level in the interwar period. However, in a longer perspective this now looks like a low-unemployment interregnum, because after the 1980s, levels again went up to between 5 and 10 per cent. The execution of detailed demand management often went wrong because of the problem of timing, which was to some extent caused by insufficient macroeconomic data and by the fact that increasingly open economies were influenced by shocks from the world market. A combination of an unanticipated positive demand shock from outside and deficit spending at home led to 'overheating'. The budgetary process, by which budgets were approved at a fixed date once a year, was not adequate for fine-tuning, which required quick adjustments to unexpected shocks. Nations like France and the UK also failed to raise productivity sufficiently, and expansionary policies therefore quickly encountered balance-of-payments problems. Trade unions and employers failed to build the co-operative institutions that developed elsewhere in Europe. Frequent changes in policy orientation contributed to the judgment that UK economic policy was characterized by policy-generated stop-and-go cycles. Until the early 1970s unemployment was generally low, but would not remain so. Early experiments in demand management ultimately faced the problem that workers and trade unions anticipated government policy responses. If trade unions knew that a wage increase that eventually created unemployment would be met by government spending to drive down unemployment, then inflationary pressures would build up. Therefore fine-tuning worked only in a political environment of centralized trade unions, which showed restraint and were forward-looking. Barry Eichengreen, the Berkeley economic historian, has argued that this worked best in those European nations, such as in Scandinavia, Austria and Germany, in which there was an established tradition of co-operation between unions, the state and employers. The relative success of demand management in the Golden Age (1950–73) depended as much on the elastic supply of raw materials, such as oil, and labour from the dwindling agricultural sector and from immigration. These forces contributed to the unique combination of low inflation and low unemployment in the period.

When and where Keynesian-inspired demand management was applied skilfully, economic fluctuations were dampened, according to the Heller report (1968) sponsored by the OECD. But the fast economic growth of the Golden Age seemingly had other sources: high profits and investments, technology transfer, increased openness to trade and, as a consequence, high total factor productivity. The gradual build-up of the Welfare State and extension of the coverage of tax-financed unemployment benefits introduced *automatic stabilizers** and at least partly relieved governments of the need to use active intervention. Welfare states are high-tax economies, and an increase in unemployment will immediately reduce government revenue and increase government outlay, which will have a stabilizing effect. Likewise, in an economic upturn high taxes and lower spending on unemployment programmes will slow down the expansion. Unlike in the Great Depression, when governments often tried to compensate increasing outlay with higher taxes, there has been general agreement, since the Keynesian doctrines were accepted, that the automatic stabilizers should be allowed to work. The advantage of automatic stabilizers is that the government does not need to get the timing right. The labour market does the timing.

However, the wage restraint offered by trade unions in exchange for secure jobs and investments in advanced technology permitting future pay rises broke down in the early 1970s. There were a number of reasons for this: exogenous import-price shocks from oil, the fact that the 'free lunches' of technology transfer were not so easily available, and the fact that the costs of financing the Welfare State were increasingly being borne by the low to middle-income earners, which meant that a gross pay rise needed to be higher to produce a given net take-home pay (pay after tax) rise. In the 1950s and 1960s it was believed that there was a trade-off between inflation and unemployment, as summarized in the so-called Phillips-curve relationship. This demonstrated that a fall in unemployment was associated with an increase in inflation and vice versa. However, in the 1970s a new pattern emerged in which both unemployment and inflation increased. With few exceptions (chiefly Germany), nations accommodated the external imbalances caused by high inflation and falling competitiveness by repeated devaluations. Some, for example Sweden and the UK, gave up currency alignments altogether and set their currencies to float in the early 1990s, just as the USA and Japan had done earlier after the final breakdown of the Bretton Woods System in 1973. Those who remained in the German-mark-dominated European monetary systems later formed the core of the euro area. Governments increasingly blamed rigidities in the labour market for the persistent high unemployment, accepting a view that had been highlighted by New Classical economists since the 1970s. By the 1980s the main preoccupation of governments became to combat high, often two-digit, inflation. Germany had a tradition of not tolerating high inflation, so an increasing number of economies, including France, Italy and Denmark, decided to peg their currency to the German mark in the 1980s, effectively abdicating from an independent macroeconomic policy. France is probably the most dramatic case because it tried the expansionary way in the early 1980s only to be forced to make a U-turn and let the Bundesbank take over its monetary policy when the expansion led to uncontrollable inflation. The full-employment goal was effectively subordinated to price stability after the difficulty of containing inflation in the 1970s, and was replaced in the 1990s by inflation targeting managed by *independent* central banks. Although unemployment has remained at a high level, one reason for this may be that generous insurance schemes prolong the job-search period of the unemployed. This may ultimately lead to better allocation of labour, but long unemployment spells are dangerous because they tend to make skills obsolete.

Inflation targeting means that an independent central bank is given the task of pursuing a monetary policy which aims at a given yearly inflation target, say 2 per cent. The logic is appealing because it suggests that a given rate of unemployment, needed to permit workers moving from one job to another, can be reached as well by a low as by a high rate of inflation. It all has to do with inflationary expectations. The reality has not easily given in to the logic, however. Unemployment has remained high in continental Western Europe by the standards set in the Golden Age.

In the new political economy framework, governments can still pursue counter-cyclical spending subject to the intervention of independent central banks if government policy threatens price stability. For members of the euro area the new regime requires a degree of fiscal policy co-ordination that is still in the making. It is, however noteworthy, that European nations outside as well as inside the euro managed to bring down inflation rates considerably in the 1990s and the first decade of the second millennium. Central bank policy is not the only cause since the competitive pressures from the elastic supply of manufactured goods from the low-wage developing nations has also held back inflationary tendencies.

10.4 Karl Marx's trap: the rise and fall of the socialist economies in Europe

Karl Marx, the economist, philosopher and social critic, author with Friedrich Engels of *The Communist Manifesto* (1848), developed a theory of history with a surprising lesson for the socialist economies, an economic experiment that ultimately failed. Marx argued that social systems thrive and expand only if they can develop technologies and sustain an increase in material welfare. His theory is a variety of a consequence explanation of institutions which we discussed in Chapter 5: institutions emerge and persist because they have beneficial effects. The demise of the socialist experiment fits well into Karl Marx's historical explanation: it failed because it did not deliver technological progress and material improvements on a scale comparable with the market economies of Europe. Deprived of a political voice, the peoples of Eastern Europe voted with their feet and brought about the collapse of the centrally planned economies, first at the border with Western Europe and finally at the core, Soviet Russia, around 1990.

Although Marx was routinely referred to as the major intellectual inspiration in the socialist economies, the social-democratic movement in Europe also considered itself as his legitimate heir, especially in its formative years at the end of the nineteenth century, before the communists broke away and formed independent parties. Socialist economies represented an almost total dominance of politics over the economy, a maximum state, while social democracy and socially minded liberals strove to balance the domain of markets and that of politics – the 'mixed economy' – which eventually turned out to be the more endurable solution.

Marx's conjecture was that communism would emerge after capitalism had lifted economies to an unprecedented level of material welfare. Although a fierce social critic, Marx in no way denied the dynamic advantages of capitalism and its global reach, and looked upon it as a necessary stage in the pursuit of the final stage of communism. Therefore, he would probably have been surprised to hear, if he had had the chance, that the first socialist economy, Russia, was a predominantly agrarian economy and something of a backwater in terms of technological, intellectual and economic development.

The Russian revolutionaries drifted naturally towards administrative control of the economy after the 1917 revolution. The nation was weakened by the First World War, internal strife and chaos. However, the government soon had to retreat from tight top-down control and re-introduce market principles in the early 1920s, only to return to planning by the end of that decade. The return to tight central planning was in no way inevitable and did not arrive until the early 1930s with the first five-year plan. The inspiration for central planning is somewhat obscure. Karl Marx certainly did not offer a blueprint for how a socialist economy should be run. One possible source of inspiration was the administrative bureaucracies that developed in Europe, and Germany in particular, to sustain the war effort, and the bureaucracies which managed public enterprises, for example the railway system. A firm is in many respects a centrally planned entity at the micro level. For example, the research department of a firm does not normally apply market prices when it supplies services to the production department of the same firm. Much later the eminent socialist economist Oscar Lange described the planned economy as a permanent war economy. A less dramatic metaphor would be to invoke the similarity with the way that a large university allocates resources among departments. Price and economic incentives have a minor role in both systems.

Four characteristics of early Soviet planning stand out: an abolition of private ownership of resources and the means of production; very high investment ratios; a strong bias towards investment in capital goods industries; and a neglect of consumer goods production. While these characteristics were unthinkable without authoritarian political rule, it is not obvious that the excesses of Stalinist repression were necessary. Despite the human losses in the 1930s repression, which took its toll of many talented people in science, industry and the military, industry expanded sufficiently to sustain a war machine that drove the Nazis out of Russia and Eastern Europe. The costs in human lives of the military campaigns were very high, a fact that has been neglected in subsequent Cold War tainted historiography. The anti-Nazi resistance in

Eastern Europe was dominated by social democrats and communists; the latter, and sometimes the former, found a natural ally in the Soviet Union, which liberated them from Nazi occupation. A transition towards a Soviet-style political and economic system was then imposed after the Second World War in the Baltic states, Poland, East Germany, Czechoslovakia, Romania, Bulgaria, Yugoslavia and Albania. Only a few of these countries had a strong tradition of parliamentary democracy. About a third of the European population were living in centrally planned economies by the mid-1950s. These nations differed somewhat in the treatment of private property. It survived longer in East German industry, and Polish and Yugoslavian agriculture was spared collectivization. The Soviet-type planning system and priorities were, however, generally endorsed. Like Russia before the revolution, the new socialist economies were predominantly agrarian with small industrial sectors. Only East Germany and Czechoslovakia had a substantial industrial base. The other new members of the socialist club had comparative advantages in agriculture, but that sector received a tiny proportion of investments. As a consequence of the high investment in industry the productivity gap between industrial occupations and jobs in agriculture was huge, which implied gains from the structural relocation of the labour force.

Structural change was one of the reasons why growth was quite high in the Golden Age, although not as high as in Western European economies that had started from similar income levels in 1950. It is reasonable to compare the Eastern European economies with those economies in Europe that shared a predominantly agrarian structure. That comparison is not favourable to Eastern Europe or Russia. Compared to Spain and Portugal, which also suffered from authoritarian but conservative rule, the annual growth of GDP per capita was two percentage points lower in Eastern Europe from 1950 to 1973, despite the fact that the ratio of investment to GDP was 10–15 percentage points higher in Eastern Europe.

The low efficiency of investments had to do with the difficulties of central planning and the political intervention at all levels of production. In a planned economy the central planning authority collected information from firms and relied on information about technical requirements for the production of goods. For example, to produce a ton of steel you would need certain quantities of coke, iron ore and man-hours. On that basis, production targets could be set and the required inputs were allocated to the firm. However, information about the required inputs was routinely distorted by managers to secure an over-allocation of resources and firms would tamper with the quality of products to attain production targets. Market pricing was not used at all in the early phase, and when introduced later it was not applied consistently. In a market system, much passing around of detailed information is unnecessary because prices alone contain the information managers need. The market is in fact an information-processing machine, which motivated Adam Smith's famous metaphor about the 'invisible hand' that the planning authorities tried to replace by a visible hand. However, the refusal to use the information provided by prices led to waste, because planners allocated resources ignoring the opportunity costs of inputs. Managers in the industrial sectors, which policymakers favoured, had virtually free access to capital, which explains the excessive investment ratios and neglect of consumers. The quality and variety of goods produced was unsatisfactory. Only excess demand for consumer goods, as revealed by rationing, made consumers tolerate the poor quality. The planners' contempt for consumers was of course ultimately based on political authoritarianism.

The difficulties associated with central planning became apparent after the first heroic years of post-war reconstruction, and attempts to introduce economic incentives based on market principles were tried. However, the half-baked nature of these reforms created new problems. In the 1970s and 1980s growth slowed down considerably. The socialist economies became indebted to Western creditors and ran trade deficits to mollify an increasingly hostile domestic population with consumer goods. In the first Cold War decades of the socialist experiment, the Soviet bloc had been cut off from imports of advanced technology. When Cold War tensions eased and technology transfer was permitted, it still did not help the socialist economies to attain the growth rates of the 1950s and 1960s. In relative terms Soviet Russia and Eastern Europe diverged not only from the USA but also from Western Europe.

Table 10.1 reveals the poor relative performance of the socialist economies. Russia's income relative to that of Western Europe falls from almost 70 per cent in 1950 to 50 per cent in 1990. Eastern Europe falls back from earning half the Western European income in 1950 to a third forty years later. Western Europe by contrast converged on the leading economy, the USA.

In the 1930s, when the world was ravaged by the consequences of the Great Depression, intellectuals studied the planning experiment in Russia with great interest and admiration. They had a vision of central planning as a crisis-free economic system. The appeal of planning faded not only in the West but also in the East as the contradictions and inefficiencies mounted. Although saved from the perils of unemployment and intensification of work experienced in the West, workers in the socialist economies were deprived of political rights as well as the consumer goods available to people in Western Europe. The system simply did not deliver, and, as Karl Marx predicted, economic systems that do not raise the material welfare will not survive. The transition in the 1990s was

Table 10.1 GDP per capita in the USA, Russia and Eastern Europe relative to Western Europe 1950–90. Western Europe = 1

	1950	1973	1990
USA/Western Europe	2.08	1.46	1.45
Russia/Western Europe	0.67	0.57	0.49
Eastern Europe/Western Europe	0.46	0.44	0.34

Source: Own estimates from data in A. Maddison, *Contours of the World Economy, 1–2030 AD* (Oxford University Press, 2007), p. 337.

not easy, but after years of negative growth most of the former socialist economies exhibited the typical characteristics of latecomers in the modernization process. With a few exceptions there was a period of technological catch-up and growth rates double of those in the mature Western European economies.

10.5 A market failure theory of the Welfare State

In the first decade of the twentieth century, government spending rarely exceeded 10 per cent of GDP and most of that spending was directed to basic state functions such as law and order, infrastructure investment and defence. Most European nations provided elementary schooling and some poor relief, but the combined costs amounted to only a few per cent of GDP. The expansion of public spending on welfare did not really take off until the extension of the franchise after the First World War and especially in the 1930s. However, as late as 1930 pension costs did not exceed 1 per cent of GDP in Germany or Sweden. The modern Welfare State, with extensive coverage including subsidized or free healthcare, education, housing, childcare and old-age pensions was born after the Second World War. Since the 1970s, welfare spending has been between 25 and 35 per cent of GDP in most European nations, of which about half is transfers and half is public consumption in health and education. Table 10.2 reveals that between 50 and 60 per cent of public spending is welfare-oriented, with an additional 10–15 per cent spent on education and research. The sum of both types of spending was close to 5 per cent of GDP a century earlier. The national differences in the direction of spending are also quite small.

What explains this significant change in the role of government and polity in modern economies?

To answer that question we must first look more closely at the nature of the Welfare State. Although it is popularly associated with egalitarianism and redistribution, the Welfare State is mainly about the inter-temporal transfer of

Table 10.2   The uses of local and central government spending in Europe in 2005. Percentage of total

Year 2005	Per cent								
	Denmark	Germany	Greece	France	Italy	Poland	Sweden	UK	Norway
Public service	15	17	27	20	24	20	17	21	13
Welfare provisions	57	63	53	59	53	53	56	54	57
Education and R&D	15	10	7	11	11	15	14	15	15
Envn. protection	1	1	1	2	2	1	1	1	1
Other	12	9	12	8	10	11	12	9	13

Source: Eurostat on line.

resources over the life cycle of households and individuals. Redistribution, meaning transfers between classes, is a minor effect of welfare spending and can be explained by the extension of the franchise, which made it possible for the majority of low and middle-income earners to tax the rich. *Progressive tax** systems, a system whereby the tax rate increases with income levels, contributes to this redistribution in the sense that incomes after tax become a little more egalitarian than gross incomes. However, it is noteworthy that economies with elaborate Welfare State systems rely more heavily on consumption taxes, which are *regressive** rather than progressive in their effect, than do economies with limited welfare provisions. The reason is simple enough. The extent of income taxes needed to fund an ambitious Welfare State would have a disincentive effect on workers.

Figure 10.2 provides a simplified exposition of the inter-temporal life-cycle redistribution of consumption possibilities. We define the *net welfare state balance* as the difference between (1) the household's contribution to the funding of Welfare State expenses from taxes and other contributions and (2) the monetary value of the household's use or extraction of Welfare State transfers and services.

We look on the Welfare State as a provider of transfers and services which helps households to smoothe consumption possibilities over their life cycle. A family will go through some predictable states as well as transitory income shocks due to unemployment and health problems. The family-formation phase is unusually demanding in terms of income needs linked to family size and schooling and reduced earnings because of child-related constraints on labour supply. The typical household starts at the family-formation phase as a net receiver from the generations that have left the family-formation and child-rearing phase behind. The sum of Welfare-State-related taxes it pays is smaller than the contribution in terms of subsidized day-care and schooling

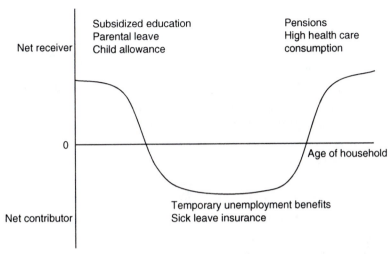

Net receiver

Subsidized education
Parental leave
Child allowance

Pensions
High health care
consumption

0

Age of household

Net contributor

Temporary unemployment benefits
Sick leave insurance

Figure 10.2   Net welfare state balance of a typical household over its life cycle

for children, child allowances and paid parental leave. As children leave school (or university) the household starts becoming a net contributor since the use of unemployment and sick leave benefits is transitory. The household remains a net contributor until it enters old age, when households become intensive public health consumers as well as beneficiaries of publicly funded pensions. In most European economies about 75 per cent of heath expenditure is geared towards the elderly. The scope of the Welfare State varies. Most European nations have a mix of pay-as-you-go pensions, that is the working-age population pays the pensions for the non-working generation, and funded pension schemes.

The life-cycle transfer is an implicit contract between generations: net contributors will become net receivers and vice versa, and the reciprocity is essential for the stability of the system. However, the fundamental question remains why citizens have delegated the life-cycle redistribution of consumption possibilities to politicians. The alternative solution would be to use the market for inter-temporal redistribution of consumption possibilities by borrowing at an early stage before becoming net savers and ending up with negative saving in old age.

I shall argue that Welfare State institutions were preferred to markets because the market alternatives were deemed inferior, for four distinct reasons. First, market solutions tend to have distributional effects which violate commonly held preferences for equal access to some essential services. Secondly, externalities and co-ordination problems would make the market solution inefficient. Thirdly, capital market imperfections are not compatible with universal access to inter-temporal smoothing of income; and fourthly: time-inconsistent preferences make most people under-invest in pension saving as well as sick leave and unemployment insurance.

Although economists as a rule use the idea that human beings are chiefly motivated by self-interest, at least as a first approximation, there has, in recent years, been recognition that they have a more complicated behavioural strategy. In a large number of situations, people tend to show concern not only for themselves but also for the welfare of others. Few people would argue that those without means should not have access to schools or healthcare, for example. Most people would also admit the need for some income redistribution. However, we should take care not to make human beings more altruistic than they are. Cross-border studies of redistributive systems indicate that ethnic homogeneity is usually positively associated with more redistribution. A drastic illustration of that phenomenon is reluctance to provide foreign aid, which amounts to less than 1 per cent of GDP, as against the more generous domestic Welfare State spending.

The second explanation focusses on inefficiencies caused by co-ordination problems and is within the domain of standard economics. From the middle of the nineteenth century, schooling became increasingly public, rather than privately provided, and also compulsory. The presence of externalities in education helped in making it compulsory because lack of schooling does not only hurt those left behind. The externality resides in the fact that the usefulness of your own knowledge is greatly enhanced by your fellow citizen's having corresponding knowledge. For example, to enter a contract with an illiterate person is time-consuming and ignorance might stop many a mutually beneficial exchange. For that reason, any private decision to invest in elementary schooling will depend on what others are doing. Such uncertainty causes a co-ordination problem. Compulsory schooling solves that problem and without it people would tend to under-invest in education.

Redistribution by means of *taxation** and income transfers also opens up a co-ordination problem. It is plausible that some types of altruistic behaviour that require substantial contributions are conditional on a mechanism that forces others to contribute as well. But in a world of voluntary contributions there will be uncertainty about what others are doing. Private charities are based on voluntary and unconditional contributions and cannot commit everybody. A public tax and transfer system is therefore called for.

Can we imagine a market solution to the type of inter-temporal redistribution that is shown in Figure 10.2? In principle, yes, but it will violate the condition that there must be universal access to it. You could think of households borrowing so as to meet the net excess costs related to family formation, that is the reduction of family income during and immediately after pregnancies, the fees for day-care institutions and schools for children. However, it is likely that capital market imperfections would make this solution far from universal. That is, a large number of people will be denied loans. Banks would be unwilling to provide credit without collateral so that only households who were considered low risk would get access to credit.

Health and unemployment insurance would, if left to markets, be associated with *adverse selection**. People with high risks would opt for insurance, which would drive up the cost, making low-risk people opt out. If risks were not pooled, that is if beneficiaries did not include both high and low-risk people, the health insurance policy would be too costly. This may explain why many Welfare-State-sponsored insurance schemes are compulsory.

Pensions are different. As noted above, pension systems in the developed Welfare States combine the inter-generational redistribution provided by pay-as-you-go systems with funded systems where individuals save for their own retirement benefits. However, it is noteworthy that funded pensions are often semi-voluntary. Trade unions typically negotiate with employers to divert a fraction of potential pay increases to pensions and members have little or no chance to opt out. It is an expression of paternalism that has its roots in the well-known problem of time-inconsistent preferences. There is strong empirical evidence that people tend to change their relative preferences for different events or states as time passes. More generally, people tend to go for immediate gratification, which makes them neglect long-run needs, or needs in a distant future. The basis of the bias, which seems to be deeply embedded in human psychology, may be evolutionary. In a harsh environment a failure to satisfy immediate needs might have endangered long-run survival. Be that as it may, time inconsistency makes people under-invest in provisions for future events such as unemployment, health problems and old age. However, people tend to be aware of their lack of self-control, that is the difficulties of making plans that are consistent with long-run interests, and seem willing to delegate decisions regarding savings for old age to politicians or trade-union representatives. It is a sort of self-imposed paternalism.

Although centre-left parties have been instrumental in advancing Welfare State solutions there is an astonishing consensus across the political spectrum in Europe that such solutions are desirable. Centre-right parties when in power do not, despite accusations to the contrary, make more than marginal changes to Welfare State provisions. Denmark is a typical example. After thirty years of centre-right coalitions interrupted by shorter spells of centre-left government since the 1980s, the public sector share of GDP remains among the highest, if not the highest, in the world.

The Welfare State is associated with high levels of taxation and the suspicion that high taxes harm growth has been advanced since its birth. The reason for this is of course the negative effect on labour supply of high taxes and generous transfers. What does state-of-the-art research say?

Unfortunately, the major studies that look at welfare spending in a comparative setting come to opposing results. Robert Barro, a Harvard economist and frequent contributor to the *Wall Street Journal*, found that there was a negative effect on growth. However, Peter Lindert, a University of California economic historian, was unable to verify that negative connection. The explanation for his unexpected result was that nations with high welfare spending had smarter tax systems, which raised more revenue from taxing consumption and less from taxing income or corporate profits.

Summary

The twentieth century saw some unlikely combinations of events. It was a century of unparalleled economic growth despite two world wars. The level of taxation reached levels which any economist living before 1930 would consider incompatible with economic growth.

However, a neat balance between the political and economic spheres developed which is fundamentally different from what things looked like at the beginning of the century. Market failures and market imperfections are now considered legitimate grounds for public action. The socialist experiment failed because it could produce neither the goods nor the liberties that the mixed market welfare economies did, that is the economies which combined a fiercely competitive trade-oriented manufacturing sector with a large Welfare State.

Suggestions for further reading

To get an idea of the optimistic mood regarding the accomplishments and possibilities of Keynesian demand management just before the eruption of the New Classical critique, read Walter Heller *et al.*, *Fiscal Policy for a Balanced Economy: Experience, Problems and Prospects* (Paris: OECD, 1968). An insider's view of how (Old) Keynesianism met the challenge from (New) Classical economics and formed New Keynesianism is Oliver Blanchard's 'What do we know about macroeconomics that Fisher and Wicksell did not?', *The Quarterly Journal of Economics* 115(4) (2000), pp. 1375–1409.

P. H. Lindert has written a comprehensive two-volume study of the emergence of social spending and the Welfare State in *Growing Public: Social*

Spending and Economic Growth since the Eighteenth Century (Cambridge University Press, 2004).

Barry Eichengreen has surveyed the political economy and economic development in Europe in the second half of the twentieth century: *The European Economy since 1945: Coordinated Capitalism and Beyond* (Princeton University Press, 2007).

The interwar period is covered in a masterly work by C. H. Feinstein, P. Temin and G. Toniolo, *The European Economy Between the Wars* (Oxford University Press, 1997).

Studies of Eastern Europe include D. H. Aldcroft and S. Morewood, *Economic Change in Eastern Europe* (London: Routledge, 1995) and I. Berend, *Central and Eastern Europe, 1944–1993: Detour from the Periphery to the Periphery* (Cambridge University Press, 1996).

N. F. R. Crafts and G. Toniolo have edited a volume of country-specific studies in *Economic Growth in Europe since 1945* (Cambridge University Press, 1996).

A modern classic is A. Maddison, *Dynamic Forces in Capitalist Development: A Long-Run Comparative View* (Oxford University Press, 1991).

11 Inequality among and within nations: past, present, future

11.1 Why is there inequality?

Inequality refers to unequal access to welfare as manifested in consumption, health, life expectancy and schooling. It is usually allied to inequality of income. However, income is not an end but a means of acquiring a good life, which has a number of attributes apart from consumption. Needless to say, income is an imperfect guide to welfare distribution because some aspects of welfare are only vaguely linked to income. For example, income inequality on a world scale went on increasing until recent decades while inequality in terms of literacy has fallen. The dramatic fall in child mortality during the last two centuries is also only remotely linked to income, and inequality in terms of life expectancy across nations has fallen. In the advanced welfare states of Europe, a growing number of services such as health, childcare, schooling and access to cultural sites such as theatres are provided at subsidized rates that again weaken the link between income and actual consumption. Despite these reservations, income inequality is an important, although insufficient, guide to welfare distribution.

The major sources of income are work, acquired or inherited wealth and, from the twentieth century onward, transfers such as pensions. Excluding property income, the income inequality we observe is closely related to skills acquired through formal education and on-the-job training. However, throughout history we have seen that discrimination can distort the relationship between skill and reward. Property income is not necessarily related to one's own efforts in the past but simply to the sheer luck of being born well endowed.

On a world scale we note that the poor in poor nations are usually much poorer than the poor in rich nations, while the rich in poor nations are almost as rich as the rich in rich nations, although less numerous. Focussing instead on inequality of mean income across nations, we can ascribe most of the difference to unequal access to good government, technology and skills (rather than access to natural resources) and to insufficient savings and investment. Poor nations remain poor because they lack the ability, in terms of institutions and education, to exploit modern technology. It is often argued that the poorest nations are poor because they are exploited by foreign investors and by unfavourable trading relations. It is true that foreign investors have been and are exploiting the fact that weak or corrupt local governments are unable to negotiate reasonable terms for economic co-operation. However, this is not the basic cause of world poverty. The disturbing fact is that the very poor nations attract neither foreign investment nor much trade. Poverty in itself is a major barrier to the escape from poverty because the resources needed to invest in education and infrastructure are hard to mobilize. Besides, corruption and a more generally poor quality of public governance are linked to poverty.

Many poor nations share the fact of having been subject to colonial rule and the question naturally arises whether their poverty has its roots in this colonial past. In one respect the colonial heritage has been particularly harmful in that the administrative units (later to become nation states) formed by colonial powers, especially in Africa, were artificial constructs which have led to endemic border conflicts in the post-colonial period, which have had negative effects on economic growth. The fact that colonized regions lacked strong local governments invited abuse of colonial power. As a consequence the terms on which colonial corporations acquired property rights in land and mineral resources were unfavourable to indigenous people. The imprint of colonial expansion on trade has left many colonies with a heavy concentration on a few commodities from extractive industries which have been and remain subject to wide fluctuations in prices. It turns out that trade volatility has a direct and strong effect on fluctuations in government revenues and economic growth. The fact that poor nations specialize in primary products, including agriculture, need not in itself be a barrier to growth. But the agricultural *protectionism** of the rich world prevents poor nations from exploiting their comparative advantages. Agriculture is not a laggard in terms of productivity growth, as has been demonstrated by agricultural total factor productivity in Europe and elsewhere: it has grown at rates on a par with or higher than in manufacturing during the last two centuries. History tells us that wealth is not built on *what* you do but how *efficient* you are at doing *whatever* you do.

11.2 Measuring inequality

There are a number of inequality and income dispersion measures and none of them are perfect. A commonly used measure is the so called *Gini coefficient**.

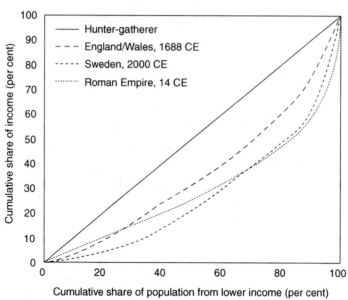

Figure 11.1   Gini distributions in economies from 10,000 BCE to the present. Own estimates based on data from B. Milanovic *et al.*, *Measuring Ancient Inequality*, NBER Working Paper No. 13550 (2007), Statistiska Centralbyrån, Stockholm, Sweden, Disponibel inkomst per konsumtionsenhet inklusive kapitalvinst efter deciler, available at www.scb.se.

It measures the extent of inequality relative to an ideal of equal income distribution in which all individuals or households earn the same. The Gini coefficient takes values from 0 – perfect equality when all households earn the same income – and inequality increases as it approaches 1. Sometimes the coefficient is presented as a multiple of 100, so that a Gini coefficient of 0.5 is equivalent to 50. While it is possible to imagine a perfectly equal society, as represented in Figure 11.1 by a hunter-gatherer economy, a Gini coefficient of 1 is only a theoretical possibility. The maximum inequality possible for a sustainable society from a purely nutritional point of view must permit the population to have at least a subsistence income, which implies that the maximum Gini coefficient in the Roman Empire was around 0.55 and that of a modern rich economy in Europe or North America will be around 0.97 to 0.98. However, there are few historical examples of actual Gini coefficients exceeding 0.6.

The principle behind the Gini coefficient is illustrated graphically in Figure 11.1. On the horizontal axis, we measure the cumulative percentage of households in the population ranked according to income – from low to high – and on the vertical axis the cumulative percentage of total income. The straight line represents a case of perfect equality, in which 10 per cent of households acquire 10 per cent of the income, 20 per cent of households get 20 per cent

of total income etc. We can think of pre-agricultural hunter-gatherer economies before the transition to agriculture some 12,000 years ago as coming close
to perfect equality. These societies lacked a pronounced social stratification
and had common access to resources. Since an income was close to subsistence there was simply no above-subsistence income for an elite to appropriate.
Agriculture and unequal access to power, property and skills allowed higher
mean incomes and hence higher inequality. Figure 11.1 also shows the income
distributions for a number of civilizations by so-called *Lorenz curves**, from
the Roman Empire to a modern Welfare State, Sweden. All these curves depart
from the straight line of an egalitarian hunter-gatherer society. The more the
curve departs the more unequal the income distribution will be and the higher
the value taken by the Gini coefficient. In the geographical core of the Roman
empire in year 14 the *Lorenz curve** indicates that 20 per cent of the top income
earners, those in the interval between 80 and 100 per cent of the population,
earn about 55 per cent of total income in society, that is above the 45 per cent
of income that 80 per cent of the population earn. The Roman mean income
underlying this estimate of the Gini is about twice the subsistence income, and
a large share of that above-subsistence income benefits a minority of rich and
very rich people. In England and Wales some 1600 years later, mean income is
about three to four times the subsistence income, but the Lorenz curve does
not differ much from that of Rome. A contemporary European distribution is
represented by Sweden in the year 2000. Income is now fifty times subsistence,
but inequality is in fact less than in England and in Rome, as indicated by a
Lorenz curve that is closer to the straight line of egalitarian income distribution. In other words, there is not necessarily an increase in inequality as income
per head increases. However, in a poor economy income distribution cannot
be very unequal. If the average income is exactly 400 $PPP (see Box 2.1, p. 28),
which we take as subsistence income, it follows that the society cannot be sustained if it is not perfectly egalitarian, as demonstrated for the hunter-gatherer
society in Figure 11.1. Only as the average income increases above subsistence
can inequality as measured by the Gini coefficient increase. Branko Milanovic,
a World Bank economist with a keen interest in income distribution in historical and contemporary economies, introduced the concept of the maximum feasible inequality an economy can experience given a rise in average
income. Assuming that a small elite, say 0.1 per cent of the population, receives
all income above the subsistence income, this implies that the rest, that is 99.9
per cent, of the population has to survive on 400$PPP per head. The higher the
average income is the higher the maximum inequality as measured by the Gini
coefficient. An informative way of understanding inequality over time will
then be to estimate the actual Gini coefficient as a proportion, a percentage,

of the maximum Gini coefficient given the per capita income. It turns out that the *actual* Gini coefficients for Rome in year 14 and the USA in year 2000 were around 0.40. Is it meaningful to say that they had the same inequality score? Not really, if we take their Gini coefficients as a proportion of the maximum inequality permitted by the per capita income. Rome 2000 years ago was in fact almost as unequal as it possibly could be given the low income per head. Its maximum Gini coefficient was just around 0.55 while the maximum Gini coefficient for the USA in 2000 was 0.98.

I have therefore calculated the ratio of actual relative to maximum Gini coefficients for economies over time and the evolution of that ratio is shown in Figure 11.2. The ratio first increases, which demonstrates that actual inequality follows potential or maximum inequality as income per head increases. But that increase levels off in the Early Modern period and falls in the twentieth century. Inequality has fallen relative to its maximum level. An explanation must focus on the distribution of skills and property. The early civilizations, say the Roman Empire or Byzantium, were characterized by large inequalities in the distribution of property and skills, but as history went on larger and larger sections of the population got the skills and access to other resources which made it possible for them to raise their income above subsistence.

While it is clear that actual inequality has declined relative to potential or maximum inequality, it is not obvious that actual inequality declined before the twentieth century. Once economies left a state in which mean income was just about twice subsistence income, when potential inequality cannot exceed 0.55, an increase in income per head tended to increase inequality, as indicated by the development in the Netherlands. Before the twentieth century, Gini coefficients were typically between 0.4 and 0.6, though the fragility

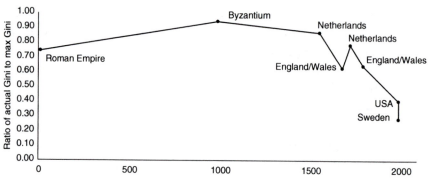

Figure 11.2 The actual Gini coefficient as a share of the maximum Gini over time. Own estimates based on data from B. Milanovic *et al.*, *Measuring Ancient Inequality*, World Bank Policy Research Working Paper, 2007.

of the income data makes strong conclusions about trends difficult. This also holds for other measures such as the share of top income earners. For example, before industrialization the richest 5 per cent of the population earned some 35 percent of total income, but only half that by the end of the twentieth century. In nations as different as France and Denmark the top 10 per cent of the population earned about half of total income before industrialization and that share fell to 30 percent during the twentieth century. There is, in other words, little doubt that inequality fell in Europe in the twentieth century. The estimates quoted refer to pre-tax income data, so the egalitarian trend is not caused by redistributive taxation and transfers. If these policies, which became of some importance after 1930, were taken into consideration the drift towards less inequality would be even more pronounced. Attempts to measure inequality after tax and transfers indicate an egalitarian effect, but it is not strong. The decline of the Gini coefficient is in the order of 0.05 units, that is from, say, 0.3 in pre-tax income distribution to 0.25 after tax and transfers, which should be compared to the much larger decline over time, from pre-industrial inequality of around 0.5 to 0.6 to contemporary inequality at 0.4 to 0.3. This finding reinforces the reservations about the redistributive effects of the welfare state discussed in Chapter 10. However, it is far from clear that the egalitarian trend will continue. A number of studies suggest that income inequality has settled at its historically low level and in some of the most egalitarian nations, such as the Nordic countries, there was a slight reversal of the egalitarian trend in the last quarter of the twentieth century.

However, in a longer perspective modern European nations are less unequal than in the past. What lies behind the historical march towards a less unequal society? The most obvious explanation is the rise of mass education in the twentieth century, which raised and equalized the skill levels of people most of whom were previously deprived of any formal schooling. Mass education and the successive extension of the school-leaving age were the result of two factors: first, the breakthrough of democracy which gave ordinary people a political voice; secondly, the demands from the ever-increasing complexity of production technology. A higher school-leaving age can be seen, at least partly, as a response to the skill shortages that followed from technological change. That explanation would fit into the so-called Kuznets curve hypothesis, named after a Harvard economist, Simon Kuznets. Admittedly, Kuznets suggested on meagre empirical grounds that inequality increased early in the industrialization and modernization phase because of initial skill shortages, only to fall when the supply of skilled workers increased. That process would generate an inverted U-shape for inequality. While researchers cannot agree on whether early industrialization actually increased inequality, there is more unanimity as regards the trends towards narrowing wage gaps in the twentieth century.

11.3 Gender inequality

Most of the income and wage data we have are of recent origin; we have very little evidence of gender-specific wage or income inequality before the nineteenth century. However, there is reason to believe that females on average were paid less than males also before the nineteenth century when pay differences were substantial. Women, on average, earned around half the male wage. When work was very demanding in terms of physical strength, pay differentials reflected the gender-specific physical demands of the job. The little evidence we have suggests that women were paid even less in agriculture, mostly because they did other jobs than men. Physical strength is less relevant in a modern economy because production technology has replaced muscles with machines. Pay differentials still persist, although they have fallen considerably, particularly in the second half of the twentieth century. The gender gap today varies between 30 to 10 per cent and a substantial part of it is due to differences in occupations, education and job experience. Economies where women have a high and lasting participation in the labour market, such as the Nordic countries, have lower gender gaps than economies where labour market participation is interrupted by long and frequent spells of childcare.

What is the role of discrimination in the earnings gap? Discrimination is usually understood as a pay differential which is not explained by differences in skills or more generally human capital. Skills are acquired through formal training, schools and universities, and on-the-job training. Both men and women tend to experience an increase in pay as a function of age or time in the labour force since employees get on-the-job training. Historically the on-the-job training effect has been stronger for men than women as far as we can judge from age-specific wage data for the nineteenth and twentieth centuries.

It is generally agreed that pay differences were smaller between males and females with comparable skills at the time they entered the labour market. The male–female gap tended to increase with increasing age, which probably reflected the fact that females did not obtain the same on-the-job training as males. Females had a disadvantage in that their work history was less regular than that of males. Before the middle of the twentieth century it was normal for females to drop out of the labour market at marriage or after the birth of the first child, which gave employers little incentive to invest in firm-specific training for females. However, as female attachment to the labour market became more permanent we would expect that difference to fall. The decline in the gender gap in the second half of the twentieth century is part of that story. However, pay differentials that we cannot ascribe to observed background factors, that is individual characteristics such as work experience and education, still persist. These discrimination effects are difficult to estimate, but there are studies suggesting a 5 to 10 per cent pay disadvantage of females relative to men with identical skills, job history and training. How can we explain that? The Harvard-based economic historian Claudia Goldin has suggested that discrimination may persist because employers fail to register the true attributes of individuals and stick to average attributes of men and females because the assessment of individuals is costly. For example, the average length of on-the-job training of men is greater than for women, because an average woman's job history is interrupted by giving birth to children. However, there are females with a longer work experience than some men. But employers who infer individuals' attributes from average characteristics fail to see that.

Critics maintain that the discrimination concept used here is too limited, since it only compares pay differentials between equally qualified men and women. They argue that traditional job choices and occupational strategies endorsed by social conventions direct women in to low-paid occupations. A large part of the gender gap was and still is due to the fact that men and women are concentrated in different occupations: women are more numerous in low-paid sectors and in low-paid functions in high-wage sectors. This pattern, critics maintain, correlates with prevailing norms and outright discrimination in the educational system or in the job market, which make women opt for jobs with low skill content and excess supply of labour, which puts downward pressure on wages. It also makes the gender wage gap sensitive to technological change if the ladder reduces the demand for unskilled labour, which it often does. While the educational system failed to given women equal access to education well into the twentieth century it is less true for the 1970s onwards, a period that saw a radical change in the educational choices of women, which are now becoming similar to the choices of men. A telling example from the Nordic countries is the fact that women constituted more than half the students enrolled at Medical Schools around the year 2000 while they were virtually absent a century earlier. Part of the reason why women increasingly opt for a lengthy education is the fact that modern birth control methods make the huge investments needed for such education less risky, since disruptive unplanned births can be and are evaded during the years of study. Since a costly education requires a long pay-off period, day-care institutions that help households to combine work and children probably help as well. There is no denying that male and female students are still not equally distributed across education and jobs. However, the trend towards a more equal access to education is probably behind the slight narrowing of the gender gap. The forces of discrimination are more elusive, as are the forces that still keep a large number of women in training for low-paid jobs.

11.4 World income distribution

Until 1800 mean income, that is GDP per capita, was in the range of 1–5 subsistence incomes, a subsistence income being understood as 400 $PPP (1990); see Chapter 2). While mean income is still at or just above subsistence level in some of the poorest African nations, it has increased since 1800 in Europe, North America and elsewhere, particularly since c.1950. Rising income and productivity differences are clearly a phenomenon of the last 200 years. L. Pritchett suggests that the ratio of per capita income in the richest economy compared to the poorest was almost 9 to 1 by 1870 and 45 to 1 in 1990. The simple explanation is that not all economies have benefited from the advantages of modern economic growth, However, the difficult part of that explanation is of course explaining why some economies, although ever fewer, continue to be unaffected by knowledge and technology transfer, because they will not open up to that transfer or because the educational and institutional pre-conditions are not present.

There is considerable confusion as to recent trends in world income distribution because different measures are used and give widely different results. An appropriate study of world inequality should follow the same strategy as the analysis of inequality within a nation, i.e. it should include all citizens of all nations in the world. This concept is called *global inequality*. That would require a database with income data for all households in the world. However, a large but shrinking number of nations, rich and poor, do not produce or have information for such estimates. With the help of existing data and supporting – but risky – assumptions it is possible to make some conjectures about the evolution of inequality among all citizens in the world from 1970 to the present. There is no clear consensus as to what has actually happened to world inequality, but there is at least agreement that it has not increased, although the assertion that it has fallen is not shared by all. As an increasing number of nations start producing more reliable income surveys we can expect more robust results in the future.

The proposition that world income inequality has not increased since the 1970s may come as a surprise, since it is often argued that it has continued to increase. However, that statement refers to an inequality concept that is not very meaningful. If we take the income per head in each nation and estimate Gini coefficients, then 'un-weighted' inequality, as it is usually called, has increased since 1950, from about 0.45 to 0.55. This approach gives the per capita income of each nation the same weight; Iceland, with a quarter of a million inhabitants, has the same weight as China or India. There is something inherently problematic about this concept, because when China and India experience a growth of per capita income of, say, 8 or 10 per cent per year it affects about a third of the world's population while an increase in Iceland is barely noticeable. Surely we need to take the size of the economies we analyse into consideration to get a more balanced view? If we do, we arrive at what is commonly called 'weighted inequality'. The basis for the analysis is still per capita income in each nation, but each nation is given a weight proportionate to its population. Using this measure we arrive at a decline in inequality, in fact the Gini coefficient falls from 0.55 in 1950 to 0.5 in the year 2000.

The population-weighted measure indicates a fall in world income inequality while the un-weighted shows an increase. Confusing? Not really.

What drives the decline in the population-weighted Gini coefficient is the fact that a number of very populous nations, such as China, India, Vietnam and Indonesia, have experienced fast GDP growth since the 1980s. Clearly, the second measure is preferable to the first.

However, an increase in average GDP per head may conceal increasing inequality within a fast-growing nation. The argument, referred to above as the Kuznets hypothesis, is that early on in the modernization phase the educated labour is scarce and so the premium on it is very high, so that most of the increase in income is reaped by a small number of people with scarce skills. While the validity of the Kuznets curve is disputed for Europe, there is mounting evidence that the recent industrialization in China and India has increased earning differentials. This might explain why we cannot detect a clear decline in global inequality if we factor inequalities within nations into the analysis. The poor nations have advanced in terms of per capita income, but that increase has been unevenly distributed among their citizens.

The findings can be neatly summarized as follows:

1. Unweighted world inequality has increased since 1800 and is still increasing, but this concept is misleading since it neglects the size of the nations which are affected by income growth.

2. Population-weighted world inequality has fallen since *c.* 1950, mainly owing to fast growth of per capita income in low-income nations in Asia.
3. Global inequality seems to be stable, the reason being that the fast increase in per capita income in low-income nations in Asia has not helped the very poor in these nations as much as the rest of the population.

11.5 Towards a broader concept of welfare

So far we have discussed exclusively the distribution of income per head, although we started by saying that income cannot be seen as a guarantee of acquiring welfare or a good life. The United Nations has sponsored an effort to estimate a broader concept of welfare which includes not only income but also other aspects, most notably literacy and school enrolment as well as health as indicated by life expectancy. The reason for including literacy in a welfare measure is straightforward: it helps a citizen to participate in social life and be informed, and to inform others using the written word. Likewise life expectancy is a guide to the general nutritional and health standards of a society and is an important aspect of the quality of life. Both life expectancy and literacy expand the choices that citizens can make; they increase human capabilities. On this basis an attempt has been made to build a so-called Human Development Index, HDI for short, which has three (weighted) components: per capita income, education and life expectancy, and can take a maximum value of 1. The choice of indicators is limited by the availability of data and the weights given to the different indicators are a bit arbitrary – which is admitted by the architects of HDI. While HDI is not an alternative to income as a welfare measure, it does convey additional information. By and large the view that the human condition is worsening and that inequalities are increasing is challenged. The reason is that health and educational standards, as measured by literacy rates, have converged worldwide despite the fact that income differences remain large.

In Figure 11.3 we look at the divergent patterns of GDP per head in constant 1990 $ (right vertical scale) and HDI (left vertical scale) for Western Europe and India.

The Figure demonstrates that important aspects of welfare as expressed by HDI develop differently from income. Comparing Europe with India, which represents a developing nation, it turns out that absolute income difference has increased while the difference in the HDI index has fallen. The reason is entirely due to the fact that India, and poor nations in general, have narrowed the gap with the rich world in terms of literacy and life expectancy.

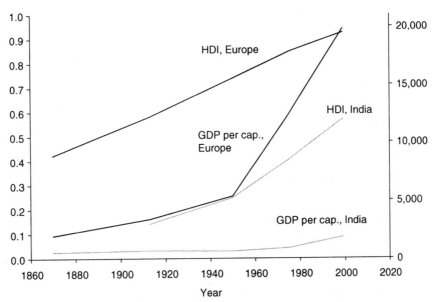

Figure 11.3 HDI and GDP per head, 1870–2000. Sources: N. F. R. Crafts, 'The Human Development Index and changes in standards of living: some historical comparisons, *European Review of Economic History*, 1 (3) (1997), pp. 299–322; A. Maddison, *The World Economy: Historical Statistics* (Paris: OECD, 2003).

11.6 Speculations about future trends in income inequality

What happens to global income inequality in the future will depend on the answers to the following questions.

1. Will all nations eventually enter a phase of modern economic growth or will a significant fraction of nations remain in a state of stagnation?
2. Will latecomers initially grow much faster, say at 8–10 per cent per year, than the rich economies until they finally settle at the lower, 2–3 per cent per year, steady rate of the mature economies?
3. Will the new industrializing nations follow the pattern of Europe and North America and become less unequal after the initial phase of increasing domestic inequality?

If the answer is 'Yes' to all three of these questions, global inequality will diminish in the future and it may in fact already have peaked.

However if the answer is 'No' to one, any one, of the questions it is not possible to make an unambiguous prediction about future trends in global income inequality.

Let us reflect more carefully about the likely answer to the three questions.

The second question is easier to answer than the other two. The historical record clearly indicates that *if* a latecomer enters the growth club, meaning basically that its institutions, educational system and property rights can respond to the opportunities of modern technology, then the initial phase of catch-up will be associated with fast economic growth. But, turning now to the first question, can we be sure that all nations will get their institutions right, manage to reform markets and open up to capital and technology transfer?

The European experience has some bearing on that question since almost all European nations now have the characteristics of modern economic growth. However, the historical record indicates that the process of joining the European 'growth club' has been uneven and lengthy. Before 1914 only a few nations in north-west Europe had actually converged on the then leading economy in Europe, the UK, and it was not until well after 1950 that the Iberian economies and Ireland started the catch-up process which happened even later for the socialist economies of Eastern Europe. As the latter case demonstrates, institutional change mattered, but increased openness was also an important factor in the case of Spain, Portugal and Ireland. So the success story of Europe is one of almost all economies finally joining the growth club. Can this be repeated on a worldwide scale? The obvious objection to generalizing from the European experience is the homogeneity of Europe in terms of institutions and culture. A glimmer of hope is the diversity of past institutional experience in two of the Asian latecomers, China and India. The latter, a populous democracy with strong vested interests fighting for privileges, has been able to generate the fastest growth in its history. The former, China, has an authoritarian political elite combining socialist rhetoric with capitalist and market principles and nervously monitoring popular protest. So why are both nations marching in the same direction economy-wise? One possible answer is that the gains from modern economic growth are now so apparent, thanks to easily accessible information technologies, that political elites, whatever their political orientation, cannot ignore them. If they do they will be reminded by their increasingly enlightened subjects that the people will not tolerate lost opportunities. But the real testing ground for the idea that all nations might enjoy modern economic growth is no longer Asia but Africa, still largely unaffected by catch-up growth and where political mismanagement still prevails in far too many nations.

The third question, finally: will the mounting inequality within modernizing and fast-growing economies in Asia and elsewhere trigger off a mass education campaign which will reduce the inequality of domestic earnings? There are strong reasons to believe that the pattern in Europe and North America will be replicated. Sustained economic growth is not likely without a broadening of the skills base. If this happens, the trend towards increasing domestic inequality in low-income but fast-growing economies may turn out to be transitory rather than permanent.

Summary

European economies were more unequal 500 years ago and even 100 years ago than today, both absolutely and relative to the maximum inequality possible. The drift towards less pronounced inequality is primarily a twentieth-century phenomenon. Europe is relatively more egalitarian than the USA and in particular Latin America. The persistent high inequality in Latin America has prompted an inquiry into the role of inequality in the growth process. One line of argument maintains that high inequality may impede growth because it stimulates political and social conflict, which causes uncertainty about the rules of the economic game, which ultimately harms investment.

The major factor in reducing domestic inequality is open access to education. Inequality related to unequal flows of income from property has shown more inertia because the accumulation of wealth is less linked to education and relies more on inheritance. Global inequality was modest until 1800, when it started to explode because an exclusive club of economies started to grow in a world of otherwise stagnant or slow-growing economies. What divided the world was unequal access to technology. An increasing number of populous nations have been able to join the 'growth club' since 1950. This has halted the trend towards increasing global inequality, which may decline during the present century.

Suggestions for further reading

A splendid introduction to the study of inequality is B. Milanovic, *Worlds Apart: Measuring International and Global Inequality* (Princeton University Press, 2005). It is worth looking at Milanovic's homepage for recent assessments of trends.

Another study by Milanovic, written jointly with P. H. Lindert and J. G. Williamson, 'Measuring ancient inequality', a World Bank Working Paper, gives valuable insight into the long-term evolution of income inequality. See also Xavier Sala-i-Martin, 'The myth of exploding income inequality in Europe and the world', in H. Kierzkowski (ed.), *Europe and Globalization* (London: Palgrave Macmillan, 2002),which discusses global inequality.

The Handbook of Income Distribution, ed. by A. B. Atkinson and F. Bourguignon (Amsterdam: Elsevier, 2000) is a very valuable companion for comparative and historical analysis, as is a recent book by Atkinson, *The Changing Distributions of Earnings in OECD Countries* (Oxford University Press, 2008).

There are a number of historical gender gap studies for Britain. See H. M. Boot and J. H. Macdonald, 'New estimates of age- and sex-specific earnings and the male–female earnings gap in British cotton industry, 1833–1906', *Economic History Review* 61(2) (2008), pp. 380–408. The reference list for this article contains a good number of relevant studies. M. Keniston McIntosh takes a long view in *Working Women in English Society 1300–1620* (Cambridge University Press, 2005). J. Burnette, *Gender, Work and Wages in the Industrial Revolution* (Cambridge University Press, 2008) is a provocative and well-researched study. The author over-states when she argues that practically no gender gap can be explained by discrimination, but it is a useful reminder that to a considerable extent wage gaps can be explained by differences in skills, physical strength and formal or informal schooling. C. Goldin's *Understanding the Gender Gap: An Economic History of American Women* (Oxford University Press, 1990) is essential reading.

Several attempts at predicting world inequality are worth looking at; see in particular C. I. Jones, 'Evolution of world income distribution', *Journal of Economic Perspectives* 11(3)(1997), pp. 19–36 and R. E. Lucas, 'Some macro-economics for the 21st century', *Journal of Economic Perspectives* 14(1)(2000), pp. 159–68.

12 Globalization and its challenge to Europe

12.1 Globalization and the law of one price

The hype around globalization in early twenty-first century political and economic debates may convey an impression that we now are in an entirely new phase of economic development. This chapter will show that the presumption is wrong. A dose of elementary economic history is often helpful when the popular media forget about the past.

Globalization is market integration on a world scale. Market integration means that domestic markets are increasingly dependent on international markets. Prices and hence factor rewards will reflect global rather than local demand and supply conditions. Globalization is the product of intensified trade, capital mobility and migration. In that process prices, interest rates and sometimes wages tend to converge and react faster to international shocks. The first wave of globalization started in the middle of the nineteenth century when barriers to trade, migration and capital mobility were abolished or weakened at the same time as the speed of information transmission increased. In most respects markets were as globalized around 1900 as they were at the beginning of the present century. In fact labour mobility across borders was less restricted before 1914 than it is now. However, there was an anti-globalization backlash early in the twentieth century with two World Wars and the Great Depression. That policy reversal affected commodity, labour and capital markets to the extent that the late nineteenth-century globalization level was not regained until the 1970s or 1980s, when the second globalization period gained momentum.

Market integration operates through trade and arbitrage and the ultimate manifestation of a fully integrated market is the *law of one price**. The law of one price proposes that the price of identical goods that are traded is the same in all geographical locations. This is strictly true, of course, only if transport and transaction costs are zero, which they are not. Transport costs have fallen but remain considerable in commodity trade. As long as transport costs are high there is a good deal of scope for domestic price variations before it pays to import (export) the good from (to) an external market. When transport and other transaction costs, including tariffs, fall, the band with its upper and lower limit within which domestic prices can vary will become narrow. For financial assets transaction costs are low and price differences are therefore close to zero for identical assets traded in different markets.

For commodities a more adequate formulation of the law of one price is that *the (absolute value) of the price difference between identical goods in two geographically separated markets is equal to or smaller than the transport and transaction costs associated with moving the commodity from one market to the other.* If the two markets actually trade the good then the price difference should be strictly equal to transport and transaction costs. If the price difference is smaller than transport cost it does not pay to trade.

Historically the major obstacles to the operation of the law of one price and to market integration have been tariffs, the high costs of transport, and the unreliability and slowness of information transmission. If you are not sure about the actual price at other locations it is too risky to trade. The law of one price operated first within regions and nations, and later in clusters of neighbouring nations as transport and information transmission improved.

The law of one price has two major implications. First, the price difference between identical goods traded in geographically separated markets will decline as transport and transaction costs and tariffs fall. This is called price convergence. Second, any deviation from the law of one price will prompt faster price adjustments so that the law is restored. Both the decline in transport costs and more efficient transmission of information are primarily nineteenth-century phenomena.

What are the economic mechanisms securing the law of one price? The short answer is trade and arbitrage. If it turns out that the price difference of a given commodity, say between Genoa and London, exceeds the transport and transaction costs it will be profitable for traders to import that good to Genoa. As a result, prices in Genoa will fall and prices in London may increase because of additional demand. By the middle of the nineteenth century all major cities in Europe were linked by the telegraph, and if information was transmitted by telegraph the price difference would be known within hours. Price adjustments will start immediately because there are usually inventories of goods in most markets in a trading network. Genoa merchants will therefore start selling their inventories, anticipating shipments from London and a lower price in the future. The price will start falling in Genoa before the new shipments arrive. If information travels by mail then the adjustment will be slower, simply because it takes longer for the information to reach merchants. A similar argument applies to the price of financial assets. If it is cheaper to borrow in London rather than Milan speculators will borrow in London rather than Milan and interest rates will increase in London and fall in Milan. It follows that integrated capital markets with few restrictions on capital mobility will tend to have converging rates of interest.

Labour markets are exceptional because restrictions on mobility are and were more persistent there than in capital or commodity markets. That is also a major reason why convergence of wage levels across nations is more subdued. Persistent wage differences remain because labour varies in terms of skills, human capital, and access to physical capital: in short, productivity. The law of one price applies only to strictly identical commodities or factors of production.

Globalization means a high inter-dependence of domestic and global price and interest rate movements. It reduces the price-setting market power of domestic industry as well as the power of trade unions to set nominal wages and negotiate costly improvements in working conditions. In a globalized world the negative link between domestic labour cost and employment is stronger than in a less open economy. The mechanisms at work are set out in Figure 12.1. Consider an industry in an economy with a downward-sloping labour demand curve and an upward-sloping labour supply curve. The labour demand curve, D, is actually derived from the demand curve for the products produced by the industry. When the economy concerned is undergoing a process of globalization the demand curve, for its products and hence for labour, turns counter-clockwise and becomes flatter: in technical jargon, it becomes more elastic as it shifts from DD to D'D'.

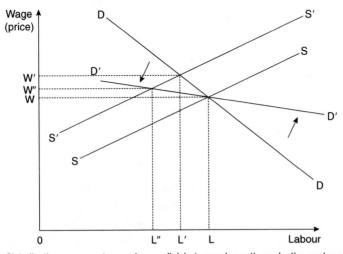

Figure 12.1   Globalization means a stronger inverse link between domestic production costs and employment

The reason is that demand for the industry's products, and consequently for labour, will be increasingly sensitive to changes in wages and hence prices as competition increases. If trade unions increase wages, a shift in the supply curve from SS to S'S', the negative effect on employment will be much larger in a globalized economy with labour demand curve D'D' than in an economy facing less international competition with labour demand curve DD. The employment effect will be 0L' – 0L". This argument holds under the 'all other things being equal' condition. A wage increase which compensates a rise in labour productivity will not shift the labour supply curve upwards at all, if we think of the wage as the wage paid per effective labour input per hour. We should not rush to the conclusion that globalization imposes welfare losses on economies because of the unemployment risk. Globalization constrains the bargaining power of trade unions simply because it limits the market power of firms.

12.2 What drives globalization?

The discussion in the previous section indicated that the major breakthrough of globalization took place in the nineteenth century, particularly after 1950, though there were tendencies towards price convergence in the world economy as far back as the seventeenth and eighteenth centuries. What were the forces that drove market integration and globalization? The short answer is *politics* and *technology*. On the policy side, tariff policy, financial market de-regulation and immigration policy were paramount. But economic policy is subject to political processes of advances and retreats. Globalization has its winners and losers and the balance of pro- and anti-globalization forces have shifted in history. Periods of trade liberalization are interrupted by free trade backlashes, leading to protectionist legislation as explored in Chapter 8. The basic reason is that trade liberalization makes prices converge, which alters the competitive position of domestic producers. Scarce factors of production which, because of their scarcity, have been well rewarded in the past lose from free trade. The adjustment required involves structural changes forcing people from their land or jobs before they find new jobs in new occupations. There was, however, a general drift towards free trade since after the Second World War and in the seventy years before the First World War. Europe's external tariff level for manufactured goods is lower now than at any time in history, and tariffs have been abolished entirely within the European Union, while agricultural protection remains high towards non-European exporters and higher than before 1930. Capital market openness has also been contested repeatedly because it constrains the monetary policy of governments.

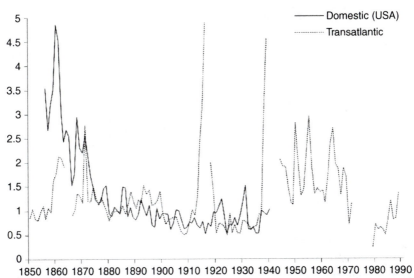

Figure 12.2   Real domestic (US rail) and transatlantic freight rates, 1850–1990 (1884 = 1). Note: Real freight rates are measured by the so-called *freight factor,* which in this case is nominal freight rates for wheat deflated by the nominal wheat price. Own estimates based on data in G. Federico and K. G. Persson, 'Market integration and convergence in the world wheat market 1800–2000', in T. J. Hatton, K. H.O'Rourke and A. M. Taylor (eds.), *The New Comparative Economic History: Essays in Honour of Jeffrey G. Williamson* (Cambridge, Mass.: MIT Press, 2007), p. 99.

The technological factors contributing to globalization are primarily those linked to transaction and transport costs. Transport costs fell in the nineteenth century, but it is not clear that they have fallen since. The most dramatic reduction in transport costs was not in transatlantic freight rates but in domestic railway rates. Previously landlocked areas of the Americas and Russia were linked to ports in the second half of the nineteenth century, which made areas such as the American Midwest part of the world economy.

Figure 12.2 suggests that real transatlantic freight rates over the last 150 years have varied, but there is no clear trend. However, railway rates declined dramatically in the nineteenth century.

Information transmission costs have fallen since the early nineteenth century while speed has increased. Speed of information is important because much of the price adjustment in global markets is driven by new information about commodity prices. The major technological breakthrough in information technology was the telegraph, which had connected major European markets by *c.*1850; and by the early 1870s the whole world was 'wired'. Before the telegraph information travelled at about the same speed as or slightly faster than commodities. As the costs fell the accessibility of information also increased, which improved the efficiency of markets. If information is hard to get it may remain private. If trade takes place and insiders refuse to share information the risk of collusion is large. In the second half of the nineteenth century a commercial press developed which published telegraphically transmitted information. By 1870 a merchant in a small city in France could read *L'Echo des Halles*, a daily paper with business news, and gain information about yesterday's prices and market conditions in St Petersburg, Berlin, Chicago and Buenos Aires. While twenty-first-century technology permits instant access to information, the great leap forward in information transmission technology was from private information transmitted by post to the telegraph and the emergence of a specialized commercial press in the middle of the nineteenth century. During the remainder of that century price differences which could not be explained by trade costs gradually declined – probably a consequence of improved access to accurate information by traders.

By the 1850s commodity market inefficiencies were showing up in fairly large price differentials, which could not be fully explained by trade costs but must have been due to excess profits linked to entry barriers to trade or imperfect information.

12.3 The phases of globalization

Three important characteristics are associated with market integration: price convergence, faster price adjustment in the domestic economy to world market events, and an increase in the volume of trade, capital flows and migration flows. By looking more closely at the timing of these indicators we can get a better picture of the globalization process in recent history; we will investigate capital markets, commodity markets and labour markets in turn.

12.3.1 Capital markets

Currency markets have existed on a European level since early medieval times, and moneychangers in major trading spots were well accustomed to dealing with hundreds of different coins. The *bill of exchange** developed to settle imbalances in trade between markets and became an instrument of credit. But was arbitrage efficient in that identical assets earned the same return (profit) at different locations? To answer that question we would need a lot of detailed and frequent data which is not readily available. However, for some major financial centres, such as London and Amsterdam in the seventeenth and eighteenth centuries, we can actually test how efficient arbitrage was. Both markets traded shares in the East India Companies, for example, and Larry

Neal, a financial history scholar, has shown that not only were price movements highly correlated but furthermore there were no systematic unexplained price differences between the two markets for identical assets. However, London and Amsterdam were the leading financial centres in the eighteenth century, with frequent and efficient postal services linking the two cities. We cannot assume that smaller and peripheral financial markets were as well integrated.

The advent of transcontinental telegraphs in the 1860s and 1870s created the pre-conditions for global capital markets. Information now travelled in minutes or hours rather than weeks.

The major advantage of international capital flows is that domestic investments need not be constrained by domestic savings, as noted in Chapter 9. Nations with large investment needs but low income and savings can therefore borrow in order to invest. It is important to stress that the impact of globalization here is to relieve economies of the potentially harmful effect of insufficient savings on growth. One measure of capital market integration is therefore the absolute size of the *current account** or net exports (exports minus imports). There is a downside, however. Although it is believed that international capital markets can discipline high-spending governments which borrow instead of taxing their citizens, history provides abundant examples of governments which default on international debt. Global capital markets allow large current account deficits or surpluses as a share of GDP. Most latecomers to industrialization benefited from foreign borrowing in their drive towards modernization at the end of the nineteenth century and the last third of the twentieth. Looking at the historical record the pattern of the current account imbalance (as a share of GDP) increased in the nineteenth century to reach an all-time high prior to 1914 – around 6 to 8 per cent of GDP in some nations – only to decline in the interwar period. Current account imbalances remained low for a long time after the Second World War, but increased again after capital market deregulation in the 1980s. The link between domestic saving and domestic investment has remained strong, which is a bit puzzling. In a global capital market an increase in domestic savings should not necessarily impact on domestic investment. Capital should flow to where rewards are highest, but there is a home bias in investment behaviour which may be explained by information asymmetries. That is, domestic investors are better informed about home market conditions than about foreign markets, to the extent that they might foresee profitable opportunities abroad. When investigating the time profile of the home bias it turns out that the world was more globalized pre-1930, with outward-looking investors. The Great Depression and the breakdown of international capital markets restored a strong link between domestic investment and domestic saving, as noted by Maurice Obstfeld and Alan Taylor. Only in recent decades has that link been weakened, so that about 25 per cent of additional savings head abroad, as against over 40 per cent in the first globalization phase before the Great Depression.

A consequence of less globalized capital markets was that current account imbalances, positive or negative, were smaller and short-lived. Economies before 1914 were permitted to run current account deficits for long periods. The Scandinavian countries and Russia, to name but a few, did so before 1914. Although current account imbalances (the absolute value as a share of GDP) are typically smaller and transitory, gross capital flows have been much larger since 1980. In the first globalization period nations were typically either debtors or creditors, with the UK, France and Germany as the major creditors and Russia, Scandinavia, the British Empire and Latin America as major debtors. At present, nations typically have foreign liabilities as well as foreign assets. Residents of a nation – say Germany – own assets in foreign countries, but foreign residents also own assets in Germany. The magnitude of the flows, specifically of short-term capital, is causing problems for developing economies. Latin America and East Asia were troubled by large fluctuations in foreign investments in the late 1990s which had severe negative macroeconomic effects. As a consequence a more sceptical view of the merits of unregulated capital markets emerged once it was perceived that economies which had implemented capital controls weathered the crisis more successfully.

We have noted two distinct periods of capital market integration: the first in the fifty years before 1914, the International Gold Standard period, and the second starting with the break-up of the Bretton Woods System in the 1970s. Is that pattern also visible if we trace the efficiency of capital markets? As hinted at above, efficiency is based on arbitrage that reduces price differences between similar assets. However, if there are restrictions on capital mobility we can expect arbitrage to be incomplete, making, say, interest rate differences between nations high. Figure 12.3 illustrates this phenomenon by showing actual USA–UK interest rate differences as well as the *standard deviation**, a measure of *variance**. A similar pattern is found within European capital markets. In an efficient capital market the interest rate difference (controlled for the exchange rate risk) should be zero. Figure 12.3 confirms that the interest rate differential was converging on zero before 1914 and was pretty close to it after 1980. The year 1914 marked the suspension of the gold standard, and in the 1980s capital markets were again liberalized after the barriers erected by the Bretton Woods System had been dismantled. In between these two periods there were large interest rate differentials, which were to be expected since there were barriers to capital mobility.

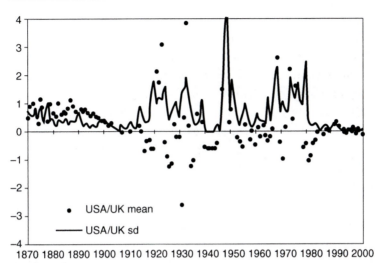

Figure 12.3 Nominal interest rate differentials between the USA and the UK on similar assets, 1870–2000. Source: Obstfeld and Taylor, *Global Capital Markets: Integration, Crisis and Growth,* p. 90.

What was the direction and magnitude of capital flows? In the nineteenth century the UK dominated and was in a sense the banker of the world, but it was joined by other lenders such France and Germany by the end of the century. As late as 1914 about half the stock of foreign capital was British, but the figure fell to about 15 per cent during the twentieth century, when the USA emerged as the major foreign investor. The stock of capital has increased not only in absolute terms but also relative to world GDP. In the early phase of the Industrial Revolution foreign investments were insignificant; it was only after 1850 that the stock of foreign capital as a fraction of world GDP increased to some 20 per cent. That share then fell in the 1930s and the Bretton Woods period; it did not regain pre-First World War levels until the 1980s, after which it exploded. By the end of the century the total stock of foreign capital was at par with the value of world GDP.

The country distribution at the receiving end has also changed dramatically. In the first globalization phase the developing world received a fair share – about a third – of foreign investments, but that share fell to about 10 per cent of all foreign investments by the end of the twentieth century. Behind this pattern lies the growing role of multinationals in foreign investment: multinational firms tend to invest in middle to high-income nations where there is a market for their goods. In the past a considerable part of foreign investments in developing nations went into raw material extraction, such as mining, and to as infrastructure investment in rail and telegraph.

All the aspects of capital market globalization which we have discussed point to the same U-shaped pattern. There is one period from about 1870 to 1914, and in some cases up to the Great Depression, with efficient capital markets and high capital mobility which permitted current account deficits or surpluses. Then comes a long period stretching from the Interwar years to just after the Second World War with low scores on capital mobility (it is restricted on the capital account), low levels of capital market efficiency as witnessed by interest rate divergence, and current accounts were allowed only short and transitory deviations from balance. As indicated in our previous analysis of the Bretton Woods System in Chapter 9, interest rate differentials in this period were a deliberate choice of policymakers. The disappointing experience of the discipline imposed by the gold standard in the interwar period made policymakers favour a degree of domestic monetary autonomy, which required capital mobility regulation. However, with the collapse of the Bretton Woods System came a revival of global capital markets.

12.3.2 Commodity markets

Like that of capital markets, commodity market globalization can be measured by price convergence, but there is a difference in that commodity trade also involves high transport costs and often tariffs. We will therefore not find that price differentials between markets separated by great geographical distances converge on zero. As an additional indicator of commodity market integration we will use the speed of price adjustments. It makes a great deal of difference whether a world market price shock takes years to affect domestic prices or only days. Domestic producers do of course have much more time to adjust in the former case and therefore enjoy some market power. There was some price convergence among markets in the Baltic area in the eighteenth century, and between the Baltic ports and European ports on the Atlantic coast. The spice trade and trade in tropical commodities also experienced limited price convergence as early as the seventeenth century. However, price differences between markets linked by long-haul trade, e.g. between the Americas and Europe, did not show strong convergence until the nineteenth century. Indeed it seems as if convergence was a nineteenth-century phenomenon; in the twentieth century prices again tended to diverge. There are two reasons for that. The reduction in transport costs petered out and for some products, particularly agricultural commodities, tariffs began to rise. For industrial commodities, which enjoy close to free trade conditions, price convergence gained momentum from trade liberalization after the Second World War.

Figure 12.4 shows convergence of wheat prices in the American and UK markets. The UK has been a major importer of wheat since the early nineteenth century and the price level was above that in the USA. Over time the

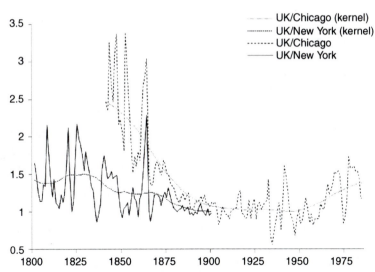

Figure 12.4   Price convergence between the UK and the USA 1800–1975. Price of wheat in UK relative to price in Chicago and New York. Data from Federico and Persson, 'Market integration and convergence in the world wheat market 1800–2000', Note: The convergence of prices is slightly exaggerated because there was a fall in the quality of British wheat relative to that of US wheat in the second half of the nineteenth century. In the nineteenth century quality-adjusted price differentials corresponded to the transport cost from the American Midwest to the UK amounting to *c.* some 20 per cent of the US price.

price differential fell, especially against Chicago, from about 2.5 times the UK price to between 1.2 and 1.5 times the UK price. It fluctuated strongly in the interwar period and tended to increase after the Second World War owing to higher freight rates and as a consequence of the UK joining the Common market (EEC/EU) and adopting its agricultural *protectionism**.

For continental Europe the price convergence was more short-lived because protectionist forces managed to impose tariffs on grain imports from the Americas, first in the 1880s and later in the interwar period. Some agricultural tariffs were increased under the EEC's Common Agricultural Policy so that in the 1980s prices in Europe were twice the level of American export wheat prices. By and large violations of the law of one price are policy-related, that is, price divergences are caused by trade policies. Price gaps on industrial goods were generally smaller than for agricultural goods in the second half of the twentieth century.

When we focus on the volume of trade and the trade/income ratio (i.e. exports as a share of GDP) we see the ratio increase in the nineteenth century from a mere 3–5 per cent to 20–25 per cent for small economies and the UK, and 10–15 per cent for larger economies. That ratio fell in the interwar years and did not regain pre-First World War levels until the 1970s or 1980s. However, the non-trading public sector increased its relative share of GDP after the

1950s, which means that trade-exposed sectors, in particular manufacturing, now have a much higher trade/income ratio measured in terms of manufacturing exports as a share of that sector's added value: between 50 to 80 per cent. Some European nations have developed formal or informal rules requiring the trade-exposed sectors to set the standard for wage increases. The rationale for this policy is to evade a situation where public sector wage explosions trigger off compensatory wage rises in the sectors exposed to international competition, which in the end would ruin their competitive stance. These wage policies can work only if there is a fair degree of central guidance in wage negotiations, however.

In a poorly integrated economy a local price shock will have a long life. Integration speeds up price adjustments and makes shocks transitory. The speed at which the shock is 'absorbed' is an indicator of the extent of market integration. Before the nineteenth century it took a very long time for prices to adjust. For example, if the price of grain increased in an important export hub such as Danzig in the Baltic, that price shock would affect the price in Amsterdam, an importer of Baltic grain, and eventually reach the Mediterranean. But there would be no strong impact on prices elsewhere until months and sometimes up to a year later. Within a region or in a small nation like the Netherlands adjustment speed was higher, but still nowhere near the speed recorded in trans-continental markets by the end of the nineteenth century. By that time most adjustments took less than a week for internationally traded goods, and on modern commodity markets it is a matter of hours.

12.3.3 Labour markets

Convergence of real wages is much more partial and incomplete than the convergence observed in other markets. The convergence mechanism is migration of labour from nations with excess labour and low wages to nations with excess demand and high wages. It turns out that the wage differential between receiving and sending nations is a powerful determinant of the size of migration flows, but there are a number of barriers to migration. There is a 'home culture bias' in the sense that workers are reluctant to move to nations where there are not many previous immigrants from their own country. Before 1850 transport costs were also prohibitively high for those who were most likely to benefit from migrating across the Atlantic. As emigration from a particular country gained momentum it reduced the initial wage gap between receiving and sending nations and eventually migration fell back from its high level.

Before mass migration, which started after c.1850, there were only small flows of voluntary migration, but substantial flows of forced migration. Within

Europe migration was often related to religious persecution, for example the expulsion of the Jews from Spain at the end of the fourteenth century, or of Protestants from France in the seventeenth century. This type of migration often included skilled workers and professionals, which helped to diffuse technology, e.g. in printing, mining and iron manufacturing, and institutional innovations. The history of financial institutions in Europe is intimately linked to migration of Italians and Jews. European migration to the New World (the Americas and Australia) was also modest until the nineteenth century. For the entire period between 1650 and 1800 the flow of Europeans to the Americas was smaller than for a single year in the late nineteenth or early twentieth century: slightly below one million. However, Europeans orchestrated a massive forced migration of Africans to the Americas – an estimated seven million of them until the slave trade was prohibited in the first quarter of the nineteenth century.

After the decline of the slave trade, Europe became the major source of emigrants for the New World. There was internal European migration from poor areas in southern and eastern Europe to Europe's industrializing core but the extent of that migration was small relative to European migration to the Americas before 1914. The first wave of mass migration started after the disturbing harvest shocks of the 1840s, at about 300,000 per year, but by the late 1870s, migration had reached some 600,000 per year. Migrants from the British Isles, Germany and Scandinavia were still in the majority at this stage; it was not until *c.*1900–1910 century that migrants from eastern and southern Europe became the majority of a total which by then was above a million per year. Most of the European migrants headed for North America, but with the increasing share of southern Europeans in the migrant flow South America became a more attractive destination owing to similarities of language and culture. The time for a steam-powered transatlantic passage had by then fallen to about two weeks; sail took over twice as long. The price had fallen so far that some of the migration from Italy was seasonal. The dull winter season in the northern hemisphere was the busy harvest season in the southern hemisphere and attracted seasonally unemployed Italians.

Mass migration reached its highest levels just before the First World War, but afterwards European migration never picked up again, partly due to immigration barriers erected in the USA and subsequently by most other nations in the New World. After having introduced a literacy test, the USA established country of origin quotas in the 1920s mainly to reduce the inflow of low-skilled immigrants from southern and eastern Europe. Since the 1930s, levels of European migration to the New World, that is the European offshoots in the Americas, Australia and New Zealand, have been similar to or lower than those of the 1840s.

The fall in European migration, both internal and external, was not unexpected. The wage gap between potential host country and country of origin had declined *because* of mass migration. That decline had already reduced flows from north west Europe by the end of the 19th century. Migration was not the only factor causing *real wage** convergence within Europe and between Europe and the New World. Trade in cheap grain entering Europe from the New World led to a fall in consumer prices which contributed to a rise in European real wages. Looking at the spread of real wages (measured by the *coefficient of variation**) of a sample of European nations and their offshoots in North America we observe that it falls in the two globalization periods, that is from 1870 to 1913 and after 1950. Before 1850 there were no signs of wage convergence – rather the reverse.

It is worth noting that what is true for this sample of nations, which impacted on each other due to intense migratory flows, capital flows and trade, would *not* be true for a wider sample of economies including developing economies. There are limits to what trade and migration can do to cause wage convergence. A significant part of wage differences across nations is related to differences in labour productivity, as noted in Chapter 11.

12.4 Globalization backlash: three cases

12.4.1 Trade openness and migration

The period of mass migration came to an end in the early twentieth century. A migration backlash was already visible in agitation in formerly labour-scarce New World economies, such as the USA, at the end of the nineteenth century, but was not widely acted on until the 1920s. The USA restricted the inflow of Asians before then, however. There is an apparent paradox in that economies which used to have open access for migrants were usually protectionist compared to Europe. It is a paradox, as noted by the economic historians Timothy Hatton and Jeffrey G. Williamson, because trade and migration have the same effects on workers' wages. A massive inflow of immigrants will constrain domestic wages because the labour supply increases. However, imports of commodities which are produced by low-paid workers abroad will push down commodity prices, and in the end constrain wages in domestic industry that is competing with imports. Restrictions on immigration were eased after the Second World War, but not to the extent that mass migration was again permitted. However, the trade policies of formerly protectionist New World nations have changed fundamentally in that tariffs have been reduced substantially.

The New World has transformed policy priorities from *protectionism* and free migration to free trade and constrained migration. Europe returned to its free trade tradition after the Second World War, but also restricted immigration. The paradox remains in that only one of the two convergence forces is opposed, but a different one in the first and second globalization periods.

Some critics of globalization maintain that it leads to a worsening of working conditions in Europe. The historical record does not support this pessimistic assessment. On the contrary, openness, defined as the share of trade in *national income*, was positively associated with good working conditions. Known as 'labour compact', working conditions include legislation on hours of work, health hazards at work, and unemployment and sick leave insurance. Figure 12.5 demonstrates this positive relationship for a sample of European nations on the eve of the First World War. Open economies, i.e. those with trade shares above 30 percent of *national income**, such as Germany (GER), the UK, Sweden (SWE) and the Netherlands (NET) score high on both trade openness and the labour compact index (a measure of working conditions and insurance coverage), while Russia (RUS), Spain (SP) and Finland (FIN) rank low on both indicators.

Figure 12.5 disproves the idea that openness means a 'race to the bottom' as far as working conditions are concerned. In the first globalization era Michael Huberman has documented a 'race to the top', which means that the most advanced labour protection standards were imitated and implemented by other economies as they became more open. It turns out that this historical pattern is not unique to the first globalization period but is also true for the second. D. Rodrik found that there was a positive relationship between the openness of an economy and welfare spending as a proportion of *national income* in a much larger sample of economies towards the end of the twentieth century. The logic is compelling. Open economies are more susceptible to shocks from the international economy, and that translates into demands for tighter safety nets.

12.4.2 The retreat from the world economy

In the early phase of globalization a particular division of labour evolved in which exports of manufactured goods came from Europe while the rest of the world, including North America, primarily exported food and raw materials. There is an erroneous belief that agriculture is not capable of fast productivity growth and rising income. However, the conditions for modernization relying on agriculture as an export sector changed after the Great Depression. Food exports suffered and there was a sharp fall in prices. Economies locked into

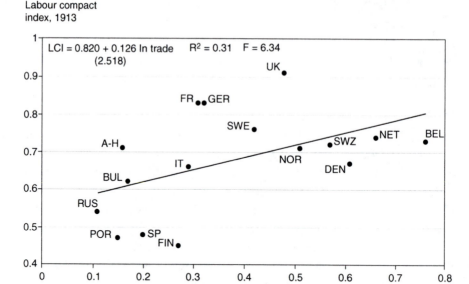

Figure 12.5   Openness and labour standards in 1913. Source: M. Huberman and W. Lewchuk, 'European economic integration and the labour compact, 1850–1913', *European Review of Economic History* 7(1) (2003), p. 29.

agricultural specialization in the first globalization period were met by *protectionism** and farm support in North America and Europe in the 1930s. Rather than dismantling protectionist policies in the general drift towards free trade since the 1950s these policies have been strengthened by Europe and the USA, although there are signs of attempts to reform and weaken farm support in both continents. Furthermore the design of farm support often increases production in Europe and the surplus output has in some periods depressed world market prices. In the developing world this experience led to a reorientation in economic policy after the Second World War. This was due not only to the experience of the immediate past but also to a belief that modernization based on food and raw material exports was not sustainable because food prices could be expected to fall in relative terms in the long run. This view gained currency in the 1950s and 1960s and inspired many developing nations to start import substitution industrialization, often aided by tariff protection or government subsidies to industries judged to need infant industry protection. Several Latin American and Asian economies became more inward looking and partially withdrew from the global economy. It is true that the frequency of major shocks to output in Latin America has been about twice that of Europe since the late nineteenth century. However, there is no evidence that the vulnerability to growth disasters is linked to the extent of openness to trade.

The results of the re-orientation of economic policy were mixed. By and large the long-run growth experience of Latin America was disappointing in the twentieth century. There were some initial industrializing spurts, as was to be expected from so-called infant industry protection. However, the infant tended not to grow up, i.e. tariff-protected industries did not become competitive internationally and protection, which was at first thought of as transitory, became permanent. Although industrial tariffs erected by developing world economies remain higher than those of Europe, they have fallen considerably since the 1970s. The group of economies which experimented with import substitution industrialization had average tariffs as high as 50 per cent as late as 1975, but tariffs have more than halved since. Industrialization based on import substitution has generally been abandoned as a viable modernization strategy. There is a reason for this. If a nation imports a certain good it may be because it does not have a *comparative advantage** in producing it.

12.4.3 The tale of the twin farm protests

In the middle of the nineteenth century vast areas of land in the Americas and Australia were occupied by settlers from Europe. Cheap, fertile land and falling transport, in particular domestic freight, rates led to a 'grain invasion' of Europe, which lowered prices of farm products both absolutely and relative to other goods. Farmers and landowners in Europe demanded protection, and got it in most nations. Denmark, the UK and a few other nations remained free traders. However, there were conflicts surrounding the free trade issue. Workers and industrialists benefited from the fall in consumer prices, and trade unions in Europe were as a rule ardent free traders. By the 1870s and 1880s landed interests in many European nations, such as France, Germany, Italy and Sweden, succeeded in restoring some protection against the New World grain invasion. At about the same time and more surprisingly, American farmers, particularly in the newly settled areas, protested against alleged economic hardship. From 1875 to 1900 there was a general fall in prices worldwide, but the conventional view is that *real* grain *prices** increased in the USA. So why did farmers in the US revolt? We need to understand that falling transport costs (specifically domestic rail rates) led to a gradual extension of the area of grain production. When rail rates fell this extended the distance between consuming centres and producing centres. American economic historians have generally dismissed the farm protests and argued that they cannot be explained by adverse economic conditions because the real price of grain did not fall, say, in Chicago, where it actually increased. However, evidence based on what happened to prices at a specific point of production or trade, such as Chicago, is misleading because the centre of production moved further away over time. The relevant grain price is a weighted average of prices in different regions, where the weights are given by the share of each region in total production. Measured in this way real prices fell! But there are regional differences. Production centres closer to the ports on the eastern seaboard, in the former frontier areas, actually experienced a rise in price. As a consequence the *relative* income of new frontier farmers fell relative to income in neighbouring states, which may have been an additional reason for the discontent in areas of recent settlement. It is well known that so-called relative deprivation is a matter of concern in protest movements. The argument is explored more rigorously in Appendix 12.1.

Summary

The story told in this chapter is that of two major waves in liberalization and globalization, namely the second half of the nineteenth century and the second half of the twentieth. The earlier globalization was characterized by an almost simultaneous liberalization of capital, labour and commodity markets, whereas the globalization since the Second World War has been more uneven and incomplete. Migration policies still remain regulatory, inhibiting the flow of migrants across continents and nations, which did not happen in the nineteenth century. The migration backlash started in the New World when migrants started arriving from nations with wage levels far below those of the host country and of the first wave of European migrants. At present migration policy is again aimed at barring migrants from low-income nations, but the European Union is a single labour market. Although commodity markets have seen an impressive dismantling of formal and informal trade barriers, agriculture remains almost unaffected by free trade and we are therefore far removed from the global food markets of the late nineteenth-century world economy. Capital markets also continued to be regulated well into the 1980s. That was largely a heritage from the Bretton Woods era, which opted for capital market restrictions in order to enhance economic policy independence for domestic governments.

All indicators of globalization, that is price and interest rate convergence, speed of price adjustment, and price convergence, suggest that the nineteenth century, and more specifically the second quarter of that century, marks the decisive breakthrough of globalization. European markets were vaguely integrated before that, but price adjustments were still very slow, and a truly international market had not yet emerged. That does not imply that there was no long-distance trade, but rather that trade was typically in non-competing goods. These were goods which were not produced in the importing nation, such as spices or agricultural goods from another climate zone, e.g. coffee. As a consequence local producers were not directly affected by competitive pressures. The trade pattern changed in the nineteenth century when commodities produced in the importing country, say grain or textiles, were also produced by local manufacturers and farmers. Faced with foreign competition, local producers had to adjust prices and domestic workers had to adjust wages, since they were threatened by unemployment if they did not. This is the essence of globalization as a process of increasing mutual dependence. A global economy opens up opportunities but is also associated with challenges. History has shown that the challenges can foster a globalization backlash and we can therefore not exclude a return to more protectionist policies in the future.

This introduction to the economic history of Europe has stressed the importance of market size, good government and openness to trade, factor flows and ideas as the dynamic forces in economic development. Globalization is the ultimate, but not necessarily irreversible, stage of that process. The fact that I am writing these lines in the spring of 2009 in the midst of a world economic crisis also highlights the speed at which a crisis that erupts in one large economy now affects all others. Policymakers seem, despite all, to have learned from history and modern economics has developed tools to stabilize fluctuations. Even a severe crisis must be put into perspective. The number of growth disasters likely to occur is about one or two in a generation. Despite the calamities following a decline in income and output of, say, 10 per cent over two to three years it is worth stressing that income per head in Europe has quadrupled between 1950 and 2000 and that institutional change and technology transfer permitted a number of populous and poor nations to start growing fast in the closing decades of the twentieth century.

Appendix: Freight rates and globalization

Figure 12.6 describes the process discussed in Section 12.4.3 more rigorously. Mass migration to the USA implies a perfectly elastic labour supply, which means that labour is willing to settle at a given price of grain. That condition generates the flat frontier price schedule. Transport costs increase proportionately with distance from the consuming centres in Europe, which is demonstrated by the constant price schedule. The price received by non-frontier farmers increases the closer they are to the ports on the eastern seaboard from which wheat is shipped to Europe. The farm-gate price depends on where the farmer is located along the *pp* schedule. The price paid to farmers in New

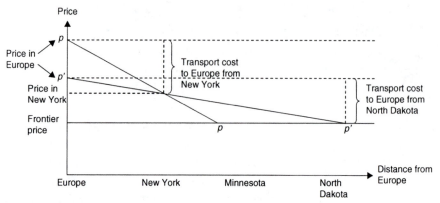

Figure 12.6 Freight rate reductions extend the frontier and increase price and income for non-frontier farmers. The figure captures ongoing research by K. G. Persson and Paul Sharp.

York state is the price in Europe minus the transport cost from New York to Europe.

The worldwide expansion of grain supply was caused by falling transport costs, which also meant a fall in the European grain price. In the figure this process is represented by the shift of the farm-gate price schedule from *pp* to *p'p'*. The frontier is determined by the intersection of the farm-gate price schedule *pp* or *p'p'* and the frontier price schedule. With the shift from *pp* to *p'p'* the grain-producing frontier is extended from Minnesota to North Dakota. The Minnesota farmers enjoy an increase in price while new settlers receive the constant frontier price, which is the new lower European price minus transport costs to North Dakota. The weighted average price falls when the centre of grain production moves away from high-price regions to the low-price frontier areas.

Suggestions for further reading

Much of the recent research in the economic history of globalization has been inspired by Harvard and Wisconsin-based J. G. Williamson and younger colleagues. Major themes in this research effort are explored in K. H. O'Rourke and J. G. Williamson, *Globalization and History: The Evolution of a Nineteenth Century Atlantic Economy* (Cambridge, Mass.: MIT Press, 1999).

M. D. Bordo, A. M. Taylor and J. G. Williamson, *Globalization in Historical Perspective* (Chicago: University of Chicago Press, 2003) contains a large number of chapters on practically all aspects of globalization.

The role of transport cost reductions, as opposed to trade policy, in globalization is played down in G. Federico and K. G. Persson, 'Market integration and convergence in the world wheat market 1800–2000', in T. J. Hatton, K. H. O'Rourke and A. M. Taylor (eds.), *The New Comparative Economic History: Essays in Honour of Jeffrey G. Williamson* (Cambridge, Mass.: MIT Press, 2007), p. 99.

M. Obstfeld and A. Taylor, *Global Capital Markets: Integration, Crisis and Growth* (Cambridge University Press, 2004) is a careful analysis of the ups and downs of capital market integration over the last 150 years.

M. Ejrnæs, K. G. Persson and S. Rich, 'Feeding the British. Convergence and market efficiency in nineteenth century grain trade', *Economic History Review* 61(1) (2008), pp. 140–71, points out that increased market efficiency contributed significantly to price convergence in the nineteenth century.

J. G. Williamson, 'Globalization, labor markets and policy backlash in the past', *Journal of Economic Perspectives* 12(4) (1998), pp. 51–72, suggests that globalization has winners and losers, which explains policy backlashes.

D. Rodrik, *Has Globalization Gone too Far?* (Washington: Institute for International Economics, 1997) warns us not to overstate the advantages and gains from globalization.

Glossary

Karl Gunnar Persson and Marc P. B. Klemp

Adverse selection a type of *market failure** that arises when buyers and sellers do not have access to the same information. Potential buyers of health insurance, for example, have more information about the state of their health than insurance firms. Healthy individuals have less incentive to buy the insurance than unhealthy individuals, so driving up the price of insurance and thereby further reducing the incentive for healthy individuals to buy it.

Agency problems see *principal–agent problem* and *moral hazard*.

Aggregate demand (also known as aggregate expenditure) is the sum of private consumption, investment, government expenditure and net exports. See also *national income*.

Automatic stabilizers have a counter-cyclical economic effect, (see also *pro-cyclical economic policy**). For example, the government deficit tends to increase in a downturn because of falling tax revenue and increasing unemployment benefits and this acts as an automatic stabilizer. See also *multiplier*.

Balance of payments the sum of all economic transactions of a nation with all other nations during a specific time period, usually a year. It is computed as the sum of the *current account* and the capital account. The latter is the net foreign investments and loans.

Bank see *fractional reserve bank*.

Barter the exchange of one commodity for another without the use of money as a means of payment. Barter reduces exchange below desirable levels because of the low probability of *coincidence of wants*.

Bills of exchange were widely used to settle payments related to trade. A bill entailed a promise by the debtor to pay the creditor at some future date. It was possible to transfer bills from one owner to another and banks would discount them, that is buy them at a discount. See Appendix to Chapter 7.

Border effect the difference in the price of a good in any two countries which is not attributable to tariffs and transport costs but only to the presence of a border. Differences in culture and language may generate additional border costs.

Cartel a coalition of firms that seeks to maximize each individual firm's profits by fixing prices, allocating market shares, fixing aggregate industry output or any other kind of collusive behaviour. The existence of *cartels* often leads to Pareto-inefficient outcomes (see *Pareto optimal*).

Coefficient of variation(s) is the ratio between the *standard deviation, sd or σ*, and the average, μ, i.e. $c = sd/\mu$.

Coincidence of wants is an event such that A, who wants to exchange x units of **a** for y units of **b**, finds B, who wants to exchange y units of **b** for x units of **a**.

Commonwealth the UK and its former colonies together with dominions such as Canada and South Africa.

Comparative advantage a concept used in trade theory whereby mutual gains from trade can be reaped when economies specialize in the product with respect to which they have a relative advantage. A nation can therefore gain from trade even if it is absolutely less efficient than its trading partner. If price ratios between goods differ across nations there is ground for trade. See the Appendix to Chapter 8.

Current account the balance of trade in commodities and services, called net exports, which is equal to national savings minus investment. See also Section 9.1 in Chapter 9.

Customs union a free-trade area with common external trade restrictions, such as the EU.

Economies of scale lower average costs in response to an increase in production. Often, if present, economies of scale are the result of the fixed costs being shared among a larger number of produced goods. Fixed costs are the costs that are not (immediately) dependent on the level of production.

Engel's law named after the nineteenth-century Prussian statistician Ernst Engel (1821–96): it proposes that the share of income spent on food declines with increasing income in cross-section samples of households. Over time it seems as if the share of food consumption in total consumption falls as per capita income increases. The *income elasticity* of demand for food is lower (often smaller than unity) than for other goods and services, according to a large number of studies.

Exchange rate, see *nominal exchange rate* and *real exchange rate*.

Extent of the market as used by Adam Smith is synonymous with *aggregate demand*.

Externality occurs when the impact of an action is not internalized by an agent. For example, a chemical firm polluting a river is causing an external effect when the firm destroys the fishing for others. External effects can be either positive or negative. The presence of externalities can lead to a *market failure**, see e.g. *tragedy of the commons.*

Fiat money typically paper bills or tokens without *intrinsic value*, but which are accepted at a positive value in exchange. The willingness of the public to accept and use *fiat money* depends on their confidence that the government and monetary authorities will ensure that *fiat money* can be exchanged for goods and services. Also called *fiduciary money.*

Fractional reserve bank a bank that keeps only a fraction of its deposits as reserves, investing the remainder in assets such as loans to the public. Virtually all modern banks are fractional reserve banks. Fractional reserve banking is possible because creditors do not in general redeem all their deposits simultaneously.

Free rider problem occurs when there are non-excludable so-called *public goods**. Since no one can be excluded from the consumption of a public good (say, the light from a lighthouse) once it is produced, people will understate their true preferences for the good, which leads to a market failure in that the good will not be provided efficiently.

GDP see *National income.*

GDP deflator a price index which is used to distinguish between the current money value of GDP and actual physical output. When the GDP in current prices has been deflated you have the GDP expressed in physical quantities. It is usually expressed as GDP at constant prices.

Gift exchange can be considered as ritualized *barter.*

Gini coefficient see *Lorenz curve**.

Income effect a rise (fall) in the price of a good will reduce (increase) the consumption of the good by reducing (increasing) the real income of the consumer. This effect of a change in price is called the income effect. Furthermore a rise (fall) in the price of the good changes its relative price. If the price of the good increases it will cause consumers to shift to other goods that are substitutes. This effect is called the *substitution effect.*

Income elasticity a measure of how responsive demand for a good is to changes in income. It is (approximately) the ratio of the relative change in the quantity demanded to the relative change in income.

Intrinsic value the market value of the metal from which a coin is made.

Law of one price stipulates that the price of a good, such as wheat of a particular and well-specified quality, will be the same in two markets if transport costs are zero. Since transport costs as a rule are positive, the 'transport cost adjusted law of one price' is the appropriate concept and it stipulates that the price differential between an identical good in two markets does not exceed the transport cost between the markets. The economic mechanisms that support the law of one price are arbitrage and trade. If the price differential exceeds transport costs it is profitable for merchants to bring the good from the low to the high-price market. The efficient operation of the law of one price assumes well-informed traders and fair to perfect competition. The *law of one price* should not be seen as a stable equilibrium for commodity markets but rather as an attractor which 'corrects' price deviations when they exceed transport costs.

Lender of last resort an institution willing to lend money when all other institutions are not or cannot. Central banks often act as lenders of last resort to minimize the risk of bank runs.

Linear regression a statistical technique used to estimate the influence of one or more variables on a given variable, everything else being equal.

Lorenz curve a visualization of cumulative distribution functions, most often used to represent income distributions. When representing an income distribution, the horizontal axis (see Figure 11.1) represents proportions of the population, and the vertical axis represents the proportion of total income that goes to the corresponding portion of the population. In a perfectly equal society, any portion of the population would always have an equally sized proportion of the total income, resulting in a straight, vertical line. Income distributions that are less than perfectly equal are represented by lines that can also be represented by convex functions. The area between the vertical line and such a line representing the income distribution in an unequal society is called the Gini coefficient and is a measure of inequality.

Market clearing price the price at which demand equals supply.

Market failure a characteristic of a market that leads to an inefficient outcome (see *Pareto efficient**). Markets can fail under the presence of an *externality**, imperfect competition, information asymmetry, a *public good**, etc. For an example of a market failure arising from the presence of an externality, see *tragedy of the commons*.

Market power the ability of a firm to influence the market price of a good, most often by a corresponding change in the quantity. A firm that does *not* have market power, i.e. which is operating under perfect competition, will lose all customers if it raises the price above marginal costs, since other firms will supply the good more cheaply. If such a firm sets prices lower than marginal costs, it will eventually go bankrupt. A monopoly, on the other hand, can raise the price of the good as it wishes, since no other firm is present to supply it more cheaply, although the monopoly will most often then produce a smaller quantity.

Moral hazard a problem that arises, when an agent does not bear the full consequences of his actions. In that case, the agent has an incentive to behave
more negligently than he otherwise would, if negligent behaviour is
more agreeable to the agent. A person insured against theft, for example,
is more likely to leave the door unlocked.

Multiplier a ratio of change in *national income** and change in expenditure.
When the government invests money in building a bridge, for example,
all of this spending becomes income for agents. Most of it will be spent
on goods and services. An initial rise in expenditure of one million euro
can thus result in a rise in GDP of more than one million euro. The true
size of the multiplier is a matter of controversy. Quite a few economists
argue it is below 1 while others insist it is greater than 1.

Mutual funds collective investment funds in which investors' money is pooled
and traded by professional investment managers.

National income Two approaches are widely used: the expenditure approach
and the income approach. While the income approach aims to describe
national income directly as a sum of disaggregated income, the expenditure
approach aims to describe *national income* in terms of what income is used
for. Since one person's expenditure is equal to another person's income, the
two approaches are equivalent when expressed as Gross National Product.
Using the expenditure approach gives the Gross National Product, *GNP*,
which is broken down into consumption *C*, investment *I*, government
spending *G*, and net exports (exports minus imports) plus net earnings
on foreign assets (earnings by nationals on foreign assets minus earnings
by foreigners on domestic assets) *N*, i.e. $GNP = C + I + G + N$.

The income approach makes up Gross Domestic Product, *GDP*, which
is broken down into the incomes of workers and the self-employed, capital income, and income of landowners. The income of workers and the
self-employed is the wage rate, *w*, times the supply of work, *L*, i.e. wL. Total
capital income is the rate of return on capital including public utilities, *r*,
times the supply of capital, *K*, i.e. rK. The income of landowners is given by
the rate of return (rental rate) of land, *i*, multiplied by the amount of land
rented, *L*. If we deduct the net income of foreigners, the income approach
therefore produces the identity $GDP = wL + rK + iL$. This is the expression used in the Appendix to Chapter 4. GDP measured using the income
approach will be equivalent to GNP using the expenditure approach if
you deduct the net earnings of foreign assets from GDP. The symbol Y
is often used in a loose sense to indicate either GNP or GDP and in most
cases the difference between the two is trivial. If an economy has huge foreign investments its GNP will be smaller than its GDP.

Neolithic revolution the initial transition from a hunter-gatherer society to a society based on agriculture. Archaeological findings suggest that this transition took place around 12,000 years ago in the Middle East.

Nominal exchange rate the price of one currency in terms of an other.

Nominal wage the wage measured in current values. See *real wage*.

Non-rival good a good with the property that one agent's consumption of the good does not reduce the availability of the good to others. Unlike a *public good* it can be excludable. A modern-day example of such a good is cable television or patent-protected knowledge.

Opportunity cost represents the value of the opportunities forgone by choosing one of several alternatives. It is measured by the value of the most highly valued of the rejected alternatives.

Opportunity income the forgone income that an agent could achieve by employing his labour in the highest-paying alternative opportunity. This term is sometimes used even when no alternative work opportunities are available. A serf, for example, unable to buy his freedom, would not be able to work anywhere except on the land held by his landlord; but we may still consider the wage income he could earn elsewhere if he did have his freedom, i.e. his *opportunity income.*

Pareto-efficiency an allocation of goods whereby no agent can become better off without at least some other agent becoming worse off. (*Pareto optimal =* highly *Pareto efficient.*)

Path dependence the notion that present economic decisions are dependent not only on present conditions but also on historically given economic decisions which constrain future choices.

Positive checks see *preventive checks.*

Preventive checks deliberate and planned fertility-reducing strategies by households. The *positive check* is a direct or indirect effect of income changes on mortality. People rarely starve to death but a sharp fall in income per head usually increases epidemics and mortality.

Principal–agent problem the type of problem that arises when an agent is hired by a principal and the former has more information than the latter, and the parties do not share the same objectives. The principal will therefore need to monitor the agent and/or design an incentive scheme so that the agent serves the interest of the principal.

Pro-cyclical economic policy a policy that reinforces the business cycle. In general, pro-cyclical economic policy tends to increase fluctuations in economic variables, while counter-cyclical economic policy and *automatic stabilizers** tend to decrease fluctuations.

Progressive tax a tax whose rate increases as taxable income increases.

Protectionism an economic policy aiming to protect domestic producers and workers, mainly by imposing tariffs or quotas on imported goods and subsidizing exports.

Public good a good with the following two properties. First, it is not possible to prevent consumption of the good, it is non-excludable. Second, consumption by one agent does not reduce the availability of the good or service to others, i.e. it is *non-rival*. An example of such a good is the provision of a lighthouse or knowledge for which patent protection has expired.

Purchasing power parity (PPP) a theory that assumes that the *law of one price* holds internationally and therefore that the exchange rate between two countries adjusts so that purchasing power of the currencies becomes equal. See also *real exchange rate*.

Real exchange rate reveals the real purchasing power of a currency at home and abroad. If we denote the *real exchange rate* by x, the *nominal exchange rate* by X, the foreign price level by P^* and the domestic price level by P, we have, formally, $x = X\frac{P^*}{P}$. For example, if the price of one \$ is £0.75, then the nominal exchange rate is 0.75. Furthermore the US price level (*GDP deflator*) is 100 and the UK price level is 75 and therefore the real exchange rate is 1. In this case each currency buys as many goods at home as abroad if exchanged to the foreign currency. The nominal exchange rate is consistent with *purchasing power parity*. If the nominal exchange rate is fixed but the UK experiences an isolated inflationary shock so that the price level becomes 100, then the real exchange rate increases to 1.33. The UK currency, £, has become overvalued since it buys more goods in the US than at home. A basket costing £100 in UK costs \$100 but at the prevailing nominal exchange rate £100 buy \$133!

Real interest rate (r) the nominal interest rate, i, deflated by the inflation rate, π, i.e. $r = (1+i)/(1+\pi)$. When the nominal interest rate and the inflation rate are small, the *real interest rate* can be approximated by the relation $r \approx i - \pi$. Essentially, the *real interest rate* is the interest rate on *real money balances*.

Real money balances the nominal quantity of money deflated by prices. See also *real interest rate*.

Real wage is the wage measured in terms of a representative basket of goods. The real wages is obtained by deflating the *nominal wage* with a consumer price index.

Regressive tax refers to a tax whose rate decreases as income increases.

Rent-seeking the use of resources to get a rent by reducing the welfare of others. For example farmers can lobby the European Commission to get subsidies that will increase farmers' income but reduce it for all others.

R&D (Research and Development) spending spending on fundamental as well as applied research. *R&D* is carried out by both privately and government-run firms and universities. *R&D* carried out by privately run firms is most often motivated by profit and tends to focus on application rather than gaining knowledge of general applicability, which is normally sought by government-sponsored institutions such as universities.

Residual claimant the agent who receives the net income, i.e. the revenue minus costs and expenses. The owners of a firm are the residual claimants, hopefully earning a profit.

Seigniorage (from the French *seigneur*) originally the fee charged by a mint for striking money. That fee exceeded the cost of minting and became revenue for the state, king or lord. Nowaday, *seigniorage* means the profit earned by the monetary authorities by issuing money.

Standard deviation (σ or sd) the square root of the *variance*.

Sterilization the act of counteracting the inflationary tendency of capital flows. When capital flows into an economy through foreign investment, foreign exchange reserves increase since the central banks buys the foreign currency in exchange for the domestic currency. This leads to an expansion of the money supply, which can fuel inflation. Therefore, central banks may choose to decrease money supply by selling bonds to the public, thereby 'sterilizing' the inflationary effect of monetary expansion. Central banks can also sterilize the effect of capital outflows by buying bonds from the public to counteract the fall in money supply.

Substitution effect see *income effect*.

Taxation see *progressive tax** and *regressive tax*.

Token a stamped coin used as a means of payment at its nominal value but not backed by intrinsic metal value equal to its nominal value, which is the case with a so-called *full-bodied coin*. *Tokens* are a variety of *fiat money*.

Total factor productivity the increase in output that cannot be ascribed to an increase in inputs. See also Section 4.2 and the appendix to Chapter 4.

Variance a statistical concept that formalizes the notion of dispersion. The variance, σ^2, of a set of numbers, denoted $x_1, x_2, \ldots, x_n$, is the sum of the squared deviations from the average, μ, divided by the sample size, n, minus 1, i.e. $\sigma^2 = \dfrac{\sum_i^n (x_i - \mu)^2}{n-1}$.

Index

CPSIA information can be obtained at www.ICGtesting.com
Printed in the USA
BVOW01*1834230914

368015BV00003B/4/P